THE COMPLETE GUIDE TO E-MAIL MARKETING:

How To Create Successful, Spam-Free Campaigns to Reach Your Target Audience and Increase Sales

BY BRUCE C. BROWN

THE COMPLETE GUIDE TO E-MAIL MARKETING: HOW TO CREATE SUCCESSFUL, SPAM-FREE CAMPAIGNS TO REACH YOUR TARGET AUDIENCE AND INCREASE SALES

ISBN-13: 978-1-60138-042-5   ISBN-10: 1-60138-042-9

Library of Congress Cataloging-in-Publication Data

Brown, Bruce C. (Bruce Cameron), 1965-
The complete guide to e-mail marketing : how to create successful, spam-free campaigns to reach your target audience and increase sales / by Bruce C Brown.
     p. cm.
ISBN 13: 978-1-60138-042-5 (alk. paper)
ISBN 10: 1-60138-042-9 (alk. paper)
1. Telemarketing. 2. Internet marketing. I. Title.

HF5415.1265.B764 2007
658.8'72--dc22
                        2007028082

EDITOR: Tracie Kendziora • tkendziora@atlantic-pub.com
INTERIOR LAYOUT DESIGN: Vickie Taylor • vtaylor@atlantic-pub.com
PROOFREADER: Angela Adams • aadams@atlantic-pub.com

Printed in the United States

Printed on Recycled Paper

We recently lost our beloved pet "Bear," who was not only our best and dearest friend but also the "Vice President of Sunshine" here at Atlantic Publishing. He did not receive a salary but worked tirelessly 24 hours a day to please his parents. Bear was a rescue dog that turned around and showered myself, my wife Sherri, his grandparents Jean, Bob and Nancy and every person and animal he met (maybe not rabbits) with friendship and love. He made a lot of people smile every day.

We wanted you to know that a portion of the profits of this book will be donated to The Humane Society of the United States.

–Douglas & Sherri Brown

THE HUMANE SOCIETY
OF THE UNITED STATES ©

The human-animal bond is as old as human history. We cherish our animal companions for their unconditional affection and acceptance. We feel a thrill when we glimpse wild creatures in their natural habitat or in our own backyard.

Unfortunately, the human-animal bond has at times been weakened. Humans have exploited some animal species to the point of extinction.

The Humane Society of the United States makes a difference in the lives of animals here at home and worldwide. The HSUS is dedicated to creating a world where our relationship with animals is guided by compassion. We seek a truly humane society in which animals are respected for their intrinsic value, and where the human-animal bond is strong.

Want to help animals? We have plenty of suggestions. Adopt a pet from a local shelter, join The Humane Society and be a part of our work to help companion animals and wildlife. You will be funding our educational, legislative, investigative and outreach projects in the U.S. and across the globe.

Or perhaps you'd like to make a memorial donation in honor of a pet, friend or relative? You can through our Kindred Spirits program. And if you'd like to contribute in a more structured way, our Planned Giving Office has suggestions about estate planning, annuities, and even gifts of stock that avoid capital gains taxes.

Maybe you have land that you would like to preserve as a lasting habitat for wildlife. Our Wildlife Land Trust can help you. Perhaps the land you want to share is a backyard—that's enough. Our Urban Wildlife Sanctuary Program will show you how to create a habitat for your wild neighbors.

So you see, it's easy to help animals. And The HSUS is here to help.

The Humane Society of the United States
2100 L Street NW
Washington, DC 20037
202-452-1100
www.hsus.org

CONTENTS

FOREWORD

By Elie D. Ashery

Legitimate, commercial e-mail has come a long way since I first started experimenting with the practice ten years ago during the Dot Com era. Back then there were no e-mail service providers to help manage the e-mail marketing process, no case studies to mimic, no books to reference, and no laws that established minimum standards. It was the Wild West to say the least.

Thanks to the many Internet marketing pioneers during that unprecedented time in digital history, e-mail marketing exploded into a multi-billion dollar industry. The main catalyst to this growth was Congress's passage of the CAN-SPAM Act of 2003, which established minimum standards for commercial e-mail. Since then, legitimate e-mail marketers have rushed to build on this foundation, creating the best practices, codes of ethics, and organizational bodies to help guide their fellow practitioners and create a clear separation between themselves and spammers (marketers who send unsolicited bulk e-mail).

Contrary to initial thought, e-mail marketing is not easy and not always cheap. Anyone can gather a list, create a message, and try to blast his or her way to success. They will find their efforts futile, as their e-mail gets magically eaten by spam filters, black lists, and other anti-spam measures, never reaching their intended recipients.

This thinking is very common among e-mail marketing neophytes and can get you into serious trouble. Will you go to jail if you send unsolicited e-mail? It is possible, but not probable. As I write this, there have only been 90 successful prosecutions using the CAN-SPAM Act of 2003, in contrast to the hundreds of trillions of spam messages that get sent every year. If you decide to send unsolicited e-mail, you will encounter a bunch of angry people, including the recipients who received your message, your ISP's systems administrator, and an anti-spam vigilante who will take matters into his or her own hands, posting information about you on blogs and calling in death threats. And I am not kidding about the latter.

So what is a legitimate marketer to do? The good news is it is not 1997, and there are plenty of resources to help you be successful and keep your nose clean, starting with this book. *The Complete Guide to E-Mail Marketing: How to Create Successful, Spam-Free Campaigns to Reach Your Target Audience and Increase Sales* will explain to you in detail what I feel are the two most important criteria for successful e-mail marketing: list building and testing. With a good opt-in list, your job as an e-mail marketer is already half done. Just as with traditional direct marketing, list quality is everything, and this fact carries even more weight in e-mail marketing. After spending numerous, painstaking hours building an opt-in list, most newbies jump at the chance to send their message to everyone on their list. This is a typical amateur faux pas that only leads to list attrition, as the opt-out requests will start pouring in.

The great thing about e-mail is that results are nearly instantaneous, and it does not take much to find out whether your campaign banks or tanks. Test everything about your message in small list samples. Test the offer, subject line, from line, images, text, everything until you feel you have achieved an optimal response rate. Eventually, you will achieve equilibrium with your e-mail marketing efforts, where success will seem to come naturally. This is where you will recognize the fruits of your labor. But do not get too comfortable. This is short-lived, and eventually you will need to continue building your list and testing your messages.

E-mail marketing is a never-ending cycle that, if done properly and ethically, can be very lucrative. I am living proof. My company, Gold Lasso, was founded with a mere $20,000 investment and grew in two short years into a multi-million dollar enterprise using e-mail marketing as its primary component in its promotional mix. Now, we leverage other marketing mediums, such as search in conjunction with e-mail; however, no other marketing medium remotely compares to e-mail with regards to facilitating customer retention.

Elie D. Ashery
President & CEO
Gold Lasso, LLC
http://www.goldlasso.com
312 Main Street, Suite 200
Gaithersburg, MD 20878
Phone: 301-990-9857 x212
Fax: 301-990-9856

Introducing Dot E-mail—The Web's First E-mail Marketing Community: **http://www.dotemail.com**

Visit his blog: **http://www.fromline.com**

Bio from the Gold Lasso Web Site. Printed with Permission from Elie D. Ashery.

Elie D. Ashery, President and CEO of Gold Lasso, is a true entrepreneur who has dedicated his career to technology and the Internet. He is responsible for the vision and strategy execution for Gold Lasso, and drives the innovation behind Gold Lasso's products and services. Elie started his career as a financial analyst and investment researcher for the Internet media sector at Newby & Co., a special situations investment research and investment banking firm. In 1997 he co-founded **Newsletters.com**, a subscriptions reseller of industry trade publications and market research. While serving as President of Newsletters.com, Elie helped raise equity financing from prominent angel and institutional investors in the Washington, D.C. area. In addition, Elie helped to implement a partnership marketing strategy that made Newsletters.com the premier subscription reseller of industry periodicals on the Internet. **Newsletters.com** was sold in August of 2000 to **MarketResearch.com**, a subsidiary of The Tribune Companies. After **Newsletters.com**, Elie served as the Vice President of Business Development for IncenSoft, a state of Maryland funded software company that specialized in the development of incentive compensation management programs. At IncenSoft, Elie implemented a successful e-mail marketing strategy that netted business from Fortune 1000 companies. IncenSoft was acquired by Synygy, Inc. in September of 2002. Elie holds bachelor's degrees in finance and accounting from the University of Maryland.

INTRODUCTION

When I was first approached with the idea of writing *The Complete Guide to E-mail Marketing: How To Create Successful, Spam-Free Campaigns to Reach Your Target Audience and Increase Sales*, I was excited. To be fair, there are several other books on similar subjects; however, I felt I had a great opportunity to introduce the e-mail marketing to the small business community, online retailers, and those with extremely limited marketing and promotion budgets.

E-mail marketing, when designed and implemented correctly, can be one of your most effective advertising, marketing, and sales tools. It can also be one of your most cost-efficient means of disseminating large amounts of information, promotional materials, advertisements, special offers, coupons, new product announcements, and relevant news to a large audience for low costs when compared to traditional print media advertising and marketing campaigns. Face it, practically everyone has e-mail, and most access e-mail daily at both work and home. E-mail marketing allows you to distribute information instantly and globally, while providing detailed tracking and reporting not possible with other forms of advertising and marketing.

Sounds great! Sign me up! Trust me, it can be great — when done properly. So let us take an organized approach to developing your e-mail marketing campaign to ensure that we fully understand all the concepts and options, develop a marketing budget to support your requirements, design optimized e-mail campaigns, ensure we follow anti-spam laws, and develop an entire portfolio for success, rather than a shotgun approach of just blasting out random e-mails. I am constantly asked by clients whom I design and develop Web sites for, "Will my Web site will be number one in all major search engines, such as Google, Yahoo, and MSN?" I will show you how e-mail marketing can help you in your quest to obtain that goal and dramatically increase your overall Web site visibility in search engines. As you know, obtaining high search engine rankings is a combination of many factors, starting with overall Web site design and culminating with an effective Web site marketing strategy. This strategy maximizes your potential for high rankings and ultimately increases revenue or Web site traffic, while balancing the constraints of often limited resources and budget. You will be surprised at how effective e-mail marketing can be in helping you achieve this goal.

In this book, we will discuss the often misunderstood world of e-mail marketing. E-mail marketing is not spam when it is done properly and legally. I do not consider those annoying bulk e-mails that bombard your inbox to be a valid e-mail marketing campaign. Those are simply a barrage of trash, spyware, and virus infected e-mails, which offer no valuable service or purpose other than to waste time, commit fraud, or cause harm to your computer network. A properly designed e-mail marketing campaign is targeted, relevant, and useful to the recipient. We will discuss all aspects of the development and design of an effective and successful e-mail marketing campaign from cradle to grave, including all of the relevant methodology to ensure your campaign maximizes overall effectiveness while staying on budget and in compliance with rules, regulations, law, and protocol. The implementation of an e-mail marketing campaign is not a guarantee of increased sales or revenue, or even an increase in Web site traffic. We will ensure that your e-mail marketing campaign has the best design and position to achieve both of these critical goals, and be a major contributing factor to the success of your business.

WHO IS THIS BOOK FOR

This book is written for anyone who has a Web site or is considering developing a Web site. The techniques in this book can be used by traditional retailers, online-only merchants, as well as a variety of other business ventures. It is also valuable for those interested in distributing information and news — not just for the sale of products. I have designed this book to be incorporated into your marketing portfolio where possible by the individual business owner (you do not need to hire an expert consultant), and to be implemented at little or not cost. This book cuts out the fluff and gives you straightforward techniques, facts, and advice. I have included advice from industry experts, as well as assembled case studies with proven successes (and failures) to highlight techniques employed by e-mail marketers. This book will guide you to success by arming you with the tools required to establish, manage, and grow a successful e-mail marketing campaign. Throughout this book you will find hints, tips, and best practices to help you save money, establish a fast, successful e-mail marketing program, and ensure you maintain 100 percent spam-compliance.

HOW THIS BOOK IS ORGANIZED

We will provide you with the following:

- **History of Online Marketing and E-mail Marketing** — An extensive history of the evolution of online marketing and the different types of campaigns/marketing strategies employed by Web site operators to promote their business through search engines, free marketing, and PPC marketing programs, as well as an in depth orientation to how E-mail Marketing fits within your marketing portfolio.

- **Introduction to E-mail Marketing** — A comprehensive introduction and overview of e-mail marketing, how it works, how it compares to and can be used in conjunction with other marketing techniques, and how to effectively design an e-mail marketing campaign for maximum success. We will show you how an e-mail marketing campaign works from start to finish.

- **SPAM, SPAM, SPAM** — We will delve into the definition of Spam, the history of Spam, the legalities of spam, and how to ensure you maintain compliance with the Canned Spam Act. In addition, we will provide you with the tools, techniques, and industry secrets to ensure your e-mail marketing campaign is SPAM compliant.

- **Opt-In and Opt-Out** — We will take an in-depth analysis of opt-in and opt-out in regards to e-mail marketing, and provide you with a comprehensive understanding of what constitutes legal opt-in and opt-out for your e-mail marketing campaigns.

- **How to Create & Grow your E-mail List** — We will show you how to create an e-mail list, how to maintain it, and how to add names to it. Equally important, we will discuss how to keep people from un-subscribing to your e-mail list.

- **How to Design an Effective E-mail Campaign** — We will teach you all the techniques you need to create basic and advanced e-mail campaigns, how to begin the process of setting up a successful e-mail program, and take a look a the wide variety of e-mail publishers you can consider using to help you manage your e-mail lists and campaigns.

- **Target and Segment Your Audience** — If you want to have success with your e-mail marketing campaigns, you must know the target audience you are seeking. By identifying your target audience, you can design highly customized and effective e-mail campaigns based on your market segment or target audience.

- **How to Write an Effective E-Mail** — We will arm you with industry proven secrets and tips from the professionals on creating well-written, profitable and highly effective e-mails for your e-mail marketing campaign. We will also provide you with a list of industry proven "do's and don'ts" when creating your e-mails.

- **The Subject Line** — We will provide you with all the knowledge you need to create the most effective subject lines in your e-mail marketing campaigns. This is often overlooked, but is the most important element that determines the success of your e-mail marketing campaigns.

- **When to E-mail, How Often, and What Time?** — We will discuss proven success formulas in relation to how often to e-mail, when have you exceeded your welcome, what days and times are most effective, and how to avoid losing potential customers with poor e-mail techniques.

- **The Future of E-Mail Marketing** — The latest techniques, industry speculation, and other tidbits which will help you ensure your e-mail marketing campaign is successful today and built for success in the future.

- **Search Engine Optimization** — SEO is critical to e-mail marketing, and we will show you why. This is a general guide to design your site for maximum SEO in relation to your e-mail marketing campaign. You will learn tips and tricks to garner the most from site visitors to increase revenues and Webs site design effectiveness.

- **Case Studies** — E-mail marketing and search engine optimization can fuel an enormous increase in online sales, generate substantial web site traffic, and increase your potential customer base. Read the results of others who have implemented successful e-mail marketing campaigns and have succeeded.

- **Industry Experts Tips & Advice** — A compilation of the best advise, secrets, hints, tips, tricks, and tidbits from the experts who do it every day.

I will provide you with the tools and knowledge to unlock the secrets of e-mail marketing, and enable you to you use to the internet and electronic media distribution to its fullest potential to promote, advertise, and market your business in a cost-effective campaign. The internet is the ultimate marketing tool — giving you immediate access to billions of people worldwide. By implementing marketing campaigns, such as e-mail marketing, you will benefit from being able to instantly reach your existing and potential customers at practically no cost. After reading this book and applying the principles and techniques contained within, you will empower your business to operate a cost-effective, and highly success e-mail marketing campaign, ensuring the maximum return on investment through the design and development of a successful e-mail marketing strategy.

You will have all of the tools and steps that you need to follow to maximize and harness the power of the Internet to promote and market your business and products through e-mail marketing, as well as provide you with some of the formulas for success in developing your overall Web site design and marketing strategy. If you follow the guiding principles contained in this book, you WILL be successful! Ideally, you should follow the principles of this book in concert with two previous books; *How to Use the Internet to Advertise, Promote and Market Your Business or Web site with Little or No Money*, and *The Ultimate Guide to Search Engine Marketing: Pay Per Click Advertising Secrets Revealed*. All three books complement each other, providing you with a wide variety of low or no cost marketing techniques, along with a comprehensive pay-per-click advertising campaign. Proper site design, search engine optimization, advertising, marketing, pay-per-click advertising, and e-mail marketing should all be part of your overall portfolio for success — and all should be used together to complete your overall long-term marketing strategy.

E-mail marketing campaigns can be exclusively designed, implemented, and managed by you. You do not need to be a professional web designer or hire an expensive marketing firm to promote and market your online business. I will tell you the secrets, the time-tested methodology, and the tricks of the trade to ensure that you design and implement a successful e-mail marketing campaign. There are many resources available to assist you with your implementation plans, and we will walk you through the best of them. If you prefer to seek professional assistance, we also provide you with a reference list of the industry leaders.

The concepts in this book are presented in a simple to understand and implement manner, so that you can easily adapt them for your organization. By following our guidelines, you will successfully (and in a cost-effective manner) reach your customers and potential customers in a way that you could not previously.

BENEFITS OF USING E-MAIL

Think about the benefits of utilizing e-mail:

- E-mail is fast and reaches your customers almost instantly.

- E-mail can be tracked, so you will know if someone opens your e-mail and clicks on the links embedded within your e-mail.

- E-mail marketing allows you to target or segment your customer base and audience not only by interests, but by geographical regions, age, sex, and a variety of other filters.

- Not only do you get to track your response rates, you will obtain higher response rates than through traditional print media advertising.

- No Stamp, no postage, no envelopes, no printing, no distribution problems, no poly-bagging.

- System Automation allows you to remove bad e-mail addresses instantly, add new e-mail addresses, let people subscribe to your list automatically, and ensure your list is up to date — can you do that (for no cost) with your print advertising lists?

- It is a proven and effective advertising method.

The key principles to remember with e-mail marketing are that you comply with spam laws, developing your e-mail client list, and design effective campaigns, which compliment your company and/or products and services. You do not want to be accused of being a spammer or have your company name associated with being a spammer. When you send out an e-mail marketing campaign, you want your existing and potential customers to be interested, to want to read your e-mail and to provide them with multiple opportunities for feedback, information exchange, and links to your Web site. You also must respect their privacy and include an automated, fool-proof way of allowing those who do not wish to be on your list to easily and quickly remove themselves from any further mailings.

Convinced yet? Here are some statistics regarding e-mail use published by numerous sources including: Google, Brightmail, Jupiter Research, eMarketer, Harris Interactive, and Ferris Research.

- Daily e-mails sent: *31 billion*

- Daily e-mails sent per e-mail address: *56*

- Daily e-mails sent per person: *174*

- Daily e-mails sent per corporate user: *34*

- Daily e-mails received per person: *32*

- E-mail addresses per person: *3.1 average*

- Cost to all Internet users: *$255 million*

If I have not convinced you yet that e-mail marketing is a simple to implement and cost-effective advertising method, read this book, follow the principles outlined, and try it for yourself. The instant gratification from seeing orders generated within minutes of sending out an e-mail blast is tremendously rewarding and satisfying. Even if you are just using the e-mail marketing campaign to distribute information, news, or articles of interest, you can reach hundreds of thousands of people almost instantly.

This book is designed to provide you with the background, tools and knowledge to succeed in e-mail marketing. I will show you the best practices and give you candid advice on how to stay out of the murky world of spam. I will not tell you that e-mail marketing will increase revenue by 1,000 percent guaranteed; although, if implemented properly, it is an invaluable tool that can and will increase revenue. I will cover spam, e-mail lists, and e-mail harvesting in great detail, because this information is critical to your overall success strategy.

The one thing I will guarantee you is that implementing a successful e-mail marketing campaign is easier than you think, and less costly than most other methods of advertising. When used with *Search Engine Optimization and Pay-Per-Click Advertising Campaigns*, you will have built the pillars of success for an overall online marketing strategy that will generate Web site traffic and revenue.

2

HISTORY & UNDERSTANDING OF E-MAIL MARKETING

The purpose of this book is not to provide you with a history lesson; however, there is significant value in understanding how e-mail came to be an integral part of our daily lives (both at work and home), as well as realizing the potential of e-mail as part of your marketing portfolio. To understand the history of e-mail, you need to know a brief history of the origins of the Internet. One of the best sources for Internet and e-mail history is from internet historian and expert Ian Peter and his Web site at **www.nethistory.org.** The following history of the Internet and e-mail is reproduced with the permission of Ian Peter.

Ian Peter's History of the Internet

The ARPANET was designed in the 1960s for the U.S. Defense Department. By the 1970s, the ARPANET connected research institutes and laboratories throughout the country, and it was through this network that the TCP/IP protocol (Transmission Control Protocol/Internet Protocol) was developed. In 1980, IP (Internet Protocol) became the official standard of the U.S. Department of Defense and by 1990, with everyone having gone over to using the newer, faster Internet backbone network, the original ARPANET was shut down. With the development of TCP/IP, HTTP (Hyper Text Transfer Protocol), and graphical interface browsers, such as Mosaic and early versions of Microsoft's Internet Explorer, the Internet as we know it today came into existence as the technology evolved beyond military and research application into commercial ventures. As fast as the Internet developed, so did the available speed of the Internet — growing exponentially beyond the days of 300 and 1,200 baud

Ian Peter's History of the Internet

modems into the years dominated by 28.8K and 33.6K modems into the broadband world where high-speed Internet (including wireless connectivity) is available in every room of your house.

E-mail is much older than ARPANET or the Internet. It was never invented; it evolved from very simple beginnings. Early e-mail was just a small advance on what we know these days as a file directory — it just put a message in another user's directory in a spot where they could see it when they logged in. Simple as that. Just like leaving a note on someone's desk. Likely the first e-mail system of this type was MAILBOX, used at Massachusetts Institute of Technology beginning in 1965. Another early program to send messages on the same computer was called SNDMSG.

Some of the mainframe computers of this era might have had up to 100 users — often they used what are called "dumb terminals" to access the mainframe from their work desks. Dumb terminals just connected to the mainframe — they had no storage or memory of their own; they did all their work on the remote mainframe computer. Before internetworking began, e-mail could only be used to send messages to various users of the same computer. When computers began to talk to each other over networks, however, the problem became a little more complex — we needed to be able to put a message in an envelope and address it. To do this, we needed a means to indicate to whom letters should go so that the electronic posties understood. Just like the postal system, we needed a way to indicate an address.

This is why Ray Tomlinson is credited with inventing e-mail in 1972. Like many of the Internet inventors, Tomlinson worked for Bolt Beranek and Newman as an ARPANET contractor. He picked the @ symbol from the computer keyboard to denote sending messages from one computer to another. So then, for anyone using Internet standards, it was simply a matter of nominating name-of-the-user@name-of-the-computer.

Things developed rapidly from there. Larry Roberts invented some e-mail folders for his boss so he could sort his mail — a big advance. In 1975 John Vital developed some software to organize e-mail. By 1976 e-mail had really taken off, and commercial packages began to appear. Within a couple of years, 75 percent of all ARPANET traffic was e-mail. E-mail took us from Arpanet to the Internet. Here was something that ordinary people all over the world wanted to use.

One of the first new developments when personal computers came on the scene was "offline readers." Offline readers allowed e-mail users to store their e-mail on their own personal computers and then read it and prepare replies without actually being connected to the network — sort of like Microsoft Outlook does today.

Ian Peter's History of the Internet

This was particularly useful in parts of the world where telephone calls to the nearest e-mail system were expensive. With connection charges of many dollars a minute, it mattered to be able to prepare a reply without being connected to a telephone and then get on the network to send it. It was also useful because the "offline" mode allowed for more friendly interfaces. Being connected directly to the host e-mail system in this era of very few standards often resulted in delete keys and backspace keys not working, no capacity for text to "wrap around" on the screen of the user's computer, and other such annoyances. Offline readers helped a lot.

The first important e-mail standard was called SMTP, or simple message transfer protocol. SMTP was very simple and is still in use; however, SMTP was a fairly naïve protocol and made no attempt to find out whether the person claiming to send a message was the person they purported to be. Forgery was (and still is) very easy in e-mail addresses. These basic flaws in the protocol were later to be exploited by viruses, worms, and by security frauds and spammers forging identities. Some of these problems are still being addressed in 2007. But as it developed, e-mail started to take on some neat features. One of the first good commercial systems was Eudora, developed by Steve Dorner in 1988. Not long after, Pegasus mail appeared.

When Internet standards for e-mail began to mature, the POP (or Post Office Protocol) servers began to appear as a standard — before that each server was a little different. POP was an important standard to allow users to develop mail systems that would work with each other. These were the days of per-minute charges for e-mail for individual dialup users. For most people on the Internet in those days e-mail and e-mail discussion groups were the main uses. There were many hundreds of these on a wide variety of topics, and as a body of newsgroups, they became known as USENET.

With the advent of the World Wide Web, e-mail became available with friendly Web interfaces by providers such as Yahoo! and Hotmail. Often this was without charge. Now that e-mail was affordable, everyone wanted at least one e-mail address, and the medium was adopted by not just millions, but hundreds of millions of people.

I can clearly recall the early days when I was stationed aboard the Coast Guard Cutter's FIREBUSH and STORIS, homeported out of Kodiak, Alaska in the early days of the Internet and e-mail. In the early 1990s, Kodiak did not have dialup service, and few of us had personal computers. Phone calls home were expensive and stressed our military income. Today in Kodiak, you can sign up for high speed broadband and have unlimited use of the internet. You can even access e-mail 24/7 while underway on Coast Guard and Navy ships, something unimaginable a decade ago. More incredible is the boom in use of personal computer users — powered by the growth of the Internet. The reliance on e-mail as a communication tool in the commercial and government sectors is enormous, so is the volume of personal e-mail traffic generated daily. When companies upgrade their servers or are experiencing problems, employees do not have access to the Internet or e-mail. In these cases, people do not know what to do, how to occupy their day, or how to carry on business without the use of the Internet and e-mail. The use of e-mail has grown so much that most intra- and inter-office communications are completed by e-mail, even when the recipient may be sitting at the desk next to you.

This was a short history of the Internet, which highlights the enormous reliance on it and the popularity and acceptance of e-mail. Suffice it to say, most people use e-mail every day of their lives, both at work and at home, thus opening an enormous potential marketing opportunity for you to directly reach millions of individuals with the push of a "send" button. Let us take a quick look at online marketing and the variety of online marketing methods which you can use to develop your comprehensive online marketing portfolio.

ONLINE MARKETING

Online marketing schemes have been around since the invention and creation of the world-wide-web. As web sites were developed into online businesses targeting increased revenues for traditional brick and mortar business, the important and prominence of online marketing became a dominating force in the industry, and e-mail marketing is a critical component to a successful online marketing portfolio. Today, there are hundreds of thousands of businesses who exist solely on the internet and do not maintain a traditional retail brick and mortar business. As a result of this boom in the commercial and retail sector of the web, online marketing techniques, such as e-mail marketing, pay-per-click advertising campaigns, and other enterprising marketing schemes have become increasingly prevalent, as well as extraordinarily competitive.

Marketing and advertising a traditional storefront can be costly and often unprofitable. Postage and mailing costs are high, and return rates on mailings are a dismal one percent of the total mailing or less. Over 200 million Americans went online in 2005, and nearly one billion people worldwide used the Internet during this same time period. Internet access grew more than 107 percent in 2005 in the United States and more than 165 percent worldwide. According to the facts from Jupiter Research and Nielson:

- The number of online users will reach 231 million in 2009, representing 75 percent of the total US population

- Online classified spending will nearly double in the next five years... from $1.9 billion in 2004 to $3.7 billion in 2009

- On average, Americans spend 14 hours online each month

- The preferred research tool of big-ticket purchases is the Internet

INTERNET MARKETING

According to Wikipedia (**www.wikipedia.com**), Internet Marketing is defined as a "component of electronic commerce. Internet marketing can include information management, public relations, customer service, and sales. Electronic commerce and Internet marketing have become popular as Internet access is becoming more widely available and used. Nearly half of the consumers who have Internet access in their homes report using the Internet to make purchases." In the early 1990's, Internet marketing was a new frontier in the advertising and sales. Commercial Web sites were nothing more than a corporate public relations presence with generalized information about a company and/or its products and services. As technology improved, and the understanding of the Hyper Text Markup Language (HTML), the predominant language for the creation of Web sites, improved, commercial Web sites evolved into little more than online brochures and catalogs of corporate product lines. These were designed to allow a potential customer to do research and explore products online. Then they could go to the brick and mortar retail outlet or place a phone call order to the company. Since there was no security available online for processing of credit cards, deployment of online sales was minimal. Thousands of companies allowed customers to place credit card orders using basic HTML order forms, which captured the un-encrypted credit card information, recklessly sending potentially harmful personal financial information throughout the internet. As awareness of credit card fraud and theft increased, savvy web customers refrained from placing credit card orders online in fear of comprising personal financial data.

Everything changed with the development of encryption methods and secure site technology. Data could be captured securely, and transmitted over the internet in an encrypted format to protect data online. Since the development of encryption technology, online purchasing has exploded, and is expected to grow exponentially in the future. Small startup companies like **Amazon.com** have grown into online sales powerhouses, and all of these industry giants utilize e-mail marketing as a successful and integral part of their marketing portfolio.

Atlantic Publishing Company (**www.atlantic-pub.com**) is a classic example of how the internet has positively affected their business and marketing operations. In the mid-1990s Atlantic Publishing Company embraced the internet with a very basic Web site, featuring a full list of their product lines, with pricing and ordering information. The Web site featured an online order form, which required the user to enter the items he or she wanted and calculate the item costs and totals. The user was sent, via a secure Web page, to the corporate headquarters for processing. Today, Atlantic Publishing Company features a state-of-the-art Web site boasting a full featured shopping cart, secure online order processing, advanced search capabilities, and simplified navigation. The internet transformed them from a catalog based business into an online publishing powerhouse, producing more than 50 original publications in 2006 on a wide-range of topics. In the late 1990's Atlantic Publishing began to compile opt-in customer lists for deployment of their e-mail marketing campaign. The e-mail marketing campaign was designed to promote their products and serve as an industry news and information service to those who chose to become members of the distribution list. This highly successful marketing campaign has issued more than 150 mailings to up to 100,00 subscribers since inception. A case study of Atlantic Publishing will be discussed throughout this book.

E-MAIL MARKETING

Wikipedia.com defines e-mail marketing as a form of direct marketing which uses electronic mail as a means of communicating commercial or fundraising messages to an audience. This definition means that every e-mail a company sends to its current or potential customers could be considered e-mail marketing.

INTERNET ADVERTISING

Advertising may be defined as any paid form of communication about an organization, its products and/or services by an identified and typically paid sponsor. As we have previously discussed, online marketing and advertising campaigns were designed to replicate existing advertising which was designed for traditional advertising outlets which included print media (newspapers, books & magazines), as well as multi-media advertising which includes television and radio. With the expansion of the Internet, and realization of the potential impact on customer sales base and revenues, online advertising was born.

In 2007, online advertising and marketing has matured and become fairly well refined. We have moved past most of the dynamic and revolutionary changes in the evolution of online advertising and are now seeking to refine existing advertising techniques to garner the most out of a company's marketing investment. Technology, population growth and the increasing number of households with broadband Internet access have pushed advances in technology in the online advertising world, generating billions of dollars in sales annually. The use of online advertising as the primary advertising within corporations is overtaking traditional advertising means.

The potential for developing highly innovative & unique advertisements which draw in potential customers is practically limitless — especially through the powerful e-mail medium. As the internet grew in size and popularity, the amount of money spent on online advertising increased, as did the desire to develop a variety of cost-effective advertising methods which promised a high return for low investment. This is where e-mail marketing fits into the overall picture. It is high-volume, high potential for return at a very low cost, albeit there are some risk factors with it such as spam and blacklists, which will be discussed later.

Joe Lepper from Brand Republic (**www.brandrepulic.com**) reported that "e-mail marketing volume has risen by 30 percent year on year and may soon match direct mail volume." Popular reasons that e-mail marketing has been increasing is because it is seen as cheap and effective. According to The Direct Marketing Association's E-mail Marketing Council's e-mail benchmarking survey shows a rise in click through rates, from six percent to eight percent. Another factor, according to council chairman Richard Gibson, is that marketers are getting better at using e-mail as a marketing tool and in targeting prospects. He said: "The considerable rise in acquisition response rates demonstrates increasing sophistication among clients in terms of their targeting and messaging. The report shows that marketers are continuing to invest in e-mail as a channel and are also taking steps to improve via their provider list hygiene."

TYPES OF ONLINE ADVERTISEMENTS

Four major areas which continue to own the majority of the online marketing share are:

- Paid search advertisement (pay-per-click)

- Banner advertisements

- Classified ads

- E-mail marketing

We will touch on each of these throughout the book so you can understand and gain exposure to each of them; however, the majority of emphasis will be on e-mail marketing to ensure that you gain the most return out of your investment as you develop and implement your e-mail marketing campaign. We will discuss a variety of other advertising methods which will help promote your online business which may be used in conjunction with your e-mail marketing campaign.

UNDERSTANDING BANNER ADVERTISING

Banner Advertising is simply a form of online advertising where web developers embed an advertisement into the HTML code of a Web page. The idea is that the banner advertisement will catch the attention of Web site visitors and they will click on the ad to get more information about the products or services advertised. When clicked, the banner ad will take the Web browser to the Web site operated by the advertiser. A banner ad can be created in a variety of formats such as GIF, JPG, or PNG. Banner ads can be static images or employ a variety of scripting code, Java, or other advanced techniques such as animated GIFs or rollover images to create rotating banner advertisements that change every few seconds. Over the past five years, Shockwave and Macromedia Flash technology have become popular to incorporate animation, sound, and action into banner advertisements. Banner ads are created in a variety of shapes and sizes depending on the site content and design, and are designed to be placed unobtrusively in the "white" space available in a traditionally designed web page. These ads can be static (embedded within the actual page), or they may be served through a central server, which allows advertisers to display a variety of banner ads on different Web sites.

When a page is loaded into a Web browser such as Microsoft Internet Explorer or Mozilla's Firefox, the banner is loaded onto the page creating an impression. An impression simply means that the Web page containing the advertisement was loaded and potentially viewed by someone who is browsing that Web site. Impressions are important to advertisers to track how many visitors loaded that particular page (and banner ad) in a set period of time. If the impression count is low, it is logical that the click through rate, and subsequent sales will also be low. When the Web site visitor clicks on the banner advertisement, the browser is then sent to the Web site, which he or she is linked through the ad. The process of a site visitor clicking on a banner ad with his or her mouse is called a click through. Click through's are important to advertisers to track how many visitors actually clicked on a particular banner ad, and how many resultant sales are generated by the banner ad in a set period of time. Unfortunately, high click through rates do not necessarily guarantee high sales.

Most banner ads currently work on a per-click system, where the advertiser pays for each click on the banner ad, regardless of whether that click results in a sale. Originally, advertisers simply paid for the ad space on a Web site, usually for a preset period of time, and hoped that someone would see the banner ad, and click on it to visit their Web site. Banner advertising is typically a very low cost investment (usually under .10 cents per click), and the banner provider or hosting company then bills the advertiser on a pre-determined basis. The key difference between banner advertising and PPC advertising is that banner advertisements are placed within the content of Web pages, while PPC advertisements are not image based, and may be dynamically generated based on search results.

Banner advertising was extremely popular in the 1990s and early 2000s, and is still commonly used today; however, it is less effective and even less popular than other advertising techniques. Banner advertising is designed to inform potential customers about the products or services offered by the advertiser; however, unlike traditional print advertisements, they offer the advantage of allowing advertisers to track individual statistics and performance at a high level.

When banner ads were originally created, they were highly successful; however as Web surfers became Web savvy, these banner ads, popup ads, and other ads were viewed as annoying and often distracting from the actual Web site content. It was not uncommon to have Web pages loaded with hundreds of banner ads on a single page. Today the standard has improved dramatically, and you typically will not find more than one or two unobtrusive banner advertisements on any Web page. Additionally, Web browsers often contain built in pop-up blockers designed to suppress many banner advertisements.

STATIC VS. DYNAMIC VS. E-MAIL

In the early days of Web site development, Web sites were static in content and were easy to build and maintain; however, they did not offer any interactive type of experience. The development of database driven Web sites created an entirely new experience for the Web site visitor, enabling him or her to enter data into a Web site and receive dynamically generated content based on the query. An example of this is **www.google.com**. Google enables site visitors to search any topic and generates advertisements based on the query.

The development of Web portals, such as **www.yahoo.com** and **www.msn. com** enabled web visitors to personalize their Web browsing experience. Personalization allows a Web site visitor to enter information such as name, age, zip code, and other personal preferences to dynamically deliver customized Web content based on the chosen individual preferences. More advanced Web sites, such as **Amazon.com** can actually make recommendations to site visitors based on his or her profile and preferences, thereby possibly increasing sales and revenue.

With most users today surfing the web on high-speed broadband, Web site developers have been developing rich media. Rich media are advertisements geared toward high speed internet browsers and can display video, audio, music, animations, and special effects. The addition of flashy advertising to interactivity has completed the online experiences where advertisers receive interactive and often entertaining advertisements disguised as music videos, games, and other interactive content, all with the ultimate goal of producing increased Web site traffic and internet sales. Although rich media may be the banner ad of the future, it still has a long way to go to replace traditional banner advertising.

Recently, **www.ecommercetimes.com** reported that rich media ads accounted for only 1.2 percent of the roughly 57.6 million impressions delivered during the period. At the top of the list for the time frame were compound image/text ads with more than 16 million impressions (27.9 percent), followed by sponsored search links with 14.6 million impressions (25.3 percent), standard GIF/JPEG with 13.6 million impressions (23.7 percent), and Flash ads with 12.8 million (22 percent). However, it is estimated that 39 percent of internet ad spending is expected to be on rich media.

Rich media has evolved in the past year into the recycling of television advertisements and incorporating full TV commercials onto the internet. Floating and expanding banners are increasingly popular, and equally frustrating to the Web site visitor. Floating and expanding ads utilize motion and appear to float across the screen, blocking the view of the actual Web site content, often requiring a click to close the ad. However, most are based on a time interval to disappear. Sound embedded in banner advertising is becoming popular. Sound bites are launched with a Web site as an additional attempt to attract site visitors to click on the specific Web site banner. Podcasts, blogs, and RSS broadcasts have become popular in recent years. Large advertisers such as Best Buy, Acura, and Volvo are already sponsoring podcasts. Mobile, or cellular marketing advertising, is growing as the population increases the use of MP3 players, cell phones, and PDAs. You need to understand the clear distinction between this type of advertising and e-mail. Banner advertisements, pay-per-click, rich media, and other similar methods all rely on the fact that you will visit a Web site, see an advertisement, pop-up, or banner ad and click on it, thus taking you to the advertiser's Web site in hopes that you will consider buying their products or reading their sales promotional information. E-mail marketing, on the other hand, is done by pushing the information into your e-mail inbox, thus the advertisement is delivered and presented to you, viewable through your e-mail client.

E-MAIL MARKETING VS. SPAM

E-mail marketing and advertising is certainly not without controversy. You will get in trouble if you abuse anti-spam laws which can lead to legal and financial penalties, including the shutdown of your Web site. Since spam is such a prevalent issue with e-mail marketing, we have dedicated an entire chapter to it.

E-mail marketing is one of the most efficient, and effective methods of online advertising today — enabling you to quickly promote your business online in a cost-effective program while targeting your desired audience — realizing almost instantaneous results. Additionally, it can also be effectively employed to help get your Web site listed at the top of major search engines.

With the background history we have provided in online marketing and advertising, you should have a good understanding of the variety of advertisement campaigns in existence, as well as a brief history of e-mail marketing.

Case Study: Matt Bacak

Given the fact that e-mail is the single most widely used application on the Web. It follows naturally that e-mail marketing is also the most powerful online marketing tool. In a 2004 survey by DoubleClick, a whopping 88 percent of consumers said that they had made an online or offline purchase as a consequence of receiving an online marketing e-mail.

To harness the sales power of e-mails and create an effective e-mail marketing campaign businesses have to understand not only the benefits of e-mail marketing but also how to create e-mails that encourage buying action amongst consumers.

Benefits of e-mail marketing campaigns:

• More effective than traditional direct marketing

• Makes it easier to track the response rate and actual success of the marketing campaign for future reference

Case Study: Matt Bacak

- E-mail marketing campaigns are extremely economical compared to direct marketing or offline marketing strategies

- The response rate for e-mail marketing campaigns is five times greater than it is for direct mailing campaigns and 25 times greater than banner ads

- There is a quick response time with almost 85% of the responses coming within 48 hours of the online marketing campaign

If you are serious about promoting your business via online marketing then e-mail marketing is definitely the most economical, efficient and effective method.

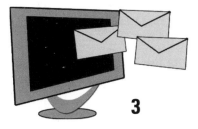

3

INTRODUCTION TO E-MAIL MARKETING

E-mail marketing is a tool in your overall online and offline marketing portfolio. E-mail marketing allows you to disseminate information about your company, products, or services to thousands of recipients with the click of a mouse key. To be fair, if you want a successful and spam-free campaign, it does take some planning, design, and organization to ensure your e-mail marketing campaign is optimized for success. If you have a personal computer and check your e-mail, then you are already familiar with e-mail marketing, since you most likely get it multiple times per day, often unsolicited and unwanted!

E-mail marketing is defined as the promotion of products or services via e-mail. E-mail is a very versatile and widely used form of communication. Thanks to advancements in technology with e-mail clients and the offer of free e-mail accounts from industry giants such as Google and Yahoo, e-mail is affordable, readily available and used by nearly everyone both at work and home. E-mail formats can be simple text-based or more complex HTML embedding graphics, and advanced Web site design techniques. The content of an e-mail can be customized based on size, target audience, and you can have scheduled deliveries, nearly automating the entire process. Of course, one the biggest benefits is that overall costs for implementing an e-mail marketing campaign are very low, especially when compared to other traditional advertising means.

You will need some in-house expertise to develop an effective e-mail marketing campaign, which includes personnel with Web design experience, as well as graphic artists who can created the embedded graphics, as well as provide input to the overall design and appeal of the e-mail marketing campaign.

E-MAIL MARKETING IS IDEAL FOR:

- Businesses with products to sell

- Businesses wishing to distribute news

- Businesses who wish to maintain contact with customers

- Businesses wishing to promote new business lines, products & services

- Businesses seeking to increase revenue

- Businesses who seek to announce special events

- Businesses who seek to offer coupons or discounts to customers

- Businesses who strive to save money on advertising costs or have a limited advertising budget

- Small, independent businesses competing with industry leaders

- Businesses seeking to expand their customer base or reach into new market areas

E-MAIL MARKETING IS NOT IDEAL FOR (NOR WILL IT WORK FOR):

- Businesses who wish to harvest e-mail names from the Web using a harvesting program to build their e-mail lists (harvesting programs scan Web sites collecting any e-mail addressed listed on their site (i.e. you@yourcompany.com) enabling them to add these harvested e-mails to their list. This is illegal, unethical, and will not be successful. Harvesting is a big business — there are companies who are profitable harvesting e-mail addresses and selling them to others. Harvesting can be targeted by keyword, allowing you to harvest e-mail from Web sites that have specific terms on them, thus targeting the audience.

- Businesses that engage in the creation of spam.

- Businesses that promote illegal activity, pornography, etc.

- Businesses that promote marketing schemes, financial scams, and other fraudulent hoaxes. (i.e. helping the son of the deposed King of some country you have never heard of before by giving him your bank account so he can transfer his billions of dollars and escape his country, letting you keep a few million for your help. Hint: this is a scam.)

- Businesses who buy CD's containing hundreds of thousands of e-mail addresses from the e-mail harvesters hoping to quickly establish an e-mail list of new customers.

E-MAIL ABUSE AND SPAM

Along with the power of e-mail comes the abuse of e-mail, commonly known as spam. Is spam e-mail considered e-mail marketing? Technically, the answer is yes, but it is certainly not responsible e-mail marketing. Chapter Four is dedicated to the understanding (and avoidance) of spam. As an e-mail marketer, spam is your biggest threat. You do not want to be accused of being a spammer. While it may often be difficult to distinguish between permission based e-mail marketing and e-mail spam, it is something you need to be very familiar with.

I have stated before that e-mail marketing should be a part of a well-balanced advertising and marketing portfolio. I recommend you diversify and implement other marketing and advertising techniques in addition to e-mail marketing. By itself, e-mail marketing has some great advantages. E-mail marketing allows you to reach out to your customers and draw them into your Web site; however, another way of drawing in customers is through PPC advertising, which is an ideal companion to an e-mail marketing campaign. It is important to keep in mind that with PPC advertising you do not pay to have your advertisement loaded on a web page, unlike other paid advertising campaigns where you pay for the campaign itself (such as in e-mail marketing) in hopes of generating customers and revenues. With PPC advertising, you do not pay to have your advertisement listed at the top of search engines and you only pay for results. In other words,

PPC advertising is entirely no cost (minus potential setup costs), even if your advertisement is viewed by millions of Web site visitors.

I wanted to touch on PPC marketing as well as other low or no cost marketing techniques which you will find in my two previous books. Of course, I have to emphasize the importance of proper search engine optimization (SEO) as an integral part of your Web design and implementation plan. We will touch on the principles of SEO later in this book. A Web site that is not user friendly, easy to navigate, and organized will not yield you the best results from e-mail marketing campaigns. You, as an advertiser, Web site owner, or corporate manager, will admire the simplicity and fast response rates through e-mail marketing campaigns.

E-MAIL MARKETING WALKTHROUGH

As you move forward with plans to implement an e-mail marketing campaign, you will follow these basic steps. Each will be explained in detail in this chapter:

- Plan your e-mail marketing campaign

- Target your audience and content

- Write and design your e-mail

- Setup your online mail distribution method

- Review your e-mail list

- Test your e-mail

- Schedule your e-mail blast

- Send your e-mail blast

- Analyze results

PLAN YOUR E-MAIL MARKETING CAMPAIGN

The biggest challenge you will face is the actual design of your e-mail marketing campaign. While there is a chapter dedicated to how to accomplish this seemingly overwhelming task, there are several principles you must decide upon before you can enter the design phase. You must determine what your desired results are and how best to capture that in a single e-mail. It is important that you identify up front what your goals and objectives are with your e-mail campaign. For example, your goal may be to distribute industry relevant news, articles, or information, or it may be to promote specific new products which you can provide. The best advice when designing an e-mail marketing campaign is to start small and think clearly. In other words, do not try to reach all of your business objectives in one single e-mail that will overwhelm and turn off any potential customers. Compile a list of the many objectives you would like to achieve, then start with the simplest and go from there — it may be as simple as an introduction to your company, a short summary of information, and a discount coupon for placing their first order. Sending an e-mail with introductions, news articles, product information, discounts, subscription offers, and other useful information will saturate your customers with information overload. Introduce them to your company, give them an incentive to go to your Web site, and let your business win them over. As you build successive e-mail campaigns, you can target products, provide industry relevant information, advice, and news, and build your e-mail client list.

TARGET YOUR AUDIENCE & CONTENT

One of the advantages of an e-mail marketing campaign is the ability to target your audience. I have an entire chapter dedicated to targeting your audience but it is important to realize that you may be able to (depending on your e-mail list) target from a wide variety of demographical or geographical information, or even limit your campaign to your specific local area.

WRITE & DESIGN YOUR E-MAIL

Writing an effective e-mail can be a challenge. I have an entire chapter dedicated to how to write an effective e-mail, which will assist you with ensuring your message is optimized for effectiveness. You will need to decide if you want to use text-based e-mail or HTML (or both). In addition, you will need to ensure your e-mail is balanced, error-free, and is properly formatted to be displayed in the recipients' e-mail client. There is also a chapter dedicated to the subject line, which is often the most confusing and important part of your campaign. How you deliver your message is critical to the success of your campaign. If your recipient does not open your e-mail, it is a failure. Therefore, you must capture the interest of the recipient to at least open your e-mail, and hopefully click through to your Web site. Obviously, if your goal is to sell products through your e-mail marketing campaign, its success hinges on the ability to actually close the deal and ultimately sell products on your site, as a result of your e-mail marketing campaign.

SET UP YOUR ONLINE MAIL DISTRIBUTION METHOD

This is detailed in later chapters, but the important message to take from this chapter is that help is out there. There are many companies which offer all-in-one solutions for managing your e-mail lists, creating and sending your e-mail campaigns, tracking statistics, and offering well-designed templates to simplify the process of designing your e-mail campaigns. We will take a close look at many of the industry leaders, as well as my personal recommendations which balance features versus cost. In addition, there are many industry professionals who will manage your entire e-mail campaign. Many of these industry experts contributed tips and tricks to help you maximize your e-mail campaign for success. We highly recommend you use either an all-in-one solution provider or one of the industry experts to manage your e-mail campaigns. Do not attempt to send out e-mail marketing campaigns through your local e-mail client or you likely find yourself suspended for spamming through your Internet Service Provider, nor should you use one of the many e-mail bulk e-mail provider who offer to send your e-mail to hundreds of thousands of recipients for one low fee. Know your service provider and have confidence in the quality of your list. Do not use overseas providers to send your e-mail to recipients who did not ask to receive it. The penalties are not worth the gain.

REVIEW YOUR E-MAIL LIST

If you have not yet picked up on it, your list is important. A quality e-mail list of opt-in recipients is a valuable asset to your company. An entire chapter is dedicated to expanding and growing your e-mail leads. Protect your e-mail list — it is valuable. We will discuss renting and buying lists in Chapter Six, as well as proven techniques to improve the quality and quantity of names on your list. Most all-in-one service providers provide you with HTML code for subscriptions, simplifying the process of allowing Web site visitors to join your mailing list.

TEST YOUR E-MAIL

One of the most important (and often overlooked) steps in the development of your e-mail marketing campaign is to test e-mails before you actually send them. You need to test your e-mails, open them in a variety of e-mail clients so that the format, appearance, etc is exactly as intended. In addition, you should test each look in the document to ensure that is works properly. If you send an e-mail with mistakes, errors, or broken lists, you will lose potential customers fast! Be sure to pay special attention to the embedded graphics in your e-mails by viewing your e-mail on a computer other than the one you created your e-mail campaign. Many times I have seen e-mails sent out using relative links instead of absolute links, which can be critical if you are pulling images into your e-mail from other Web servers. An absolute link defines a specific location of the Web file or document including the protocol to use to get the document, the server to get it from, the directory it is located in, and the name of the document or file, such as:

<a href="http://www.myWeb site.com/graphic.png"></a>

A relative link will not work in an e-mail because, unlike a web page on a web server, it does not already know the domain URL and where the document or image is located. An example of a relative link is:

<a href="graphic.png"></a>

Since the domain name and HTTP:// is not included with this, the recipient e-mail client does not know where to pull the graphic file from, and thus it will not be displayed in your e-mail. Bottom line — use absolute links when developing e-mail marketing campaigns. When you are satisfied with the quality, quantity, and functionality of your e-mail, it is time to schedule it.

SCHEDULE YOUR E-MAIL BLAST

Chapter 11 provides a detailed analysis and recommendations for when is the best day/time to blast your e-mail campaigns; however, this is based on industry analysis and is not a guaranteed of improved performance. You know your customers, and this guide will help you determine the most effective time and day to schedule your e-mail blasts.

SEND YOUR E-MAIL BLAST

The act of sending your e-mail is actually the simplest. By utilizing an all-in-one solution provider or e-mail campaign manager this will be scheduled far in advance. You will not have to do anything except wait for results once your e-mail campaign is developed, tested, scheduled, and actually launched.

ANALYZE RESULTS

Similar to testing your e-mail before actually sending it, analyzing the results is often overlooked. You must analyze the results if want to understand what is effective, and what is not effective for your business. All-in-one solution providers will supply you with plentiful data including volume rates, bounce rates, open rates, and click through rates. We will discuss each of these in detail throughout this book. Understanding what is working, and what is not is critical as you develop and refine your e-mail marketing campaign.

E-mail marketing is, of course, limited by the size of your advertising budget, but is one of the most cost-effective methods of advertising you will find. We will discuss costs, volume, and overage rates in later chapters so you can properly budget and plan for your e-mail marketing campaign.

Case Study: Manoj R. Source

E-mail marketing is one of the affordable ways to market products and services. This is because it's very popular and has the best reputation in bringing targeted traffic to Web sites. E-mail marketing can be used to build rapport with your customers, send out promotions, or make special offers.

Your e-mail can be as easy as writing a plain announcement or you can add some bells and whistles and make it a newsletter. However e-mail marketing is not just like sending e-mails to your friends and relatives. Here are some simple tips in doing e-mail marketing in the best way possible.

1. Join the "Can Spam" campaign

E-mail marketing is not at any rate tantamount to spamming. You are not supposed to send information that your e-mail list will not have any valuable use for.

Case Study: Manoj R. Source

2. Open rate

Your e-mail might get lost with the hundreds of e-mails that inbox owners are confronted with everyday. Improve your subject line by using extra white space creatively, adding text symbols, starting each word with a capital letter, asking compelling questions, not making any unbelievable claims, and not using the word FREE.

3. Don't use hype

Not including any too good to be true statements is not only applicable to your subject line. Your e-mail content must never embody any promise your business can't keep. Make your offer genuinely of value to your recipients.

4. Do not sell yourself cheap

If you inform your customers regarding discounts, minimal discounts are not that effective compared with substantial discounts. But never offer discounts that are lower than your profit. It will defeat the purpose of this e-mail marketing effort.

5. Inform people about events

It's not about contradicting the advice that you should keep an e-mail short and sweet. This tip is on including seminars, conferences and other events in your e-mail. Businesses that require training benefit much from this method. With these RSVP-requiring e-mails, repetition is important. Just make sure that an ample interval is considered before sending out a reminder e-mail.

6. Inform your audience

Sending newsletters and postcards provides useful information for your subscribers. These are the best forms of reaching out to your customers or prospects. You should keep the information short, simple, and direct to the point for this feat to be effective.

With these simple ways of going about your e-mail marketing endeavor, your business will prosper within a short period of time.

4

SPAM, SPAM, SPAM!

Wikipedia.com states that, "E-mail spam is the most common form of internet spamming. It involves sending unsolicited commercial messages to many recipients. Unlike legitimate commercial e-mail, spam is generally sent without the explicit permission of the recipients, and frequently contains various tricks to bypass e-mail filtering."

We mentioned earlier that most spammers buy bulk e-mail addresses from un-reputable resellers, or through a variety of means such as harvesting them from Usenet postings, domain name DNS listings, or Web pages. They may also use commonly used e-mail addresses with your domain such as (sales@, admin@, support@, service@, etc) or use specialized Web spider software to steal e-mail addresses from Web sites and other lists.

Another major concern with spamming is the spoofing of e-mail addresses. Spoofing is a method for concealing the identity of the sender, and making you believe the e-mail is in fact from a reputable business. With spoofing, the spammer modifies the e-mail message so it appears to come from another e-mail account. Spoofing can occur with any e-mail account or domain name. For example, you may get an e-mail from Bruce Brown with the e-mail address of bruce@email. com), which may be a legitimate e-mail account, thus avoiding spam filters and giving you, the recipient, peace of mind believe that the e-mail is a legitimate e-mail from a reputable or known source. Spoofing can cause you a multitude of headaches. As the recipient of the e-mails you can become bombarded by spoofed e-mails, many which appear to be legitimate. Dealing with spoofed e-mails is frustrating and time consuming. As the Web site or domain name owner it is much worse. Typically, bounced e-mails are sent back to the spoofed domain e-mail account — yours! You may find that you are receiving replies, bounced e-mails, and nasty grams for an e-mail which you never sent. The main goal behind spoofed e-mails is to release privacy information or passwords to third parties who will use them against your business. If you suspect spoofing of your e-mail accounts or want more detailed information about spoofing, you should contact the Cert Coordination Center at **www.cert.org**.

Most spammers are after privacy and/or financial data, or offer illicit activities such as pornography, get rich quick schemes, pirated software, or overseas business scams. The best combatants against Spam are anti-spam filters, junk mail filters, and specialized software at the e-mail server and the mail client to protect your e-mail accounts.

PHISHING

Another major threat is phishing (not to be confused with fishing). Phishing is actually a variation on the word "fishing" which means that "phishers" will throw out baited Web sites hoping someone will "bite." **Webopedia.com** defines phishing as, "The act of sending an e-mail to a user falsely claiming to be an established legitimate enterprise in an attempt to scam the user into surrendering private information that will be used for identity theft." Typically, this Web site will asks the visitor to enter personal information such as social security numbers, credit card numbers, etc. This Web site, however, is false and is only there to steal the visitor's information. In 2003, eBay users received an e-mail that was supposedly from eBay. This e-mail told them that their account was about to be suspsended and requested that they visit the Web site link contained in the e-mail and enter in their personal information. The Web site that the customers were taken to appeared like the official eBay site, thus further making customers think that the e-mail was legitimate. The phisher who created the site collected the customers' information and used it to steal their money.

The key difference between operating legal permission-based e-mail campaigns and spam is the use of permission-based or opt-in e-mail lists. Spam or junk e-mail is e-mail that is sent to one or more recipients who did not request it. We will discuss the differences in detail between opt-in and opt-out lists in the next chapter, but it is important that you have a clear understanding on what spam is and how it can affect your business.

CAN-SPAM ACT

The CAN-SPAM Act of 2003 (Controlling the Assault of Non-Solicited Pornography and Marketing Act) establishes requirements for those who send commercial e-mail, spells out penalties for spammers and companies whose products are advertised in spam if they violate the law, and gives consumers the right to ask e-mailers to stop spamming them. The law, which became effective January 1, 2004, covers e-mail which has the primary purpose of is advertising or promoting a commercial product or service, including content on a Web site. A transactional or relationship message — e-mail that facilitates an agreed-upon transaction or updates a customer in an existing business relationship — may not contain false or misleading routing information, but otherwise is exempt from most provisions of the CAN-SPAM Act according to the Federal Trade Commission.

The Federal Trade Commission (FTC), the nation's consumer protection agency, is authorized to enforce the CAN-SPAM Act. CAN-SPAM also gives the Department of Justice (DOJ) the authority to enforce its criminal sanctions. Other federal and state agencies can enforce the law against organizations under their jurisdiction, and companies that provide Internet access may sue violators, as well.

Several years ago, a former client, chose to launch an ill-advised e-mail campaign. He bought numerous e-mail lists from mostly un-reputable list clearing houses and imported more than 100,000 e-mail addresses into their e-mail management program. He set off on his campaign and launched multiple e-mails with some very surprising and disturbing results. Instead of receiving his e-mail campaign with open arms, he had an almost 40 percent bounce rate (not uncommon for harvested lists), and nearly another 30 percent had requested to be removed or had removed themselves. Many of these unsubscribe requests were extremely nasty and threatening. Within a week he found out the e-mail marketing provider had shut down his account for suspected spam activity, and a few days later his Web site hosting company had terminated his Web site under threat of legal action from the backbone provider. This meant that his entire online business was shut down within days for being accused of spam. Luckily, he had backups of his entire Web site and was able to move his domain name to another Web hosting company and re-establish his Web site; however, this process left him essentially out of business for nearly 72 hours and permanently out of the e-mail marketing business.

One tip you may find invaluable to your Web based business is when you establish a new Web site, often you buy the domain through your Web hosting company.

Thus, they purchase it and typically put it in their name, meaning they are the administrative and technical contact on it. This means that only they can access it to change important information such as DNS entries. If you find yourself in a disagreement with a Web hosting company and need to move fast, you will find yourself dead in the water if your Web hosting company controls your domain names. Always buy your own domain names. Register them for you or your business and put yourself as the administrative, technical, and billing point of contact with a good e-mail address. The only domain name registrar I recommend is GoDaddy (**www.godaddy.com**). They have the best prices, best service, and most advanced control panel, giving you 100 percent control over all your domain names within a single, easy to navigate interface. In fact, if you want to consolidate all of your existing domain names from multiple registrars you can do that into one **GoDaddy.com** account and you will even add a year onto each registration just for moving them to **GoDaddy.com**. Though not really related to the subject of spam, this tip will ultimately save you headaches and heartache down the road.

Let us take a close look at what the CAN-SPAM Act is actually comprised of.

CAN-SPAM ACT REQUIREMENTS

- **Bans false or misleading header information.** Your e-mail's "From," "To," and routing information — including the originating domain name and e-mail address — must be accurate and identify the person who initiated the e-mail.

- **Prohibits deceptive subject lines.** The subject line cannot mislead the recipient about the contents or subject matter of the message.

- **Requires that your e-mail give recipients an opt-out method.** You must provide a return e-mail address or another Internet-based response mechanism that allows a recipient to ask you not to send future e-mail messages to that e-mail address, and you must honor the requests. You may create a "menu" of choices to allow a recipient to opt-out of certain types of messages, but you must include the option to end any commercial messages from the sender. Any opt-out mechanism you offer must be able to process opt-out requests for at least 30 days after you send your commercial e-mail. When you receive an opt-out request, the law gives you ten business days to stop sending e-mail to the requestor's e-mail address. You cannot help another entity send e-mail to that address or have another entity send e-mail on your behalf to that address. Finally, it is illegal for you to sell or transfer the e-mail addresses of people who choose not to receive your e-mail, even in the form of a mailing list, unless you transfer the addresses so another entity can comply with the law.

- **Requires that commercial e-mail be identified as an advertisement and include the sender's valid physical postal address.** Your message must contain clear and conspicuous notice that the message is an advertisement or solicitation and that the recipient can opt-out of receiving more commercial e-mail from you. It also must include your valid physical postal address.

Penalties for each violation of the CAN-Spam Act are subject to fines of up to $11,000. Deceptive commercial e-mail also is subject to laws banning false or misleading advertising. Additional fines are provided for commercial e-mailers who not only violate the rules described above, but also:

- Harvest e-mail addresses from Web sites or Web services that have published a notice prohibiting the transfer of e-mail addresses for the purpose of sending e-mail

- Generate e-mail addresses using a "dictionary attack" — combining names, letters, or numbers into multiple permutations

- Use scripts or other automated ways to register for multiple e-mail or user accounts to send commercial e-mail

- Relay e-mails through a computer or network without permission — for example, by taking advantage of open relays or open proxies without authorization

The law allows the Department of Justice to seek criminal penalties, including imprisonment, for commercial e-mailers who do or conspire to:

- Use another computer without authorization and send commercial e-mail from or through it

- Use a computer to relay or retransmit multiple commercial e-mail messages to deceive or mislead recipients or an Internet access service about the origin of the message

- Falsify header information in multiple e-mail messages and initiate the transmission of such messages

- Register for multiple e-mail accounts or domain names using information that falsifies the identity of the actual registrant

- Falsely represent themselves as owners of multiple Internet Protocol addresses that are used to send commercial e-mail messages

Additional rules have been added to the CAN-SPAM Act by the FTC. These rules involve labeling sexually explicit commercial e-mail and also the criteria for determining the primary purpose of a commercial e-mail. See the FTC Web site at **www.ftc.gov/spam** for updates on implementation of the CAN-SPAM Act.

Most recipients of bulk e-mail, spam or unsolicited advertisements view them as unwelcome, unpleasant, or offensive. However, there are many mailing lists which deliver solicited (opt-in) useful information to recipients based on a variety of subjects they have expressed an interest in and have given their permission to allow companies to add their e-mail address to bulk mailing lists. The key to utilizing e-mail as a tool for marketing or advertising is to build your customer lists using opt-in methods (or double-opt-in) to ensure that your e-mail lists comply with the requirements of the CAN-SPAM Act. We will fully discuss opt-in and opt-out in the next chapter.

According to **Wikipedia.com**, "the California legislature found that spam cost United States organizations alone more than $10 billion in 2004, including lost productivity and the additional equipment, software, and manpower needed to combat the problem." Spam has had many direct effects on businesses including the consumption of computer and network resources, the time spent correcting the issues, and the time spent dismissing unwanted messages. These costs do not include the various costs associated with actually sending the spam and the costs related to stopping the spam. In addition, these costs do not take into further account the costs of the crimes, such as identity theft, that are a direct result of spam.

SPAM TOOLS

Luckily there are numerous, reputable resources available to assist you with identifying and combating spam, spoofing, and phishing, and I have outlined the best of them for you:

- http://spam.abuse.net — Contains an ongoing listing of spam related news, articles, and information;

- http://www.ftc.gov/spam — The official spam site for the Federal Trade Commission. Outlines the laws for consumers, businesses, and current penalties for violation Anti-Spam laws. You can file spam complaints by clicking the "File a Complaint" link on the home page.

- http://www.spamlaws.com — I like this site because it has all the most recent legislation and laws from the United States, Europe, and other countries, as well as state laws and selected case history.

- http://www.cauce.org — The Coalition Against Unsolicited Commercial E-mail. A group whose primary purpose is to advocate for a legislative solution to the problem of unsolicited commercial e-mail.

- http://www.spamcop.net — SpamCop determines the origin of unwanted e-mail and reports it to the relevant Internet service providers. Reporting unsolicited e-mail also helps feed spam filtering systems including, but not limited to, SpamCop's own service.

In addition, there are several commercial, off-the-shelf, or web-based products which can help you combat spam, in addition to filters in Microsoft Outlook and Outlook Express. These include, but are not limited to:

- Bullguard Internet Security Suite 7

- AVG Internet Security 7.5

- Norton Internet Security 2007

- Vanquish 4.0

- Kaspersky Personal Security Suite 1.0

- Yahoo! Mail

- SpamCatcher 4

- OnlyMyEmail Personal

- InBoxer 2.0

- Vanquish Anti-Spam 3.0

- SpamBully

As an e-mail marketer, it is critical that you understand what is, and what is not spam, spoofing, and phishing so you can avoid it. You do not want to be associated with being a spammer. You may be wondering how you get started building a good e-mail list when you can simply buy one and get started. I will cover how to grow your e-mail list in Chapter 6, and there may be times when buying names is actually okay, but I will give you some other advice to help you acquire e-mail addresses which will be a valuable asset to company.

This book is designed to make sure that you implement a successful, cost-effective e-mail marketing campaign. With spam being in the spotlight, there has been an ongoing debate about the true cost and effectiveness of e-mail campaigns and the effect of spam regulations on the success of e-mail campaigns. The next few articles in this chapter highlight many of these issues. Although some take a hard stance against the profitability of e-mail marketing, I present them as alternative opinions. If done properly and carefully, your e-mail marketing campaign can be effective and profitable for your business.

Case Study: Gold Lasso

How to Handle Spam Complaints

U.S. Congress passed the CAN-SPAM Act of 2003 for implementation on January 1, 2004 to address the issue of unsolicited commercial e-mail (UCE) or spam. Since the act's implementation, organizations have updated their e-mail marketing strategies to comply with the regulations. Consumer concern and attention on the proliferation of spam, despite the government's passage of the CAN-SPAM act, has led to both legitimate and illegitimate complaints lodged against commercial e-marketers.

Organizations using e-mail marketing as a part of their overall communications plan can utilize a variety of tactics to effectively manage and reduce spam complaints. The purpose of this document is to:

Case Study: Gold Lasso

- Educate organizations and marketers on the basics of the CAN-SPAM Act by weeding through the jargon and presenting the basics requirements. Marketers should understand and be qualified to discuss their organization's compliance with service providers and other members of their staff and leadership.

- Define spam complaints and summarize the consequences of receiving them.

- Provide solutions and tips for organizations to reduce spam complaints.

Provisions – Short and Simple

The Federal Trade Commission (FTC) is the government regulatory body responsible for implementing the CAN-SPAM Act and managing complaints lodged against e-marketers. The main provisions of the CAN-SPAM Act, or Controlling the Assault of Non-Solicited Pornography and Marketing Act, are summarized below:

- It bans false or misleading header information. The e-mail's "from," "to," and routing information must be accurate in the header. This includes the originating domain name and e-mail address.

- It prohibits deceptive subject lines. The subject line cannot mislead the recipient about the contents or subject of the message.

- It requires that the e-mail gives recipients an opt-out method that must be available for 30 days after the commercial message is sent. After receiving an opt-out request, the marketer has 10 days to comply.

- It is illegal for the marketer to sell or transfer the e-mail addresses of people who choose not to receive messages, even in the form of a mailing list, unless they transfer the addresses so another entity can comply with the law.

- Commercial e-mail must be identified as an advertisement and include the sender's valid, physical postal address.

Penalties

The FTC assesses fines for each violation of CAN-SPAM of up to $11,000. The Act also stipulates additional fines for commercial e-mailers that:

- Harvest e-mail addresses from Web sites or Web services that have published a notice prohibiting the transfer of e-mail addresses for the purpose of sending e-mail. Harvesting is defined as trolling Web sites to

Case Study: Gold Lasso

- Generate e-mail addresses using a dictionary attack — combining names, letters, or numbers into multiple permutations.

- Use of scripts or other automated ways to register for multiple e-mail or user accounts to send commercial e-mail.

- Relay of e-mails through a computer or network without permission — for example, by taking advantage of open relays or open proxies without authorization. An open relay is an SMTP e-mail server that allows outsiders to relay e-mail messages that are neither for nor from local users. This method is often exploited by spammers and hackers. An open proxy is an Internet proxy server which is accessible by unauthorized users, specifically those from elsewhere on the internet.

Additionally, the law allows the Department of Justice (DOJ) to seek criminal penalties, including imprisonment, for commercial e-mailers who do, or conspire to:

- Use another computer without authorization and send commercial e-mail from or through it.

- Use a computer to relay or retransmit multiple commercial e-mail messages to deceive or mislead recipients or an Internet access service about the origin of the message.

- Falsify header information in multiple e-mail messages and initiate the transmission of such messages.

- Register for multiple e-mail accounts or domain names using information that falsifies the identity of the actual registrant.

- Falsely represent themselves as owners of multiple Internet Protocol (IP) addresses that are used to send commercial e-mail messages.

Spam Complaints: What are they? How do you deal with them?

When a recipient officially accuses a commercial e-mailer of sending unsolicited e-mail it is considered a "spam complaint." Complaints can be lodged through the FTC or through an online complaint service such as SpamCop (**www.spamcop.net**). The major Internet Service Providers (ISPs) also provide a report button that allows the recipient to lodge a complaint when they receive a message.

In reality, e-marketers will receive spam complaints regardless of the tactics they use to prevent them. The acceptable industry standard is one complaint per 1,000 messages. If the complaint-to-message-sent ratio passes that threshold, future messages may be blocked and the e-mailer can be blacklisted.

Case Study: Gold Lasso

The first step in managing spam complaints is to have access to any complaints lodged against the organization. Periodic reviews of spam complaints allow marketers to monitor a campaign and take steps, as necessary, if levels of complaints increase or delivery rates fall due to spam filters. E-mail Service Providers (ESPs) are able to provide this data; however, organizations should be aware of simple steps to ensure access to complaints:

- Register the above addresses with **abuse.net**, a clearinghouse for registered abuse addresses used by many network administrators and tools to route complaints to the proper destination.

- Register for a feedback loop. AOL's feedback loop, for example, is set up as part of its whitelisting process.

- Provide complaint instructions in privacy and anti-spam policies. Often less tech-savvy recipients want to complain to the organization directly, but do not know how. A general best practice is to link to an online privacy policy from the e-mail's footer.

Proactive management of your complaints is essential to avoid blacklists and effectively communicate via e-mail.

What are the steps marketers can take to avoid spam complaints?

Brand Subject Lines

If the recipient's mail system offers a spam complaint button it is often available when the message arrives in the inbox allowing a recipient to delete the message before it is read. Branding the subject line with the organization's name or recognizable terms will increase the likelihood the recipient will open it and respond to the call to action in the message.

Add Unsubscribe Information to the Header and Footer

Consider adding unsubscribe information and instructions to both the header and footer of the e-mail message to avoid recipients using the "report spam" button (if available) as a means to unsubscribe/opt-out of a list.

Request Recipients Whitelist Domain Name

Include instructions for recipients to whitelist the organization's domain name allowing it to pass through spam filters. Customization of profiles allow the recipient to customize his or her profile and manage the messages he or she will receive. Also, inform the recipient how his or her e-mail address will be used and the volume of messages expected.

Case Study: Gold Lasso

Avoid Spam Triggers

Create messages using content and formatting that does not trigger spam filters. Avoid bold fonts; large, red-colored fonts; poor quality images; use of all capitals in the subject line or body of e-mail; use of words such as "free, trial, money, quote, sample, membership and access;" and excessive punctuation (!!!). Instead use relevant terms in the subject and body and include the date and/or issue number of newsletters or e-zines.

Spam Checkers

Discuss the use of spam checkers with your ESP. Spam checkers test the message for spam triggers prior to distribution to the designated list.

Relevance

Ensure the message is relevant to the recipient to increase readership and response. It may include segmenting the distribution list and personalizing the content instead of sending a mass e-mail.

Verifying Opt-In Status

Using an opt-in list is an essential element of e-marketing. Unfortunately, it does not mean recipients may not lodge complaints. If a complaint occurs from a recipient that has opted-in to receive messages, send an apology message but show the means and date of their initial opt-in status. Based on the opt-in information verify if they want to continue subscribing to the list.

Conclusion

Although the FTC implemented the CAN-SPAM Act more than two years ago, its requirements must remain on the forefront of an organization's e-marketing strategy to avoid excessive spam complaints. If ignored, excessive complaints can lead to failed message delivery and ultimately, the organization may find itself on a black list.

Reviewing any complaints lodged as well as the delivery data from e-marketing campaigns is the first step to addressing potential problems before they get to the level of action from the FTC or DOJ. It is also essential to ensure the recipient perceives marketing messages as "legitimate."

GOLD LASSO, LLC
Corporate Headquarters: **301-990-9857 Phone**
312 Main Street, Suite 200 **301-990-9856 Fax**
Gaithersburg, MD 20878 **www.goldlasso.com**
info@goldlasso.com

Case Study: Federal Trade Commission

Operation Secure Your Server

Campaign Urges Organizations to Close Open Relays and Proxies to Prevent Them from Unwittingly Sending Spam

The United States Federal Trade Commission and 36 additional agencies in 26 countries today announced "Operation Secure Your Server," an international effort to reduce the flow of unsolicited commercial e-mail by urging organizations to close "open relays" and "open proxies." As part of the initiative, the participating agencies have identified tens of thousands of owners or operators of potentially open relay or open proxy servers around the world, and the agencies are sending letters urging the owners and operators to protect themselves from becoming unwitting sources of spam.

Open relays and open proxies are servers that allow any computer in the world to "bounce" or route e-mail through servers of other organizations, thereby disguising the real origin of the e-mail. Spammers often abuse these servers to flood the Internet with unwanted e-mail. Their abuses not only overload servers, but also could damage an unwitting business' reputation if it appears that the business sent the spam.

"Operation Secure Your Server" provides businesses with simple, inexpensive ways to protect their computer systems from misuse. The FTC suggests that businesses consider these questions to determine whether their proxy servers are vulnerable:

- Does your proxy allow connections from un-trusted networks such as the Internet?

- Are you using the most current version of your proxy software and hardware?

- Have you applied the latest available patches or upgrades?

- Are you using proper access controls for your server? Is someone regularly checking for unauthorized uses of your proxy server?

- Do you have and monitor an "abuse@<yourdomain>" e-mail account where people can report abuses of your proxy server?

"International cooperation is going to play an important role in combating spam, as this project clearly demonstrates," said Howard Beales, Director of the FTC's Bureau of Consumer Protection. Moreover, "government cannot solve the spam problem on its own; everyone with an Internet connection must do their part to make sure that they are part of the solution and not part of the problem."

Case Study: Federal Trade Commission

The FTC has created a Web page, **www.ftc.gov/secureyourserver,** that contains information for businesses on how to protect themselves from becoming unwitting distributors of spam. In addition to the agencies' letter, which is available in 21 languages, the site contains business education and links to other resources.

The FTC and agencies in Albania, Argentina, Australia, Canada, Brazil, Bulgaria, Canada, Chile, Colombia, Denmark, Ecuador, Finland, Hungary, Jamaica, Japan, Lithuania, Norway, Panama, Peru, Romania, Serbia, Singapore, South Korea, Switzerland, Taiwan, and the United Kingdom are sponsoring this initiative.

This year's "Operation Secure Your Server" follows on the heels of last year's campaign against open relays, when the FTC and participating national and international agencies identified businesses with potential open relays, urged them to close the relays, and sent information on how to do so.

Case Study: Linda Formichelli

Erica Shames knew something was wrong when her latest advertising campaign resulted in ten new subscriptions for her regional lifestyle magazine, Susquehanna Life — and more than four hundred complaints.

"As a one-person operation I'm always looking for cost-effective ways to increase my readership," Shames explains. "So I thought it was fortuitous when I received an e-mail from a company called IMC Marketing that said they could e-mail my ad to 250,000 people for only $199. I put together an ad and the company promised to send it out on the following Monday. I was so excited!"

That Monday, the complaints started trickling in. "Some asked how I got their e-mail address. Others wrote nasty letters and reported me to the FCC, the state District Attorney and my Internet Service Provider, who gave me a big reprimand," says Shames. "I felt like a little kid getting slapped in the face and not understanding why. I had never heard of spam until people started reacting to my ad." (IMC Marketing declined to be interviewed for this article.)

Spam is the popular term for unsolicited commercial e-mail that's sent in bulk. The name most likely comes from a Monty Python skit featuring a group of Vikings in a restaurant who repeatedly sing an annoying song consisting mostly of the word "spam." By the end of the skit the spam song, which started out as background noise, becomes so loud that it completely drowns out the other participants.

Shames isn't the first small business owner to be burned by spam. Short on funds

Case Study: Linda Formichelli

and looking for ways to stretch their advertising dollars, many small business owners are being duped by bulk e-mail companies into believing that spam is a low-cost, highly profitable and acceptable way to advertise their products and services.

Myth #1: Bulk E-mail is Low Cost

Well, it's not really a myth — bulk e-mail is incredibly inexpensive. It seems like a gift from the small business gods: Cash strapped entrepreneurs can send an e-mail ad to millions of potential prospects without buying an expensive direct-mail list and without the cost of printing, paper and stamps. But the reason e-mail mailing lists are so cheap — and the drawback for small business owners looking to reach a particular market — is that they're completely untargeted. Bulk e-mail companies use software to "harvest" the e-mail addresses of Internet users from personal Web pages, discussion forums and newsgroups — kind of like pulling random names from the phone book. No e-mail address is safe: Even non-U.S. e-mail addresses are harvested and sold on lists, as Erica Shames learned when recipients from as far away as France and Hong Kong asked to be removed from her mailing list.

How would your customers like to receive a direct mail ad from you — postage due? Another reason that spam is so inexpensive is that it shifts the cost from the advertiser to the recipient. Some e-mail users pay for the time they spend downloading e-mail, which means they're paying for an ad they didn't ask for. And the bulk of spam is so great that $2 to $3 of every e-mail user's monthly bill goes to spam-fighting efforts and equipment upgrades by their Internet Service Providers.

Myth #2: Bulk E-mail is Profitable

"Earn Thousands!" trumpet the ads for bulk e-mail companies. That wasn't Erica Shames's experience. Out of the 250,000 people her message went to, Shames received only ten orders — a less-than-dismal .004% response rate. Since she paid $199 for her mailing list, it cost Shames $20 for each of the $15 subscription orders she received. "It could have cost her a lot more," says Kelly Thompson, founding member of the Forum for Responsible and Ethical E-mail (FREE), a spam prevention advocacy group. "If her Internet Service Provider had had a policy of not allowing spam from his system, as many ISPs do, she could have lost her e-mail connection and Web site. The $500 to $1,000 it costs to build a Web site is no small expense for a small business owner."

Myth #3: Bulk E-mail is an Acceptable Way to Advertise

That spam is acceptable is a myth propagated by late-night infomercials, traveling conferences and, yes — commercial e-mail. In a survey of 1,036 Web users by the

Case Study: Linda Formichelli

San Jose, CA-based firm World Research, 43% say they hate spam and 25% say it bothers them. Only 7% claim they "love to get spam." Bigger companies know that bulk e-mail is a good way to trash their reputations, which is why you'll never get an unsolicited ad from IBM or Wal-Mart in your mailbox. I'd never buy anything from a company that sends me spam," says Craig Maher, an illustrator in Poughkeepsie, NY whose AOL account gets four to five spam e-mails per day. "Most of the spam I get is for porn Web sites or pyramid schemes, so even if a spam is from a legitimate company, the negative association is there."

You may think, "Even if only seven percent of Internet users 'love to get spam,' that's still a lot of potential customers," but take heed: Not only is spam annoying to the vast majority of your target audience — in some cases, it's illegal. "It's now illegal to send spam with forged sending information or a misleading subject line to Washington State residents," says Dan Zerkle, the legislative contact for FREE. (Even bulk e-mail companies know that spam is unacceptable, which is why they almost always falsify sending information so the e-mail can't be traced.) Similar laws that went into effect in California on January 1, 1999 require senders of bulk e-mail to include a valid e-mail address or toll-free number, and specifies damages of fifty dollars per message if you violate an ISP's acceptable use policy. A Nevada law lets residents sue spammers for $10 per unsolicited message. Such laws target not only the people who hit the SEND button, but also those who "cause the e-mail to be sent" — so you can be looking at a business-destroying lawsuit even if it's a bulk e-mail company that actually sends the message.

The fact that spam shifts the cost of advertising from the sender to the recipient, wreaks havoc on Internet Service Providers and breaks several state laws is enough reason to reconsider using it. But for the small business owner, the most compelling fact is that the majority of Internet users — and your potential customers — loathe spam.

"There are no spamming success stories," says Zerkle. "I've never heard of a legitimate small business that spammed more than once, because they find that the bad faith it creates is like a wrecking ball to their company." Asked if she has any advice for small business owners considering adding bulk e-mail to their marketing arsenal, Erica Shames has this to say: "Do not get involved in this at all."

Linda Formichelli is the co-author of *The Renegade Writer: A Totally Unconventional Guide to Freelance Writing Success and The Renegade Writer's Query Letters That Rock*. You can reach Linda at **www.lindaformichelli.com.**

A great resource for more articles dealing with spam and the CAN-SPAM Act is **www.articlealley.com.** The following articles may be of particular interest to you:

- *The Features and Benefits of Anti-Spam Software* by Arvind Singh — **http://www.articlealley.com/article_103148_11.html**

- *How to Avoid Spam Complaints in Your E-Mail* by John Lynch — **http://www.articlealley.com/article_1258_13.html**

5

OPT–IN AND OPT–OUT

To maintain spam compliance and ensure your e-mail list is both fully compliant with the law and also contains those subscribers who actually want to receive your e-mails, you need to understand opt-in and opt-out.

The underlying principle behind opt-in is very simple: If I have expressly given you permission to add my e-mail address to your e-mail list, then I have "opted-in" to your list.

OPT-IN AND OPT-OUT CONCEPTS

Here are some definitions which may help you understand the concepts we will discuss:

- **Single Opt-In:** E-mail addresses are added to your e-mail list through a subscription (such as completing a "join our mailing list" form, sending an e-mail to a subscription e-mail address, checking a box on an order to add your e-mail address, or providing your e-mail address to customer lists through business reply cards, at conferences, or other online or offline methods of allowing your e-mail address to be added to an e-mail list. Your e-mail address may also be added to multiple lists simultaneously by submitting your e-mail address through one of many free offer and other promotional based Web sites. This is a simple process, and is not validated or confirmed. In other words, your e-mail address is added to one or more e-mail lists and you do not have to perform any specific actions to confirm that it has been added. Often, the subscriber is sent a welcoming e-mail and instructions on how to unsubscribe if he or she did not intend to join the e-mail list; however, this is often not the case.

While an opt-in list is effective and simple to manage, there are some potential drawbacks to maintaining an opt-in list:

- **Subscription Errors** — It is not uncommon for subscribers to mistype their e-mail address, making the e-mail address unusable. An invalid e-mail address will bounce back when sent, or worse, may actually be delivered to someone who did not join your list. Mistyping a single character in an e-mail address can cause e-mail to be undeliverable or sent to someone else.

- **Invalid Submissions** — Because of the prominence of spam in today's environment, many individuals may fill out Web forms and other subscription vehicles and enter a false or invalid e-mail address to avoid being added to potential spam lists. As with the subscription errors, an invalid e-mail address will bounce back when sent, or worse, may actually be delivered to someone who did not join your list.

- **False Subscriptions** — Submitting someone else's e-mail address to one or more lists. This really accomplishes nothing other than cause the recipient the frustration of receiving e-mails he or she did not really subscribe to, and also causes him or her the effort to remove himself or herself.

- **List Poisoning** — This is when invalid e-mail addresses are intentionally added to your e-mail list. In most cases, these will simply bounce back and should be removed from your list, but it does cause you extra administrative work to deal with these addresses. If your list is excessively poisoned, it may be rendered useless for its intended purpose. Another way lists are poisoned is by intentionally adding anti-spam e-mail addresses to your list, so that when you e-mail is sent to your list, these "anti-spam" e-mail address trigger "spam-traps" which can automatically put your IP address on a "blocklist" that keeps the sender's messages from getting through many mail servers.

- **Notification Opt-In** — E-mail addresses are added to your e-mail list through a subscription (such as completing a "join our mailing list" form, sending an e-mail to a subscription e-mail address, checking a box on an order to add your e-mail address, or recipients are added to a list through a single subscription act. A welcoming e-mail is immediately sent to the subscriber with instructions on how to unsubscribe if they did not intend to join the e-mail list. This is very similar to single opt-in with the exception that the welcoming and opt-out e-mail is always sent. The main advantage of this over single opt-in is that you are notified of the list subscription and are given the opportunity to remove yourself from any e-mail lists to which you have been subscribed.

- **Double Opt-In (Closed Loop Opt-In)** — E-mail addresses are added to your e-mail list through a subscription (such as completing a "join our mailing list" form, sending an e-mail to a subscription e-mail address, checking a box on an order to add your e-mail address, or recipients are added to a list through a single subscription act. A welcoming confirmation e-mail is immediately sent to the subscriber with instructions on how to unsubscribe if he or she did not intend to join the e-mail list. The recipient must then confirm his or her subscription to be activated and added to the e-mail list. This is typically done through a hyperlink embedded within the confirmation e-mail. When the subscriber enters his or her e-mail into the "join our e-mail list" form, for example, he or she is immediately sent an e-mail confirmation. He or she must click on the embedded hyperlink to "confirm" his or her subscription or he or she is not added to the list. This means the person who wishes to join your list must complete two steps to activate his or her subscription (initially joining the list, and then confirming that subscription).

While a Double Opt-in list is the most Spam compliant, it is not without its problems. In the case of a Double Opt-in list, most of the problems are for you, not the recipient:

- **Complexity** — Double opt-in is more complex, and requires a more advanced system to manage the double opt-in process. Thus most small businesses or those with limited budgets often find this system is not affordable or readily available. You will discover in later chapters that many all-in-one service providers include double opt-in.

- **Negative Impact** — As you now know, a person who wishes to join your list must complete two steps to activate his or her subscription (initially joining the list, and then confirming the subscription). While this seems pretty simple, the fact is that the percent of individuals who actually complete the double opt-in is very low. In fact, you can expect to lose as much as 50 percent of your potential e-mail customers through double opt-in when compared to single opt-in (this is not due to opt-out, but simply the fact that individuals do not complete the double opt-in process). Often the confirmation e-mail is captured by spam or junk filters and is never even delivered to the recipient so they can confirm the subscription.

- **Opt-Out** — Opt-out is the process where the e-mail recipient requests that a list owner take his or her name off of the list and ensures that he or she is not sent any future e-mails. In the previous chapter on spam, I outlined that one of the requirements of the CAN-SPAM Act is that it requires that your e-mail messages must give recipients an opt-out method. You must provide a return e-mail address or another Internet-based response mechanism that allows a recipient to ask you not to send future e-mail messages to that e-mail address, and you must honor the requests. You may create a "menu" of choices to allow a recipient to opt-out of certain types of messages, but you must include the option to end any commercial messages from the sender. Any opt-out mechanism you offer must be able to process opt-out requests for at least 30 days after you send your commercial e-mail. When you receive an opt-out request, the law gives you ten business days to stop sending e-mail to the requestor's e-mail address. You cannot help another entity send e-mail to that address or have another entity send e-mail on your behalf to that address. Finally, it is illegal for you to sell or transfer the e-mail addresses of people who choose not to receive your e-mail, even in the form of a mailing list, unless you transfer the addresses so another entity can comply with the law.

When you craft and send your e-mail campaigns, you must comply with the CAN-SPAM Act and always include a method for opt-out. Most all-in-one providers do this for you by automatically adding opt-out features to each e-mail blast that you send.

Case Study: Federal Trade Commission

"Remove Me" Responses and Responsibilities: E-mail Marketers Must Honor "Unsubscribe" Claims

Some marketers send e-mail as a quick and cheap way to promote their goods and services. Be aware that the claims that you make in any advertisement for your products or services, including those sent by e-mail, must be truthful. This means that you must honor any promises you make to remove consumers from e-mail mailing lists.

If your e-mail solicitations claim that consumers can opt-out of receiving future messages by following your removal instructions, such as "click here to unsubscribe" or "reply for removal," then the removal options must function as you claim. That means any hyperlinks in the e-mail message must be active and the unsubscribe process must work. Keep in mind:

- You should review the removal claims made in your e-mail solicitations to ensure that you are complying with any representations that you make.

- If you provide consumers a hyperlink for removal, then that hyperlink should be accessible by consumers.

- If you provide an e-mail address for removal, then that address should be functioning and capable of receiving removal requests. It may be deceptive to claim that consumers can "unsubscribe" by responding to a "dead" e-mail address.

- Any system in place to handle unsubscribe requests should process those requests in an effective manner.

The Federal Trade Commission Act prohibits unfair or deceptive advertising in any medium, including in e-mail. That is, advertising must tell the truth and not mislead consumers. A claim can be misleading if it implies something that's not true or if it omits information necessary to keep the claims from bring misleading.

Other points to consider if you market through commercial e-mail:

- Disclaimers and disclosures must be clear and conspicuous. That is, consumers must be able to notice, read or hear, and understand the information. Still, a disclaimer or disclosure alone usually is not enough to remedy a false or deceptive claim.

- If you promised refunds to dissatisfied customers, you must make them.

6

HOW TO CREATE & GROW YOUR E-MAIL LISTS

The biggest challenge you will face is creating and growing an effective mailing list. There are a wide variety of techniques for how to grow your e-mail list and I will cover each of them, giving you candid advice and proven techniques for ensuring that your list will grow over time. One of the challenges every e-mail marketer faces is creating and growing an "effective" list. There is no point in having a list with hundreds of thousands of e-mail addresses which are not relevant to your e-mail message or are invalid e-mail addresses which will constantly bounce back as undeliverable. The most effective lists are those which contain only individuals who expressly wish to receive your e-mail marketing message and may potentially act based on the message you send. Realistically, depending on the type of e-mail marketing message you send, you can expect between a one to ten percent return; however, the two to four percent range is typical.

There is considerable debate, as well as a push, for changes in regulations of e-mail marketing and the handling of Spam, such as the creation of a "do not e-mail" list, similar to the nationwide "do not call" list used for telemarketers. Obviously, this is a hotly contested issue and would require significant changes in the management of e-mail lists.

One of the questions you must answer is what demographics you wish to collect for your e-mail list. While capturing an e-mail address is the most basic, it may not be the most effective if you wish to target your e-mail blasts by region or other demographic data. You can collect a wide-variety of demographic information, but keep in mind if you try to collect too much data, you will turn off potential subscribers who don't wish to fill out a lengthy subscription form or provide too much personal data. At a minimum, if you are going to collect more than just an e-mail address you should collect the first name, last name, gender, and state of the subscriber so you can use this information for e-mail targeting in your campaigns.

PROVEN METHODS TO GROW YOUR E-MAIL LIST

Let us discuss some of the ways you can grow your e-mail list. Remember, this list is not inclusive of all methods, and a little creativity can go a long way in creating an effective e-mail list.

- **Collect E-mail Addresses on Your Web site** — This is the best method of growing your e-mail list. If you have visitors on your site which have an interest in your products or services, it is an ideal time to capture their e-mail address. You can simply place a subscription form on your home page (or other pages) which is clearly visible and readily accessible. Since this form is directly on your Web site, you know that subscribers have an express interest in your products and/or services,; therefore, this is a highly effective means of acquiring excellent quality e-mail addresses. Signing up for relevant e-mail lists is a great thing to do if you want relevant news, information, or promotional material sent to your account. As long as you know what you are signing up for, and the company complies with the CAN SPAM Act, you can have information delivered right to your inbox. One of the best Web sites I have found is **dealnews.com** which lets me sign up for e-mail notification of product sales, based on highly selective criteria that I choose. This is an example of a terrific subscription based service which offers value to me, the subscriber. I never miss out on a great deal because I signed up for this list…your list needs to also offer something of value if you want to have people sign up, and stay on your list.

- **Collect E-mail Addresses From Customer Orders** — If you sell products through your Web site, you are most likely already collecting e-mail addresses which are a great source for your e-mail list. However, you still need to ask permission to add this e-mail address to your list. A simple method of doing this is placing a question directly on the Web site order form asking the customer, "Do you want to join our e-mail list?" You can customize this to provide a brief description of what the list contains (i.e special promotions, etc) as an incentive to get people to sign up. Once individuals check the yes box, you will still run the e-mail address through your double opt-in process to ensure that you list is completely anti-spam compliant and all subscribers have performed a double opt-in process.

- **Collect E-mail Addresses through Offline Methods** — If you produce traditional media products or marketing campaigns such as print advertising, flyers, brochures, catalogs, business cards, paper order forms, and other means of disseminating and collecting information from potential customers then you have an opportunity to ask them to join your e-mail list. Since mailings, catalogs and other print media is often sent to hundreds of thousands of recipients, you have an ideal target audience for which to collect e-mail addresses. If they are returning something to your company, it is as simple as asking them to check a box and fill in their e-mail address, or you can put your Web site address on the print media to notify them to visit the URL if they wish to join your e-mail list. Either way, there is no additional cost asking for this information, and even if you only get a ten percent return on a mailing of 100,000 individuals, you have just added 10,000 quality e-mail addresses to your list. Alan's North Carolina B-B-Q of New Port Richey, Florida (which incidentally has the best B-B-Q around) simply asks customers to sign up to be on their mailing list to receive news, special promotions, and coupons. Alan enters the e-mail addresses into his customer database and uses an opt-in manager to ensure that all of his e-mail customers are double opt-in, even though they have already put their name on the list in the restaurant. You can find Alan's North Carolina B-B-Q at **www.alansncbbq.com**.

- **Collect E-mail Addresses through Surveys** — Online surveys are a great way to attract interest and draw in potential customers. Since you have captured their interest in a survey, this is a great time to also ask them to join your e-mail list and capture their e-mail address. You can also do the same thing for print survey's, why not ask them to join your e-mail list right on the survey, you not only get to add a quality e-mail address to your e-mail list, but you can also draw them to your home page, and potentially hook a new customer with your products and/or services.

- **Collect E-mail Addresses through E-Newsletters** — Obviously you use your e-mail list to distribute your e-mail marketing campaigns, such as e-newsletters. One of the great things about e-newsletters is that you can include subscription forms on the newsletters and also incorporate a "forward to a friend" feature which allows recipients to easily forward to those who may also have an interest in reading them, thus exponentially increasing your target base distribution and potentially subscriber list. Also, you should take your e-zines or e-newsletters and publish them on your Web site — this does two things for you:

  o Publishes your historical e-newsletters online so that customers can read back issues which may have relevant information. By including subscription information on them, you may draw in e-mail subscribers who never actually received your e-newsletter via e-mail.

  o Lets you place a keyword rich HTML formatted e-newsletter on your Web site, which will be scanned and indexed by search engines and spiders, so your e-newsletter can work for you by increasing your overall visibility in search engines. It is important to include proper HTML formatting, including meta-tags in each HTML newsletter to maximize the effectiveness within search engines.

- **Collect E-mail Addresses through Promotions & Giveaways** — Promotions, free offers and giveaways are a great way to attract attention, draw in new customers, and acquire new e-mail leads. Some caution needs to be taken when you offer free products though. First, the use of the word "free" in e-mail subjects is a standard target for spam filters — so your message may be flagged as spam before it ever gets to its intended target. Secondly, when you offer something for free, you can expect a lot of interest by people who have no real interest in your product lines and may not be collecting quality e-mail addresses. It is standard practice for many companies to collect e-mail addresses and personal information in exchange for a free product or sample. From experience, free offers usually generate tremendous response. A former client of mine, Daymark Food Safety Systems (**www.daymark.biz**), which is a manufacturer of unique dissolving labels for the food service industry offered a free sample of their dissolving labels along with a free water pistol (so you could squirt the label with water and watch it dissolve). The free offer was picked up by many of the e-mail lists and blogs which promote free offers to their subscribers. Within a matter of hours, Daymark was flooded with requests for their free water pistol and label promotion. The majority of these submissions were simply for the free water pistol and they had little to no interest in the labels. Since they were not in the food service industry, they were not likely to ever become a customer. Free is great to attract interest, but be ready for some unexpected and potentially overwhelming responses. Qualify your free offer in advance to target your true audience and you can save yourself some time, money, and headaches.

- **Collect E-mail Addresses by Purchasing E-mail Lists** — This is the most controversial subject, and there is no definitive answer on the subject of buying e-mail names or lists, although I would recommend you avoid it. It is highly discouraged and may in fact be illegal. A simple Google search reveals hundreds (or more) companies which sell targeted e-mail lists, often for an extremely low cost. Some offer up to one million e-mails for as low as $199. They also claim to be completely CAN-SPAM Act compliant. So the question is how they can be CAN-SPAM compliant and this be legal? Technically, it is a convoluted subject, one I would avoid as an e-mail marketer, and I personally find it questionable at best how a company can have "spam compliant" e-mail addresses and sell them to another company and still consider them as "spam compliant." I do not believe your use of another company's e-mail list meets the requirements for anti-spam laws since those subscribers have not opted-in to your company's mailing list. However, you will find e-mail lists for sale are readily available. Most of these lists have some serious drawbacks, which may include:

    o **Price** — They are typically very expensive. Unlike direct mail lists which are both affordable and readily available, e-mail lists come at a higher premium.

    o **Quality** — Expect nearly 50 percent to bounce immediately. I have found most of these purchased lists to be low quality, often harvested e-mail addresses which will quickly land you in trouble with the CAN-SPAM Act.

If you are having trouble creating and acquiring e-mail addresses to your list and wish to pursue buying e-mail addresses, I recommend you pursue what is known as co-registration instead of outright purchasing of e-mail lists. Co-registration is when you join forces with another advertiser, marketing company, or Web site which collect permission-based name and e-mail addresses to sell to other companies. Essentially, your company information, products, subscription information, or other type of data is placed on their Web site asking them to join your (and possibly many other) e-mail lists. If someone chooses to join your list you are then charged for this "lead," typically costing between .50 to upwards of $2 per lead. Again, be warned, most of the co-registration networks utilize contests and other promotional material to entice someone to give them their e-mail address in exchange for free products, contest registrations, etc. You typically get very low quality (or invalid) e-mail addresses.

Co-registration is not a low-cost solution; however, it can be used to quickly generate thousands of e-mail names, which are opt-in and spam compliant. There are hundreds of co-registration networks or solution providers which offer this service. Many will re-sell these names to you as bulk e-mail addresses for a flat rate fee; however, you will still have to deal with anti-spam issues, as well as the effect of utilizing potentially low quality leads in your e-mail marketing campaign.

- **List Exchange and Rental** — This differs from buying a list because instead of importing the e-mail addresses into your e-mail list you rent a list and have someone else send your e-mail message using their list. You will need to do your homework to ensure that you stay away from "junk lists" which we have already discussed and are mostly harvested e-mail addresses. You can verify the quality of rental lists by validating the opt-in source records for the list you plan to use. Keep in mind these must be obtained by traditional means including subscriptions, market research, surveys, etc. Ensure that you receive tracking and other detailed delivery reports as part of the list rental agreement and ensure that the list brokers comply with the CAN-SPAM Act by honoring all opt-out requests. List exchange is very similar to list rental, except instead of a monetary transaction for a list rental, you actually exchange list services. In other words, your actual lists never change hands, but you use your list to e-mail their e-mail marketing campaign, and the use their list to e-mail your e-mail marketing campaign, thus significantly increasing both distributions at little to no cost (the only cost may be if the list sizes are significantly different in comparison).

- **Collect E-mail Addresses Through Viral E-mail Campaigns** — A viral e-mail campaign is a type of campaign which is typically used for petitions, and requires you to complete a form, then forward it to a specific number of persons. This campaign hopes that each person then forwards it to ten more and so on thus expanding across the internet like a "virus" (although not necessarily the bad type of virus). These campaigns are not very successful, yet you can garner some e-mail addresses if your viral campaign requires registrations, or filling out a Web form to participate in a poll, campaign, or other similar technique. The quality of the leads is questionable at best, and many people will immediately hit the delete key upon receiving a viral e-mail; however, you may find that viral e-mails can spread quickly across the globe reaching a wide audience base.

- **Collect E-mail Addresses Through Banner Advertising** — The days of banner advertising are past us. Many sites use banner advertising as an method to generate income; however, it has been surpassed by the more effective pay-per-click advertising market. Banner ads will cost you money (typically) to have them placed on other Web sites hoping that they will attract attention of the site visitor so that they click on them, travel to your Web site, and ultimately sign up for your subscription e-mail list. If you can get free banner ads, it is not a bad option, but do not expect a significant return, as most Web site visitors have become trained to ignore banner advertising.

- **Collect E-mail Addresses Through Discount Offers** — I think this is one of the most effective ways to attract potential customers, and hopefully convert them into return customers. If your goal is to both collect permission-based e-mails for your e-mail list and build customers, you need to specify the terms of the offer very clearly, such as offering a 25 percent discount on any product on your Web site. One of the terms of your offer may be that they join your e-mail list, thus converting not only a sale, but also a quality addition to your Web site. You can then use the e-mail list to solicit repeat business by sending your preferred customers another discount certificate, drawing them back to your Web site. Trust me, everyone loves a discount, free shipping, and other promotional gimmicks to attract customers — so why not offer them, and ask them to join your e-mail list. If they are satisfied with your products and service provided to them, you may have just made a repeat customer for life.

- **Collect E-mail Addresses through Associate and Affiliate Programs** — I like affiliate programs. They are a no-brainer to the affiliate. For example, Atlantic Publishing Company (**www.atlantic-pub.com**) offers a free affiliate program for their wide ranging products (those actually published by Atlantic Publishing Company only) on topics such as real estate, mortgages, personal finance, Internet, food service, and series of books on how to open operate selected businesses. You can become an affiliate for free and earn a flat 20 percent commission for every sale through your Web site. Since you now earn money for essentially doing nothing other than listing products on your Web site, the affiliate sponsor is hoping you will send out your affiliate links to all your friends, business associates and others hoping they will buy the products, but through your affiliate link, earning you the 20 percent commission. The affiliate sponsor is looking for customers, and also subscriptions if you wish to join their e-mail list. If you host an affiliate program you can even ask your affiliate to include a subscription form to your e-mail list on their Web site as part of the affiliate terms.

> SPAM: Atlantic Publishing Company has a zero tolerance policy for SPAM. Any Affiliate accused of SPAMMING will be immediately removed from our affiliate program. The only recourse you will have to maintain your affiliate relationship is proof of 'opt in' that will undermine the validity of the Spam complaint. Valid SPAM complaints will result in the immediate termination of your account and forfeiture of any commissions owed you.

Make sure that if you host an affiliate program, you have a solid anti-spam policy to protect you in case one of your affiliates decides to promote your affiliate link through less than reputable e-mail distribution lists.

HOW TO KEEP PEOPLE FROM UNSUBSCRIBING FROM YOUR E-MAIL LIST

There is no secret formula which you can use to keep people from unsubscribing to your list; however, a little common sense can go a long way to solve this problem. The main reason people unsubscribe from a mailing list is that they are not receiving the material they expect or desire. If I signed up for an e-mail list of e-mail marketing and all I got is clothing offers, I will unsubscribe from the list. If I sign up for an e-mail list of laptop computer reviews and if I never actually get reviews of laptop computers — I am gone! You have to give your subscribers what they signed up for. If that is news, information, new product releases, etc, then that is your primary focus. You can always add additional information which may be of interest, but you must provide them with what you told them they would be getting when they first signed up with your e-mail list. Keep your list active, at least quarterly or more frequently, or it will be forgotten quickly. Keep your information fresh, relevant, and interesting. If your e-mail is of no value in reading, does not benefit the reader in some way, or is completely off-target, your e-mail subscriber will jump ship quickly!

Times are changing in regards to the concept of buying e-mail addresses. It is commonplace to see companies selling e-mail lists that they claim are spam compliant or 100 percent opt-in. Five years ago, most of these offers were simply scams containing thousands upon thousands of illegally harvested e-mail addresses. In contrast, you will find that there are many highly respected and reputable companies which offer list rentals and even purchase of lists to other companies seeking to start or expand e-mail marketing efforts.

You will find the scams continue, many list rentals and sellers are still selling harvested e-mails. They typically operate off-shore servers which are shut down and re-started under another domain overnight so you need to be cautious, check references, and do some research before you sign up with someone for list rentals or purchase. You do not want to be targeted as a spammer on your first attempt at e-mail marketing. Here is some advice to ensure that you do not end up on a spam blacklist:

- **Check references** — Ensure that the company you choose to use has been in business for a period of time, has established customers, and a good record with spam compliance.

- **Ensure you only use opt-in e-mail lists** — Do not buy harvested e-mail addresses. They are only going to land you in trouble, bombard you with complaints, and ultimately cost you money and business. You will do your business much more harm long-term by buying 500,000 e-mail addresses for $99. When you rent a list, obtain something which guarantees the list is entirely opt-in. If you do choose to buy e-mail addresses, even though they claim to be 100 percent opt-in – run through another opt-in process and re-validate them. You will likely lose up to 50 percent of your list if the list is in fact valid, and possibly more than 90 percent if your list is harvested. Keep in mind that old e-mail lists often contain e-mail addresses which account for a 50 percent loss in bounced addresses.

- **Ensure that each e-mail contains an easy-to understand opt-out method** — Ensure this actually functions as advertise and you may consider adding your e-mail address for them to contact you directly if they have concerns or to manually remove their e-mail address from your list. There is a large population out there that believes that by clicking on the "remove" links the are simply validating that their e-mail address is valid.

- **Do not sell your e-mail lists** — Rentals and co-registration is fine, but do not lose the trust of your subscribers by selling them out.

- **If you ask someone to joins your list, then they only want to be on your list** — Do not assume this is opt-in and add them to dozens of other junk lists. If you want to build and maintain trust, only add subscribers to the list they actually join.

A great source to read more about making a great e-mailing list is the article "Making Effective Use of Your Mailing List" by Richard Rutherford, which can be found at **http://www.articlealley.com/article_80003_3.html.**

7

HOW TO DESIGN AN EFFECTIVE E-MAIL CAMPAIGN

Writing the e-mail masterpiece is not as difficult as you may believe. While there are certain challenges you may have to overcome, the actual creation of the e-mail blast is probably easier and less time consuming than developing and growing your actual e-mail list. Throughout this chapter, I will cover the basic essentials and give you candid advice on how to create effective e-mail campaigns that work! Chapter 9 guides you through the process of actually creating your e-mail blasts and I will arm you with many valuable tips and recommendations to ensure your e-mail is designed properly and is optimized for maximum effect, however you must design your marketing plan and campaign before you can begin the process of creating your e-mails.

What is the most commonly asked question of an e-mail marketing specialist? It is simple, and has been the number one question for years, and likely for many more years to come. The question is a variation of this theme: Can I buy a list of e-mail addresses which I can use to start my e-mail campaigns? The answer to this is typically no, unless you follow some of the methods I covered in Chapter 6 on how to grow your e-mail list. You will quickly discover that renting or buying e-mail lists typically fails to return the results you expect, and in fact will get you in hot water fast with anti-spam laws. You need to build a quality e-mail list, and it can take some time, even years to do so. Having a quality opt-in list ensures that you have clearly established a relationship with your customers and they eagerly accept your e-mail communications with them.

E-MAIL CAMPAIGN BASICS

Here are some of the basics you need to review as you design your e-mail marketing campaign:

- Identify your audience so you know who you are targeting and why. You will often find your target audiences varies depending on the type of e-mail you may send, and often you will have multiple e-mail lists based on segmented target audiences.

- Establish the purpose and nature of your e-mails (i.e. newsletter, advertising, coupons, product announcements, press releases, articles, or a combination of any of these).

- Choose your format (HTML, text or both). A subject of great debate. Ten years ago text was king. Five years ago you should have used both text and HTML. Today, I would use HTML primarily, Text as an alternate.

- Who is responsible for your e-mail development efforts? Are you going to manage all aspects of your campaign, will you use an all-in-one service provider? Will you create, edit, format, and test your actual e-mail's or will you contract this out to an e-mail marketing specialist? Who will manage the administration of your program (opt-ins, opt-outs, scheduling, reports, etc).

- What is your short and long range plans? Do you intend to do e-mail blasts on a regular schedule (i.e. weekly) or randomly?

- Ensure whatever method you use to manage your lists is 100 percent opt-in to maintain compliance with anti-spam laws and always include a method for anyone to opt-out of your lists at anytime.

- What methods will you use to gather e-mail addresses and grow your current e-mail list? At a minimum, you should include a sign-up form on your Web site, prominently featured on your home page, and you may consider additional "Join our Mailing List" forms on your shopping chart checkout pages, in your customer e-mails, order notification or any other media which you use to exchange information with current and potential customers. You may even want to include this information on print media such as brochures, business cards, etc.

Do not forget about asking customers to join your list during phone conversations, at trade shows and other industry events.

- Use co-registration and rented lists to grow your customer base. By this I mean do not steal the e-mail addresses from rentals and co-registration lists, but as you send your e-mail blasts through co-registration and rental lists, be sure to include something to get them to sign up onto your e-mail list, thus growing your e-mail list with quality e-mail addresses.

- Discuss the technical requirements of your marketing plan. This covers a wide variety of items such as managing your e-mail lists, sending the actual e-mail blasts, bandwidth constraints, ISP policies, e-mail software, HTML development expertise, automation of opt-in and opt-out techniques, required hardware (i.e. e-mail servers). Do not discount the expertise of the individuals who will be required to manage and administer your program, including the development of your actual e-mail blasts.

DEVELOPING AN E-MAIL MARKETING CAMPAIGN

One of the steps you must complete is to design the overall objectives, purpose, mission, and goals of your e-mail marketing campaign. This can cover everything from increasing sales, growing customer base, raising product awareness to distributing newsworthy industry related information, distribution discount coupons, or promotional offers or hundreds of other possibilities. The fact is that you have full creative control of your campaign, and you can do almost anything you want with your e-mail marketing program. Ideally, you need to do the following:

- **Develop a high level e-mail campaign strategy** — This is simply your corporate vision or goals in respect to your e-mail campaigns. Typically, this is derived from the CEO corporate vision, mission statement or annual goals (i.e. increase sales in a particular product or market segment, develop or promote a new business line, etc). The corporate goals determine the priorities which drive the e-mail marketing campaign strategy. Often times in small businesses you wear all the hats from CEO to e-mail marketing campaign manager;

therefore, you determine your strategy, which helps you ensure that your e-mail campaigns are relevant and directly tied to achieving your corporate vision.

• **Develop a comprehensive implementation plan** — E-mail marketing is significantly more than just sending out e-mails. You must identify what type of e-mails, what the content is, what the theme or message is, what the desired results will be, and who the recipients are. For example, you may have a variety of potential e-mail audiences for your products and you may want to target them separately. For example, if your products are automobile parts you may wish to target wholesalers, distributors, retailers and private consumers in separate e-mail campaigns all with the purpose of brand awareness, growing your customer base and increasing sales, however your message to each of these groups would be significantly different than the other one. Your campaign may be extremely ineffective if it generically designed for all target groups, instead of four distinctly different, yet customized, and relevantly targeted e-mail messages. Your plan does not necessarily need to address the design issues, but should address the high level plan of type of e-mails, target audience, frequency, e-mail content, and e-mail goals. You may wish to send multiple e-mail campaigns to each group targeting completing different desired results (i.e. brand awareness vs. developing customer base).

• **Target the right audience** — I touched on this briefly in the previous paragraph, and because targeting is such a critical success factor in the overall success or failure of your e-mail marketing campaign, I have dedicated an entire chapter to this topic later in the book. Failure to properly target the right audience with the right e-mail message is the number one mistake made in e-mail campaigns. Sending generic e-mail messages to everyone in your e-mail list may be completely appropriate in certain circumstances; however, it may cause significant problems, loss of existing and potential customers, and loss of revenue. For example, sending an e-mail message to your entire database about promotions to increase reseller revenue will not be well received by end-use consumers who are looking for the best bottom line deals, and you may cause them to look elsewhere.

• **Track and evaluate your results** — Make incremental changes in both corporate philosophy and e-mail campaign management based on statistical results. You must analyze your statistics (click-throughs, bounces, opens, etc) to know if your e-mail campaign is successful. Essentially, you need to know how many e-mails were sent and delivered to your recipients, what percentage of your subscribers opened each e-mail, who opened and clicked through each e-mail on any of the embedded links in each e-mail, which links generated the most click-throughs (and which did not generate any), and how many individuals removed themselves from your list (or who joined your list). Understanding what works and what does not work is critical to refining the process and increasing the effectiveness of your e-mail marketing campaigns. Do not be afraid to tweak your e-mails and re-evaluate the results. Your e-mails should have a clearly stated purpose (i.e. new product release announcement, etc) and should have an expected action of the recipient (i.e. click to buy this product, click to read this article, click for more information, fill out a web-based form, etc).

HTML VS TEXT FORMAT

The first question you need to address is to utilize HTML based e-mail or text-based e-mails. Several years ago, this was a fairly pertinent question as many e-mail programs were text-based and could not handle HTML based content. Today, that is not the case, as the majority of all e-mail applications (Outlook, Outlook Express, Thunderbird, AOL, Yahoo! And Google) all effectively handle and interpret HTML code and present it in the proper format to the reader. While the trend several years ago was to cater to text-based e-mail applications, this evolved to mostly HTML based e-mails; however, the issue is convoluted and not entirely clear cut — just because these e-mail program read HTML does not mean that they are configured to allow it, plus Microsoft Outlook 2003 by default turns off the download of images in e-mails. The Department of Defense, Department of Homeland Security and several private corporations have enacted security restrictions on receiving HTML formatted e-mail messages. They strip the HTML coding and convert the e-mail to a text based format. If your are only blasting with HTML formatted e-mail messages, our message will be received at DOD + DHS facilities as scrambled HTML code, which is practically unreadable. This means there is some advantage to sending both HTML and text based e-mails to recipients or HTML with an alternative link to text versions of the e-mail.

Let us take a step backward. HTML formatted messages are simply Web pages, which are sent through an e-mail server and re-assembled and presented to the recipient in their browser. The advantage to HTML is that you can use highly customized formatting, embedded graphics, and other dynamic features which require HTML coding. Text-based messages are straight text. They have little to no formatting which is presented in both text and HTML based Web browsers in an easy-to-read format. HTML allows you to use customer fonts, colors, graphics, and interactive rich-media technology. Text-based e-mails are simple text, little formatting, no graphics, no colors or special font formatting, but does allow you to embed absolute hyperlinks in the text. So which is better? Actually, I recommend both if possible. Most all in one providers allow you to craft both text and HTML formatted messages.

The key to determining which format to send primarily depends on you e-mail list. Typically you allow those who subscribe to your list to choose which format to receive, either HTML or text. If you do not have a preference selected in your e-mail list, the guidance ten years ago was to go with text based messages, five years ago you needed to use both HTML and text based since some text-only e-mail readers were still being utilized. That is no longer the case. Most e-mail applications are HTML capable, and that is the format I recommend you use. You will not find many e-mail applications which are not HTML friendly unless you are using a 1990s vintage e-mail program. That said, a text-based alternative is still readily accepted and may be preferred by some users. As I mentioned earlier, some companies and government may actually force your HTML formatted messages back into text based format. In outlook, the recipient may convert the message back to HTML format, which makes the subject line (covered in chapter 10) all the more important if you expect the recipient to identify your e-mail when presented with the html code in a text representation.

There are times when you want to use text and/or HTML based on your customer preferences (if they can specify a preference), the type of message your sending and the volume of e-mails you want to send. Ideally, you should prepare both an HTML and text based e-mails for your e-mail campaigns; however, HTML is the more prevalent today. Giving your customers the choice of HTML or text helps you to ensure that they receive their personal preference.

The decision is entirely yours, however here are some advantages and disadvantages to utilizing HTML based e-mail:

- **Advantages**:
  - ° Professional appearance, visually pleasing
  - ° You can embed graphics into your e-mail
  - ° You can use a variety of colors, fonts, styles
  - ° Your e-mail can-be interactive with web-forms
  - ° E-mails are statistically more effective

- **Disadvantages**:
  - ° E-mail client may not support HTML format
  - ° Some companies/government may not allow HTML format
  - ° Graphics intensive e-mail are slow to load
  - ° Outlook 2003 blocks graphics by default
  - ° More likely to contain viruses & Trojan horses
  - ° Graphics are blocked by default in Microsoft Outlook & others

OPTIONS FOR E-MAIL MARKETING SERVICE PROVIDERS

I recommend you consider using an all-in-one service provider to transmit your e-mails, provide tracking, manage your lists and perform maintenance such as managing bounces, importing new e-mails and other tasks if you want to automate most aspects of the e-mail campaign management. Keep in mind, this does not relieve you from creating your actual e-mail creative — you will still need to this, although they will provide you with templates to simplify the process. These tasks can be daunting on your own without utilizing an automated system, and it is not realistic (nor typically allowed by your ISP) to host your own e-mail lists on your local PC or domain. You essentially have four choices, you can:

- Utilize an all-in-one service provider which provide you with self-managed tutorials for you to perform all management tasks, but are provided with templates, help guides, and many of the tasks are automated such as sending the e-mails, tracking the results, providing detailed statistics, managing e-mail lists and provides templates for creating e-mail blasts. This method can be less costly, but will require you to manage your accounts, create your e-mail blasts, manage your lists and schedule your own e-mail blasts. The service provider actually sends out your scheduled e-mail blasts using their service, with your lists.

- Utilize an e-mail marketing specialist who will perform all tasks for you, including the management of lists, creation of all e-mail blasts, sending e-mail blasts, tracking, reporting, and performing all maintenance tasks associated with your account. This is essentially a full-service provider solution, you do nothing more than tell the specialist what you need, and when to send it, and they do all the work creating the e-mail blasts, manage your accounts, manage your lists and track all the results. While much simpler for you, it is more costly.

- Purchase a Commercial Off-The-Shelf program which can automate your e-mail campaign management on your own e-mail servers or POP3 mail servers. Arial Software features a suite of products designed to manage your entire e-mail marketing program. We will discuss the high quality products of Arial Software later in this chapter. Arial Software's robust products certainly make this an appealing option if you want total control of your e-mail campaigns, and want to eliminate the recurring monthly costs associated with an all-in-one solution provider.

- Do it all yourself, including the management of lists, creation of all e-mail blasts, sending e-mail blasts, tracking, reporting and performing all maintenance tasks associated with your list. You can do this with a simple Microsoft Outlook and built in contact manager/address book; however, most ISP's do not allow you to perform e-mail marketing or bulk e-mails as part of their terms of service. This is certainly the most cost-effective, but may not be efficient or even realistic. If you have a very small business, with a limited customer base and have 500 names or less on your e-mail list, you may be able to manage your entire campaign, but again need to check your local ISP policies and terms of service regarding e-mail use. You can do your e-mail campaigns at no cost at all. This is also an option to consider for a new Web site or business seeking to grow your list. Once you grow it to a certain level, you may opt to use one of the all-in-one service providers to automate most of the processes involved in managing the e-mail lists and creating campaigns or upgrade to a robust products which can provide you with total control of your campaign, such as those offered by Arial Software.

ALL-IN-ONE E-MAIL MARKETING SERVICE PROVIDERS

There are many all-in-on service providers, and I have used several of them with superior results. All of the ones listed here are reputable, cost-effective and easily manageable without hiring specialists:

- **Topica.com** — Topica's Online Marketing and Sales Solution seamlessly integrates time-tested, performance-based advertising services (PBA) with a sophisticated yet easy-to-use hosted application (ASP), which combines data integration and analysis features, conversion optimization tools and industry-leading e-mail marketing capabilities. Together, they provide a reliable and extremely cost effective way to create new leads, turn them into paying customers and generate maximum value from them. Topica.com provides customized solutions for:

  - **Internet Retailers** — Everything to optimize online retail sales.

  - **Online Publishers** — Targeted content and lead generation to grow an online community.

  - **Direct Marketers** — Get your offers to the inboxes of those most likely to respond.

  - **Interactive Agencies** — Drive success across the full range of online services you offer your clients.

I have used Topica for years and have found them to be a great fit for a small business who wants to use an all-in-one solution provider to manage their lists and e-mail campaigns. Topica is very simple and flexible to manage an use, and in fact the only real negative I have regarding Topica is their technical support response rate, which often takes days. The other obvious disadvantage for any of the all-in-one solution providers is the recurring monthly fees for using their service. **Topica.com** offers an abundance of services at relatively low cost, plus the offer a significant discount if you sign up for a yearly contract. Pricing with **Topica.com** is based on the number of e-mails you send out each month, not the number of e-mails on your list. Additionally, Topica offers annual plans with 25 percent discounts on their pricing, making them very cost-effective for small business ventures. You can send out HTML, text, or multi-part e-mails, and when subscribers join you list, they can select which type they prefer to receive. There is a wide variety of user-friendly templates which simplify the process of creating your e-mails. This means you do not have to be a HTML expert to create professional looking HTML e-mail blasts. If you prefer, you can use your own custom HTML e-mails as well using another HTML editor such as Microsoft Frontpage, Microsoft Expression Web, or Macromedia Dreamweaver. Keep in mind that many programs, including Frontpage may insert additional code into your HTML e-mails; therefore, it is critical you test each e-mail before you schedule an e-mail blast. Topica automatically provides opt-out on each outgoing e-mail message and even allows subscribers to update their account online. The reporting and delivery tracking is excellent, providing you with real-time statistics, deliveries, bounces, and open rates. You can even track clicks and links to see how often each link within your e-mail is clicked on. You can easily import lists, including demographic data, and one of the best features is you can hold multiple lists within your single account if you have lists which target different segments of your business (such as retailers vs wholesalers). You can personalize e-mails and segment/target them based on demographic data.

- **EmailLabs.com** — EmailLab utilizes technology, cutting edge features, and provides flexible programs that will enable you to increase revenues, enhance brands, strengthen customer relationships, and streamline sales and marketing processes. EmailLabs provides you with the ability to upload your existing opt-in lists and synch with your database to automatically update changes to your lists. You can add opt-in forms to your site, manage un-subscribes, store files and images in the content library, and use custom templates to speed message creation, or use the provided built-in HTML editor. You can send messages immediately or schedule them for specific send times as well as trigger automatic e-mails based on customer activity, on your Web site, or in response to your e-mail. EmailLabs provides real-time, detailed reports on your messages and campaigns, including opens, click-throughs, bounces, un-subscribes and more. Improve your campaigns based on results as well as a multitude of advanced features such as API integration, dynamic content, triggers, segmentation, third-party integrations, and more.

- **Jangomail.com** — Jangomail is another industry leader in e-mail marketing. Their Web site states that they provide all the standard features of most e-mail service companies, like open tracking, click tracking, HTML/plain text messaging, personalization, unsubscribe/bounce management, data import/export capabilities, e-mail list hygiene capabilities, and a double opt-in option; however, they also provide extra special unique features such as:

- **24 hour support** — Emergency support is available to all customers.

- **100 percent branding control** — You will never see a "Powered by JangoMail" footer or tagline appended to the bottom of your e-mails. You are in full control of the look and feel of your e-mails. You can even control where CAN-SPAM requirements like an unsubscribe link and your postal address go, so that even these elements can be fully integrated into your e-mail's design.

- **Advanced HTML editor** — To help you compose HTML e-mails, JangoMail includes a powerful browser-based HTML editor that supports such advanced HTML capabilities as cascading style sheets (CSS), real-time spell checking, a Microsoft Word document cleaner, and one-click buttons to insert CAN-SPAM compliant footers, unsubscribe links, and forward-to-friend links.

- **Advanced personalization.**

- **Specify all properties of your e-mail message**, down to the header level details.

- **Foreign language capabilities.**

- **JangoMail claims to be the only e-mail service provider that has built a distributed**, rather than centralized, network of e-mail senders across the world allowing for complete fault-tolerance and redundancy across our SMTP e-mail senders. Additionally, JangoMail personnel review SMTP log files on a daily basis to ensure optimal deliverability of customers' e-mail messages, and they develop and maintain relationships with ISPs, and participate in a wide variety of white listing programs.

- **Connect to external databases in real time** — JangoMail claims to be the only web-based e-mail service provider that can connect to desktop and Internet databases in real-time.

- **Tracking down to the recipient level** — JangoMail's reporting module tells you who has unsubscribed, bounced, replied, forwarded, opened, and clicked through to your Web site on a per e-mail campaign basis. You can even track an e-mail recipient's movement through your web site after clicking a link in an e-mail message.

- **Constant Contact (www.constantcontact.com)** — Constant Contact is highly respected and provides a robust, yet simplified interface providing you with total control over your e-mail marketing program. Constant Contact enables you to create and send top-notch e-mail newsletters and promotions with no technical expertise. They excel at making the process easy for you — including list management and reporting, and they also provide free live support. You have a wealth of robust features including an e-mail campaign, pre-designed e-mail templates, advanced HTML editing functionality, customizable visitor sign-up form for Web site, bounce and unsubscribe management, list segmentation functionality, e-mail tracking and reporting, and e-mail delivery management, among others.

This list is certainly not inclusive of all of our recommended all-in-one service providers, and is merely and introduction to some of the industry leaders. Throughout our case studies and industry expert hints and tips chapters, you will be introduced to many more highly reputable and well-respected industry leaders in e-mail campaign management, all of whom have earned my respect for their honesty, integrity, and professionalism.

E-MAIL MARKETING SPECIALISTS

There are dozens of highly respectable companies who provide superior quality service for their customers as they manage complex and highly successful e-mail marketing campaigns. Gizmo Graphics Web Design (**www.gizwebs.com**) has been managing the e-mail campaigns for Atlantic Publishing Company (**www. atlantic-pub.com**) for more than six years. Producers of the Food Service Professional E-zine and a variety of other targeted e-mail publications, they have produced more than 350 e-mail campaigns, which have produced the desired results of increased sales, brand recognition, and distributing industry related news and information to segmented customer lists. Gizmo Graphics Web Design provides a fair price for above average service, even though e-mail marketing is not their primary business line. In my case studies and industry expert advice Chapters I have included a short profile of each company and E-mail Marketing Specialist for your review and consideration as you determine the appropriate e-mail marketing management technique for your company. Every company or individual profiled in this book is highly recommended, reputable and a proven industry leader.

MASS E-MAIL MARKETING SOFTWARE

There are numerous mass e-mail marketing applications on the market; however, the clear industry leader in my opinion is from Arial Software. Founded in 1993, Arial Software, LLC is widely considered the industry leader in e-mail marketing software designed exclusively for relationship building through personalized e-mail messaging. E-mail Marketing Director is professional desktop e-mail campaign software used by marketing companies, newsletter publishers, volunteer coordinators, tourism bureaus, veterans groups, neighborhood associations, event planners, churches, service clubs, schools, and more. More information on E-mail Marketing Director can be found at **http://www.arialsoftware.com/emailmarketingdirector.htm**, and I am going to give you an in depth introduction to the capabilities of -E-mail Marketing Director as an alternative to utilizing an all-in-one solution provider.

E-mail Marketing Director was recognized in 2006 with a top award for the software's ease of use, its quick installation, and for giving marketers "everything you need to create a professional e-mail campaign." **TopTenReviews.com** gave E-mail Marketing Director its Gold Award 2006 in the e-mail marketing category as the best of ten software products reviewed. The award cites the software's numerous features, its ease of installation and setup, ease of use in e-mail creation, and its e-mail campaign status reporting as the reasons for the strong review ratings and Gold Award.

"E-mail Marketing Director software is popular with small to medium-sized businesses needing to compose, design, and deliver their own e-mail newsletters, alerts, coupons, announcements, and any other permission-based e-mail messages to their customers and subscribers. E-mail Marketing Director is user-friendly and breaks the entire campaign creation process into three easy steps, on three different tabs," said **TopTenReviews.com**. "The layout of the software makes the entire process simple and pain-free."

E-MAIL MARKETING DIRECTOR OVERVIEW

Arial Software states that "E-mail Marketing Director takes the ten years of proven, bulletproof e-mail automation technology found in our higher-priced products and puts it in a streamlined, astoundingly easy to use software product that allows anyone to create and deliver personalized e-mail marketing campaigns."

E-mail Marketing is full of robust features, including:

- A built-in database supporting an unlimited number of lists.

- Easy to use database filtering logic so you can select only qualifying people from your list.

- Automatic bounce handling and unsubscribe handling.

- Built-in e-mail delivery system that may, in some cases, free you from some of the e-mail limits placed by your ISP.

- SSL protocol support.

- Built-in, professionally-designed e-mail newsletter templates that bring impressive professionalism to your e-mail messages.

- E-mail message personalization.

- Allows you to import, export, and edit subscribers' records.

- Save, view, and reuse an unlimited number of e-mail campaigns.

- IMAP support for bounces/unsubscribe processing.

- Segmented sending which allows a campaign to disconnect and reconnect per ISP specifications.

- Over 200 professionally-designed e-mail templates.

- Built-in advanced HTML editing maintains style sheets, sets advanced page and link properties, and can be configured to spell check e-mail messages. E-mail messages can also be edited in Dreamweaver, PageMaker, or FrontPage HTML programs.

- Enhanced unsubscribe processing. Exclusive hands-free processing now removes e-mail un-subscribers from all mailing lists in the built-in database.

- Database-wide bounce checking. Imported lists can be checked against a cleaner list for one-step e-mail bounce filtering.

- Accelerated importing for larger data batches. Use accelerated importing for larger lists of e-mail subscribers and standard import to maintain unique formats and characters.

- Easy access campaign metrics. Campaign performance logs and trace files are available from the main menu and reports screen.

- Online help files.

- E-mail campaigns can be sent with a working unsubscribe link automatically inserted in the message. The software automatically flags recipient addresses which have unsubscribed, no matter what list they are on.

- Campaign plotting calendar lets you coordinate scheduling of your e-mail campaigns throughout the year using a clear graphic display.

- E-mail Marketing Director can slow e-mail campaign sending speeds in accordance with your mail server maximum speed, or to match your ISP bandwidth or other Internet access limitations. Outbound e-mail campaigns are easily throttled by messages per hour and help keep you compliant with your service provider.

- Alternate server port support. The software offers support for servers that require a different port (other than the standard port 25). This allows E-mail Marketing Director to account for any increased protection your ISP may impose in the future to protect against unauthorized mail sending, e-mail hijacking, and IP spoofing.

WHO IS E-MAIL MARKETING DIRECTOR FOR

As I mentioned earlier, E-mail Marketing Director is my choice if you want to have total control over you e-mail campaigns and do not want to deal with the recurring fees and potential overage charges from all-in-one service providers. E-mail Marketing Director has a minimal learning curve and can be installed and configured in a matter of minutes. In fact, Arial Software claims you can send your first e-mail campaign in under fifteen minutes, and sending subsequent campaigns takes mere seconds.

WHAT CAN YOU DO WITH E-MAIL MARKETING DIRECTOR?

You already know the power of e-mail marketing, and the potential impact in brand name visibility and increased profits, as well as cost savings when compared with traditional direct mail campaigns. So what can E-mail Marketing Director do for your business?

- Send order follow-up e-mails to customers

- Deliver e-mail newsletters to readers

- Send news alerts to subscribers

- Broadcast important reminders to members

- E-mail your suppliers, dealers, or wholesalers

- Conduct public relations campaigns

- E-mail your local customers and invite them back to your retail establishment

- Send coupons or special offers to your customer base

- Ensure your e-mail campaigns maintain 100 percent spam compliance

Another product which has realized tremendous success is eLoop™ from Gold Lasso (**www.goldlasso.com**). eLoop™ was designed specifically for the marketing professional to effectively integrate e-mail as part of their promotional mix using a closed-loop concept.

eLoop™ is a Web-based e-mail marketing system is comprised of three distinct tools (modules), out-bound messaging, data management, and data collection. These tools provide all the functionality needed for a professional marketer to develop a successful e-mail marketing program with very little technical knowledge. All of eLoop's™ tools are integrated providing seamless functionality and easy data flow. eLoop's™ modules consist of:

- **Out-Bound Messaging** — For a simple text message to a dynamic HTML version, eLoop™ provides a message editor that is as easy to use as a word processor and gives you complete control of your message's design and layout. In addition, the Out-Bound Messaging tool provides a host of campaign scheduling features and campaign automation including Gold Lasso's proprietary Action Based Messaging™ (ABM) system, where campaign recipients receive follow-up messages based on links clicked and forms completed.

- **Data Management** — eLoop's™ Data Management tools provide you the ability to build a customized database to import or collect any data necessary to personalize your messages or segment your lists appropriately. Extensive list management options enable you to build lists based on complex algorithms with multiple data variables. eLoop's™ Data Management tools comes complete with automated list cleansing features such as e-mail automated de-duping processes, merge/purge and e-mail validation.

- **Data Collection** — eLoop™ has extensive data collection features for building landing pages, surveys, and opt-in lists. All data from your Web forms can be fully customized and the data collected is housed and linked within your eLoop™ database. Also, the data can be used for additional list building and message personalization.

OTHER MASS E-MAIL APPLICATIONS

Arial Software is not the only show in town; however, they do earn my recommendation. Other reputable companies also produce very high quality, robust applications, including:

- PHP Mailer (**http://phpmailer.sourceforge.net**)

- HotCast Mass Mailer (**http://www.legitima.com/hotcast**)

- Nesox E-mail Marketer (**http://www.nesox.com**)

Case Study: www.arialsoftware.com

E-mail marketing: Know Your ISP

When it comes to using an installed e-mail marketing software solution, your best delivery option is through an SMTP mail server.

Typically, when you sign up with an Internet Service Provider (ISP), they provide a number of e-mail addresses you can use plus use of their outgoing (SMTP) mail server.

There are thousands of ISPs across the nation and worldwide; however, and it is almost impossible to know how each of them behaves toward bulk delivery of e-mail.

It is therefore incumbent on you, the ISP customer, to know the rules and regulations of your ISP with whom you contract.

Some ISPs may block access to all other outgoing mail servers using the standard SMTP port 25. Sometimes they limit outgoing bandwidth, because spikes in bandwidth usually indicate high volume mail traffic.

Many ISPs spell out their e-mail restrictions on their Web site, typically as part of their user licensing agreement. If the restrictions placed on e-mailing by your ISP are unsatisfactory, you should change ISPs; after all, they are competing for your business.

Pressure them to provide the services you need to run your business more effectively.

General rules about ISPs

As a general observation, the larger the ISP, the more restrictive they are towards e-mailing. Large ISPs typically lack the flexibility to accommodate everyone adequately, so they basically provide a broad range of services geared toward the general masses, not your small business. A bulk e-mail marketer is not part of the general mass of Internet users, however, and requires special consideration.

We at Arial Software are constantly asked which ISPs we recommend;

Case Study: www.arialsoftware.com

unfortunately, it is impossible to recommend any company because many ISPs are typically serving local or statewide. National ISPs include large companies like Cox Communications, BellSouth, and Verizon Online. As mentioned, these ISP "big boys" typically have many limits on sending e-mails because of their huge volume of customers and their catering to this segment. Smaller ISP companies, with more control over individual configuration, may be more willing and able to accommodate your e-mail needs.

Samples of ISP rules

Here are some examples of e-mail requirements from a few larger ISPs.

Cox Communications

Cox Communications allows bulk e-mail marketing, but you need to follow their rules. These include using valid from, reply to, and return path addresses within e-mail messages. For lists over 1,000 e-mails, you must send them during low traffic times, usually between the hours of 11 p.m. and 4 a.m. Central time.

You'll also need to get written permission from Cox to engage in bulk e-mailing through their servers. Cox Communications has several regional offices and locations so you will want to contact the one providing service in your area for specific questions. For more information visit the Cox Communications e-mail policy links below.

Cox Communication E-mail Policy Links

Mass E-mail/Bulk E-mail **http://support.coxbusiness.com/sdcxuser/cbs/default. asp?theArticleView=9ec915aa-fc2c-409a-9beb-2ffd884a457e**

E-mail Relay **http://support.coxbusiness.com/sdcxuser/cbs/default.asp?theArticleV iew=bd5d144c-d57c-47b4-9f2e-13fe493a7b52**

POP/SMTP Settings **http://support.coxbusiness.com/sdcxuser/cbs/default.asp?the ArticleView=6c69c244-f64b-458c-bdff-d97837458d97**

Mass Mailing Request Form **http://massmailing.coxmail.com/**

BellSouth

BellSouth doesn't post their bulk e-mail information online, so you will most likely need to call your nearest BellSouth representative and ask them specifically what their e-mail marketing policies are. Building an ISP relationship with BellSouth would be well worth your while, because if you are determined to be a spammer it could cost you up to $5.00 per e-mail, according to BellSouth's Acceptable Use Policy.

Case Study: www.arialsoftware.com

BellSouth Policy Links

Outbound Mail Server list **http://help.bellsouth.net/bellsouth/asp/contentview. asp?sprt_cid=94e61cd2%2Dc1a9%2D44fa%2D84b0%2Db36c5d7a9bc5**

Acceptable Use Policy **http://home.bellsouth.net/csbellsouth/s/editorial. dll?fromspage=cg/legal/legal_homepage.htm&categoryid=&only=y&bfromind=354 &eeid=3761384&eetype=article&render=y&ck=**

Verizon Online

Verizon Online explicitly states that they do not support sending to e-mail distribution lists, which sounds like they do not allow bulk e-mail through their servers.

Verizon Online Links

To find Verizon information and support, go to **http://business.verizon.net/help/** and enter your state. To find the name of the mail servers click on the "E-mail" link on the right, and click "E-mail settings and server names" under the business column.

GoDaddy.com

GoDaddy, a popular web domain name reseller, is also a Web host that provides full services for managing your company domain, including e-mail services. GoDaddy limits e-mail marketers to sending 250 e-mails per day, per e-mail account. Additional sending packs for larger lists can be purchased from GoDaddy in increments of 50 e-mails.

GoDaddy Links

E-mail FAQ page **http://help.godaddy.com/article_list.php?topic_id=168**

Earthlink

Earthlink's bulk e-mail policies are a little vague. Their Web site does not provide a number on what the e-mail limit is. Their limits change daily, based on the amount of traffic through the mail server. If you get the following message "error 554: **www.earthlink.net/go/bulk** - Outbound message limit exceeded," then you know that you've exceeded the limit for the day, and you'll need to follow the link and provide additional information.

Earthlink Links

Acceptable Use Policy (AUP) **http://kb.earthlink.net/case.asp?article=10959**

Case Study: www.arialsoftware.com

Commercial E-mail Policy **http://www.earthlink.net/about/policies/commercial/**

SMTP Rate limiting information **http://kb.earthlink.net/case.asp?article=85283**

High Usage E-mail Alert form **www.earthlink.net/go/bulk**

AT&T Yahoo! (sbcglobal.net)

AT&T Yahoo! business packages have effective outbound e-mail packages when using an installed e-mail marketing software product. You must ensure that you have the right business account package. If you try to send commercial bulk -e-mails using a residential e-mail account, you will likely run into a few roadblocks along the way.

AT&T Yahoo! links

Bulk E-mail practices **http://support.sbcglobal.net/article.php?item=6292**

POP and SMTP mail server settings **http://support.sbcglobal.net/article. php?item=287**

About Arial Software

Founded in 1993, Arial Software is widely considered the leading developer of permission-based e-mail marketing software used for delivering e-mail newsletters, customer specials, automatic responses, exclusive offers, and more. Arial Software products are used by corporations, retailers, universities, and other organizations to deliver personalized messages directly to subscribers, customers, prospects and members. Arial Software customers include XM Satellite Radio, The Children's Place, DirtDevil.com, Terra Lycos, and more. More information can be found at **http:// www.arialsoftware.com.**

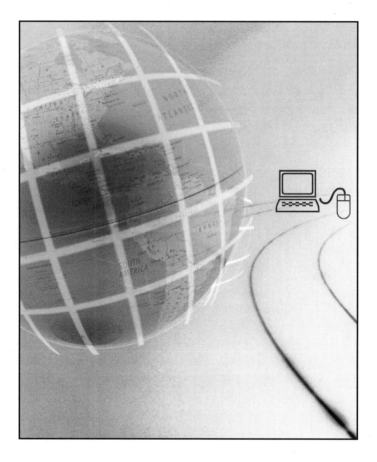

8

TARGET & SEGMENT YOUR AUDIENCE

Targeting your audience is a fairly simple concept. You want to send e-mails to the recipients who will most likely respond to your e-mail. Targeting is critical for some lists, and not so much for others.

WHEN NOT TO USE TARGETING & SEGMENTATION

I mentioned Alan's North Carolina B-B-Q in an earlier chapter about collecting e-mail addresses through customers in their restaurant, and I will use them to prove some points. Primarily, they are only targeting customers, or potential customers, and use the e-mail list to send out promotions and coupons to draw customers back in or acquire new customers. If someone is one their list, the assumption is they are likely already a customer and they probably want to receive discount coupons from the restaurant. How do you target people within that list and why would you want to? In this case, since the list is comprised of customers and the sole purpose of the e-mail list is to promote specials, distribute coupons, and announce new menu items, Alan only creates one e-mail per month to distribute to his list. Alan's list is very small and he uses his personal computer to manage his customer base. Gizmo Graphics Web Design does the creative work for him and produces an HTML based e-mail for distribution. However, there still remain potential areas to target, depending on the demographic information collected at the time of signup. In this case, Alan is collecting an e-mail address only (no demographic data); therefore, targeting a segment of his e-mail list is not productive. Demographic data should be collected when possible to help you if you choose to use it for targeting your list.

WHEN TO USE TARGETING & SEGMENTATION

Atlantic Publishing Company produces books on a wide variety of subjects. For purposes of this book, I am going to use them as a very basic example of targeting. They use targeting to segment their mailing lists between the variety of interests of their subscribers. For example, if you are a real estate professional, you may be interested in the release of the new book *How to Buy Real Estate Without a Down Payment in Any Market: Insider Secrets from the Experts Who Do It Every Day*, but would not necessarily be interested in a release on catering or bar and beverage management.

For simplicity's sake, let us say they have 100,000 names on their e-mail list. 50,000 are interested in food service related topics and 50,000 are interested in real estate topics. If they were to send an e-mail through an all-in-one service provider to all 100,000 subscribers announcing the release of the book *How to Buy Real Estate Without a Down Payment in Any Market: Insider Secrets from the Experts Who Do It Every Day*, they can expect approximately 50 percent of their list recipients to have little to no interest in it. In addition, they may actually see an increase in unsubscribe requests by individuals who expect e-mail related to food service, but are instead getting real estate information.

Additionally, and even more importantly, they just paid to send 100,000 e-mails to their list recipients when they could have realized a 50 percent cost-savings by targeting the list to the real estate specific recipients. Targeting allows you to narrow the recipient list to those who you think will have the most interest and are most likely to respond to your e-mail. If Alan's North Carolina B-B-Q started distributing e-mail's to their customer list on unrelated topics, they would soon find very few names left on their list.

The more targeted your e-mail message is, the higher the likelihood is that it will be successful. Since most e-mail programs and all-in-one solution providers give you the capability of creating targeted e-mails, you can create highly customized and personalized messages targeting only those who are most likely to act on the e-mail message, thus increasing return on investment and decreasing costs. Statistics support that personalized and targeted e-mail campaigns realize improved results when compared to generic e-mails. **Topica.com** offers a wide variety of targeting and segmentation options based on any field or combination of fields for which you have collected data including:

- Demographics or Interests

- Campaigns Opened or Clicked

- Campaigns Not Opened or Clicked

- Time Delta from Demographic Date (Renewals)

- Purchased Items

- Amount of Purchase

- Recency of Purchase

- Shopping Cart Abandonment

PERSONALIZATION

Personalization is simply the process of customizing your e-mail blasts with customer data, thus making them more personalized to the recipient. In other words, your e-mail blast to me might start with Dear Bruce..... instead of no greeting or a generic introductory greeting. So what is the value in personalization? There are several reasons to personalize which include increase recognition by customers, the "friendly" factor of receiving a personalized e-mail instead of a generic e-mail, potential increased return on investment, many recipients expect it, and may be turned off when they do not receive personalized e-mails. In general, using personalized e-mail softens the e-mail and promotes a "friendly" exchange of information.

I have read numerous surveys which indicate most Web site visitors do not mind spending up to five minutes filling out forms of personal data (name, e-mail, address, etc) to join a mailing list or get promotional information. This may have been true a few years ago, but I find it very difficult to believe that anyone is willing to share a significant amount of personal information beyond their name and e-mail address, and perhaps the state they are residing in. You need to decide how much personal data you wish to collect, and how to use it. However, be warned, there are risks in asking for too much information – you will lose potential list subscribers who do not want to spend five minutes filling out their life history on your Web site, and even more who feel like you do not need to know this information. With the prevalence of identity theft, the trend (and safest action) is to reveal less than more about yourself.

My recommendation is to require the e-mail address, and try to collect first name, last name, and state at a minimum, where possible. You can certainly collect more data if you want, but make the fields optional so the list subscriber can choose what they want to reveal to you. Also, when using the personalization in an e-mail be careful of overuse. Using Dear Bruce – is fine in the introduction, but do not use it (or the recipient's name) in every paragraph. The overkill will drive away potential customers faster than anything.

COLLECTING DEMOGRAPHIC DATA

The great thing about Web based forms is you can capture any data that is entered, and then use that data to target and personalize your e-mails. As I mentioned earlier, you can collect a wide variety of data elements, but you may lose potential subscribers if your subscription form is too lengthy and time consuming to fill out. **Topica.com** recently expanded the personalization feature in their all-in-one solution by providing up to 12 unique fields including both single-select and multiple-select category fields such as name, city, state, etc. and other behavioral or demographic data, such as product purchased or area of site visited can also be used for personalization. Most solution providers allow you to customize the degree of personalization and demographic data you wish to collect.

However, in light of the volume of potential demographic data you can collect, go with the minimum and ask for an e-mail address and name, and then only what other data you believe is critical for use in your e-mail campaign. There is no point soliciting or collecting data you don't intend to utilize in your campaigns. The golden rule is the less information you ask for, the better the chance that someone will fill your subscription forms and join your e-mail list. As you develop a relationship with your e-mail subscribers, you can always try to solicit more information later. Build the relationship first, then expand your demographic to extra information such as address, gender, age, income, marital status, etc. No matter what, if your e-mail subscriber list only contains e-mail addresses, you are way behind the power curve.

MAINTAINING MULTIPLE LISTS

One of the best features of e-mail marketing is the ability to perform list segmentation or sub-lists. If you have a variety of e-mail lists for different product lines or which target different customer needs you can use multiple lists within in a single account allowing you to maintain one cost-effective account but still maintain lists separately within your account. This is ideal for companies who have collected e-mail addresses only, for years, and do not possess the demographic data to allow for automated segmentation or targeting within their lists. They can continue to develop e-mail campaigns based on their targeted lists, and maintain each list within one single account.

A common question I get is, "How can I personalize e-mails or send targeted e-mails if my list only contains e-mail addresses?" The answer is you cannot. There is no magic program which will "know" the name of the recipient of e-mail addresses on your list, nor can you determine demographics data based solely on an e-mail address. Establish a rapport and trust with your existing subscribers, and if you want you can ask them to provide demographic data (on an optional basis) at a later date.

Case Study: Gold Lasso

When e-mail was first introduced as a viable marketing and communications vehicle, organizations used it to send mass messages to large databases of contacts. It was a fast, cost-effective tool. Since then, e-mail has become a more complex marketing medium as a result of both regulatory and market demands requiring marketers to update their use of this medium.

Audiences today favor demassification and personalization of the marketing messages they receive. Demassification refers to the process of breaking down the mass market (those large lists of contacts) into focused, segmented groups based on preferences, lifestyles, purchasing trends, values, and priorities — to name a few. The focus has shifted from a "one size fits all" model to content that is relevant and specific to the intended recipient.

Personalization commands the user's attention with tailored messages and products. It builds familiarity by utilizing consistent templates that employ a similar "look and feel" to what the end user is used to seeing. These attributes help establish a bond with the recipient that will, if executed correctly, promote loyalty through increased customer service.

Case Study: Gold Lasso

Incorporating personalization into e-mail marketing campaigns increases response rates, instills trust in the organization and the messages it sends and builds a relationship with the end user that encourages them to become an active contact.

With all the advantages to this tool, why are more marketers not using it? Most e-marketers do use personalization on some level whether it be using the first name in the message greeting or sending different messages based on geography or membership status. The most successful marketers work with their e-mail service provider (ESP) to delve deeper into their database metrics and build campaigns that uncover the essential information needed to personalize messages effectively. The challenge to successful personalization is availability of data, time and cost to collect useful data and understanding the technical aspects employed by ESPs to personalize campaigns.

The purpose of this paper is to review general concepts behind personalization, further investigate its advantages, discuss the challenges to personalizing campaigns, and provide solutions to overcome the challenges.

Gold Lasso, LLC

312 Main Street, Suite 200

Gaithersburg, Maryland 20878

Phone 301-990-9857 Fax: 301-990-9856

http://www.GoldLasso.com

DEMYSTIFYING THE CONCEPT OF PERSONALIZATION

A simple Google search provides many documents written by marketers that give definitions of personalization including:

- The process of gathering user-information during interaction with the user, which is then used to deliver appropriate content and services, tailor-made to the user's needs. (Source: Personalization of Web Services: Opportunities and Challenges — **http://www.ariadne. ac.uk/issue28/personalization/**).

- Building customer loyalty by building a meaningful one-to-one relationship. (Source: Doug Riecken. *Personalized Views of Personalization.* Communications of the ACM, 43(8): 27-28, August 2000).

While the word choice varies, the concept is the same — building customer loyalty and satisfaction by gathering and using data tailored to the customer's needs, preferences and values. Online vendors frequently use this concept. If you visit **Amazon.com** and look up fitness DVDs with or without purchasing them, the next time you visit the page you will see Amazon has automatically recommended other fitness DVDs based on your recent search.

You will also receive a personalized confirmation page if you purchased a DVD with additional items related to your search. Personalization occurs in different ways in an e-marketing campaign. Some ways include:

- **List segmentation** — dividing marketing lists based on pre-determined factors to create targeted messages to each segment

- **Content** — tailoring the text of the message to fit the list segment

- **Subject line** — creating a subject line that is personalized to the recipient, grabs his or her attention, and increases the likelihood he or she will read the message

- **Address line** (i.e. Dear [Insert name],) — including the recipients first name in the greeting

- **Signature** (insert a name and personal signature) — including an electronic signature from the person sending the message

- **Type of message** — a recipient may sign up or be qualified to receive certain publications such as e-newsletters or e-zines

Segmentation of the distribution list is a key component of personalization. Many organizations purchase or build marketing lists that include hundreds or thousands of names from different backgrounds, interests, professions, etc. Dividing, or segmenting, the list by pre-determined factors will help guide the development of a personal message. The segmenting factors are determined by the goal and scope of the e-marketing campaign.

Example:

ABC Association is conducting an e-mail marketing campaign to increase attendance at its annual educational meeting. After reviewing attendance statistics for the past three years, the marketing director concludes that only 50 percent of their current membership base attends the meeting. ABC Association currently has 95 percent of their members e-mail addresses in its database. The membership represents different industries (allied healthcare professionals, automotive service workers, nursing industries, financial planners, etc) with varied professional interests, socioeconomic backgrounds, educational needs, and technological skills. ABC's marketing director works with their ESP to segment the list and subsequent messages based on the following factors:

- **Geography** — contacts within driving distance to the three day meeting location receive messages focused on the one day rate and their ability to choose the day based on their educational program needs.

- **Activity levels** — members who had participated in other events or purchased publications already had a connection to the organization. They received messages targeted toward educational content and encouraging their continued learning and professional development through attendance at the three-day meeting. If they have had no history with ABC except for their membership, they received an introductory message highlighting the importance of attending the meeting.

- **Membership type** — those members that fall into a vendor category (service providers to the industry) receive messages recruiting them to exhibit and sponsor social and networking functions.

- **Educational content** — the content of the meeting was divided into tracks based on professional experience levels (i.e. beginner, intermediate, advanced). Contacts received messages targeted to their perceived experience level based on their years in the industry.

It is important to note the difference between personalization and customization. Customization allows the user to proactively configure a Web site and/or create a profile. Personalization occurs when the marketer actively gathers information from the user or analyzes their activity and profile.

Common Terms

- **Call to action:** In an e-mail message, the link or body copy that tells the recipient what action to take.

- **Content:** All the material in an e-mail message except for the codes showing the delivery route and return-path information, including all words, images, and links.

- **Cookies:** A collection of information, usually including a username and the current date and time, stored on the local computer of a person using the World Wide Web, used by Web sites to identify users who have previously registered or visited the site.

- **Demographics:** The characteristics of human populations and population segments, especially when used to identify consumer markets.

- **Dynamic content:** E-mail newsletter content that changes from one recipient to the next according to a set of predetermined rules or variables, usually according to preferences the user sets when opting in to messages from a sender. Dynamic content can reflect past purchases, current interests, or where the recipient lives.

- **Landing page:** A Web page viewed after clicking on a link within an e-mail. Also may be called a microsite, splash page, bounce page, or click page.

- **Personalization:** A targeting method in which an e-mail message appears to have been created only for a single recipient. Personalization techniques include adding the recipient's name in the subject line or message body, or the message offer reflects a purchasing, link clicking, or transaction history.

- **Psychographics:** The use of demographics to study and measure attitudes, values, lifestyles, and opinions for marketing purposes.

- **Segmentation:** The ability to slice a list into specific pieces determined by various attributes, such as open history or name source.

- **Signature:** A line or two of information found in the closing of an e-mail usually followed the sender's name. Signatures can include advertising information, such as a company name, product, brand message, or marketing call to action (subscribe to a company newsletter with the e-mail subscribe address or Web registration form, or visit a Web site with the URL listed).

- **Subject line:** Copy that identifies what an e-mail message is about, often designed to entice the recipient into opening the message. The subject line appears first in the recipient's inbox, often next to the sender's name or e-mail address. It is repeated in the e-mail message's header information inside the message.

CHALLENGES AND SOLUTIONS

Personalizing e-marketing campaigns allow organizations to effectively target and capture potential contacts. The most notable benefits of personalization include:

- **Increasing response rates** — Statistics indicate that personalized messages lead to higher response rates from users to the marketers "call to action." The call to action is the desired action from the message. It could be a click through to the organization's Web site or an invitation to attend an event.

- **Building relationships** — Building a relationship with the user increases the likelihood the user will purchase services or products, continue to read and act on messages, visit the organization's site, and stay on as a long-term customer or member.

- **Promoting security with customers** — The volume of spam in the recipient's general inbox requires marketers find creative ways to ensure the recipient reads the message. Personalizing the message with relevant information increases customer's security with the organization. Personalization helps marketers legitimize their messages to the reader.

Despite the opportunities available, organizations still face challenges to personalizing e-campaigns. The challenges a marketer faces vary depending on their level of e-marketing expertise, e-mail client, etc. The organization's ESP is typically able to deal with these challenges rather easily. Gold Lasso defines the top three challenges as unavailability of data, timeliness and cost to collect data and technical aspects.

Challenge: Unavailability of Data

In this case, the marketer or organization does not have data to segment their distribution list or personalize the message.

Solution: Incorporate surveys, polls, or response forms to build database.

The first step is to use any data available, even if it is just a first name, to begin personalizing the message and campaign. For example, if the organization is a non-profit membership association it likely has names and member ID numbers for billing purposes. That information can be used to initially personalize. By using the name and ID number, the sender builds security with the recipient who recognizes the confidential information as a legitimate message. Incorporating templates that contain the organization's logo and general "look and feel" will help build a brand with the recipient as well. However, gathering data should be the main focus to overcoming this challenge.

Gold Lasso recommends using quick surveys, polls, or response forms in the e-mail and on the landing pages that can be merged with general databases and used in future campaigns.

Challenge: Timeliness/Cost to Collect Data

In this case, the organization believes they do not have the time or budget to gather the data needed to personalize the campaign.

Solution: Consult with the ESP to develop tactics to gather data in current campaigns. Collecting data for personalization can occur in every campaign that is sent. For example, if a non-profit membership association conducts online membership renewal, the data collected (i.e. name, contact information, industry, title, etc) can be used to personalize messages later in the year at a relatively low cost. The key is to discuss options with the ESP instead of assuming the technology costs too much money. In the end, the return on investment (ROI) could far exceed the initial cost.

Challenge: Technical Aspects

In this case, the organization does not understand, own or utilize technical solutions available to personalize the message.

Solution: Educate yourself on the main aspects of personalization and work with an ESP to handle the technology. If e-marketing is not your primary profession, turn to someone who is an expert (such as an ESP) to help you create an e-marketing plan that incorporates personalization. The technology around this medium changes frequently. The ESP's job is to stay up-to-date with technology changes and communicate that to the client.

CONCLUSION

Personalization is a key tactic to improve the success of an e-marketing campaign. Personalized messages encourage the recipient to read the content and respond to the call to action. More importantly, personalized messages serve as a tool to build a relationship between the marketer and the recipient that can ultimately lead to consumer loyalty. In an environment where consumers are inundated with choices, employing a tool that promotes continued interaction is essential.

Personalization also helps increase perception that the marketer is a viable information source. This helps to decrease spam complaints and ensure the delivery of the message. The overall concept of demassification is dynamic, much like the personalized message itself. It will continue to evolve as techniques for gathering information improve. The goal is to understand its benefits and stay up-to-date with technology available to use this beneficial marketing technique.

9

HOW TO WRITE AN EFFECTIVE E-MAIL

This is essentially the heart and soul of an e-mail marketing campaign. I will show you how to craft an HTML and text based e-mail, and reveal time-tested techniques for ensuring that your e-mail is well-written, effective, and designed to maximize the potential return from recipients. Your e-mail (or e-mail creative as it is also known), is a critical part of your campaign. The subject line is the first thing that a recipient will see, followed by your actual e-mail. Your e-mail blast is the direct communication from your company to each of your recipients, and often serves as the initial contact from your company to a potential customer. Therefore, you want to ensure it is professional, effective, and error-free. We all know what junk e-mail and spam looks like, as there is no doubt we receive some daily. Your e-mail creative must be designed so it does not look like amateur spam. Likewise, a poorly designed e-mail creative will not inspire confidence in the recipient, and will typically not result in landing sales.

HTML VS TEXT FORMAT

I covered this in the last chapter, but I will recap it here for you again. You need to decide on whether you wish to pursue your e-mail campaign using HTML, text, or both. I recommend you do both where possible. HTML formatted messages are simply Web pages that are sent through an e-mail server, re-assembled, and presented to the recipient in their browser. The advantage to HTML is that you can use highly customized formatting, embedded graphics, and other dynamic features which require HTML coding. Text based messages are straight text, little to no formatting which is presented in both text and HTML based Web browsers in an easy-to-read format. HTML allows you to use customer fonts, colors, graphics, and interactive rich-media technology. Text based e-mails are simple text, little formatting, no graphics, no colors or special font formatting, but they do allow you to embed absolute hyperlinks in the text. Most all in one providers allow you to craft both text and HTML formatted messages, so use both when feasible to allow to you reach all of your potential customers.

HTML formatted messages are more professional in appearance, and do have a significantly higher open and response rate than non-HTML formatted messages.

HOW TO DESIGN AN HTML E-MAIL

The fact is that most e-mail applications support HTML based e-mail and that is the preferred format most people want to receive their e-mail by. I recommend you focus your efforts on HTML e-mail and use text based e-mail as an alternative for those who only wish to receive text based e-mails or whose e-mail client does not support HTML formatted messages.

When designing an HTML e-mail you should follow the same principles of Web site design. You should follow the rules for search engine optimization when you design your e-mails and incorporate meta-tag data and keywords into the design. Many companies place their e-mail newsletters, articles, and other e-mail blasts on their Web sites and I highly recommend you do this. There are several reasons which may include:

- Allowing your articles, newsletters, etc. to be available to anyone visiting your Web site.

- Your HTML formatted e-mail blasts will be picked up by search engines and indexed — this is why you need to follow the rules have provided for basic search engine optimization. Essentially, you will be using your e-mail campaigns (when properly designed with search engine optimization techniques) to increase your overall Web site rankings with search engines.

I recommend you design HTML e-mails in a Web design application, such as

Microsoft Frontpage (its replacement Microsoft Expression Web) or Macromedia Dreamweaver. You do not need the latest version for creating your e-mails and there are numerous other alternatives. I do not recommend you attempt to use Notepad or any other non-graphical user interface application, nor should you use Microsoft Word. Also, keep in mind that many programs, including Frontpage, may insert additional code into your HTML e-mails; therefore, it is critical you test each e-mail before you schedule an e-mail blast. Although there are dissenting opinions on the use of Frontpage for e-mail campaigns, I have used it for years with tremendous success. Go with the 2003 version or the replacement Microsoft Expression Web.

The process for actually creating your e-mail blast is exactly the same as designing a Web page, and with Microsoft Frontpage, the learning curve for non-experenced Web designers if very small, and most novice users can craft a professional looking e-mail campaign. Microsoft Expression Web, the Frontpage replacement, is more complicated (although far superior) to Frontpage; therefore, you may have to keep Frontpage or another familiar HTML editor for the creation of your e-mail campaigns. If you want to ensure you have a professional campaign, there are numerous e-mail marketers and Web design companies who are cost-effective and highly reputable throughout this book. Let us look at some HTML e-mail design basics (I will walk you through the process later in this chapter):

- Do not embed graphics into your actual e-mail blast. Instead, place your graphics on a Web server and call the graphics by a URL embedded into your e-mail. Embedded large graphics can cause significant download problems for recipients.

- When designing your HTML e-mail, use absolute URL's for all of your graphics or hyperlinks. A common mistake when designing is to use the relative URL, which may work fine when designing and testing, but will not work when delivered. For example, a relative URL may be "/emailblast/images/radio1.jpg", as long as you are on your Web server this relative location is understood and the images will be served properly; however, if you are not on the server (i.e. you are reading the e-mail in your e-mail client), the URL will fail and the image links will be broken. Use the absolute URL such as: **http://www.gizwebs.com/ emailblast/images/radio1.jpg.**

- I recommend you design your e-mail blast with a combination of HTML formatting (tables, text, colors, etc) and embedded graphics instead of creating your entire creative in a graphics program and sending that graphic creative as your entire e-mail campaign. However, if you choose to send a large graphic as your e-mail campaign you can still apply SEO principles, and you should slice your e-mail to facilitate download speed. All graphics software such as Macromedia Fireworks and JASC Paint Shop Pro allow you to take an image, slice it into pieces, and export it into an HTML document with absolute URL's calling each sliced portion of the image. I will walk you through this entire process later in this chapter.

• Where possible, minimize the use of graphics to improve download speed. Use HTML coding, tables, background colors, etc to design your e-mail without graphics when possible.

There are many resources available on how to craft and style and effective e-mail and I will highlight most of them in this chapter. Additionally, I have added a wealth of articles, tips, tricks, and other advice from the industry experts. By compiling this relevant advice into one book, you now possess the best advice from the experts who do it every day. Your goal when creating an e-mail is to catch the attention of the recipient, captivate them with interesting and relevant content, and provide them with the ability to complete an action (fill out a Web form, follow a hyperlink, provide information, place an order, etc).

TOOLS AND ADVICE FOR CREATING YOUR E-MAIL MASTERPIECE

Let us walk through the basic tools and advice for creating an effective e-mail:

• **Software Tools for Creating HTML e-mail:**

  ○ Microsoft Frontpage

  ○ Microsoft Expression Web

  ○ Macromedia Dreamweaver

  ○ There are others which will work fine

  ○ Do not use Microsoft Word or any other word processor

º Do not use Notepad — it will work fine, but significantly increases the complexity

- **Software for creating Graphics**

  º JASC Paint Shop Pro

  º Macromedia Fireworks

  º Adobe Photoshop

- **Design an Effective Creative/Layout** — You need to place special emphasis on the overall design and layout of your creative. Use SEO techniques and Web design fundamentals (there are dozens of resources on the Web). Your goal is to captivate the reader, get him or her to open your actual e-mail blast, and then have him or her follow your desired action. There are dozens of Web sites dedicated to how to properly format the text of an e-mail, news article, or newsletter. These Web sites can guide you through the process of writing an e-mail masterpiece, as well as utilizing the dozens of tips and articles contained in this book. For now, we will concentrate on the actual format and layout of the e-mail, not the content. You will find the layout may be the easier task, while designing the content is a much bigger challenge.

- **Use HTML Tags for Proper Formatting** — I have read many opinions which tell you to remove all or most HTML tags from your e-mail. Remember, an HTML e-mail is essentially a Web page, so you should use the basic HTML tags to properly format your e-mail. An HTML capable e-mail application will know how to read, interpret, and properly display your e-mails. Browser-based e-mail clients, such as Gmail and Yahoo! will also read and properly display HTML e-mails. Additionally, this simplifies the process of taking your HTML e-mail and turning it into a page on your Web site for references, news articles, newsletter archive, etc (remember, you want these to be indexed by search engines, so the use of keywords and proper HTML formatting is important). Keep in mind if you use a commercial product for your e-mails which states which HTML tags are allowed, you should follow that guide. In absence of any restrictions, I recommend at a minimum that you should include the following HTML tags:

- ° DOCTYPE

- ° <HTML></HTML>

- ° <BODY></BODY>

- ° <HEAD></HEAD>

- ° <LINK>

- ° <TITLE></TITLE>

- ° Do not include scripts (javascript, VB scripts), Java, Java applets, other applets, frames, or comments in your e-mail creative

- **Use HTML tables** — Specify the maximum width in pixels so you have a predefined workspace and incorporate content within your tables. The use of tables will greatly improve your layout and final presentation.

- **Host images on a Web server** — Do not embed images directly into an HTML e-mail creative. Many e-mail programs strip out an embedded image and your e-mail will not display properly, additionally embedded images affect the download and display times, negatively impacting your potential success rate. Additionally, many spam filters will block the embedded images or cause your e-mail to be sent directly to a junk mailbox. When you are sending an image file which is large and hosted on a Web server, slice the image into smaller parts to facilitate the download process.

- **Again, use absolute URL's for all of your graphics or hyperlinks.**

- **Use a white background on all table cells** — Fill in these cells with graphics and text. Colored backgrounds tend to cause problems with some e-mail clients and can conflict with font colors. If you want to use a background image to fill the empty space outside of your HTML table it may work; however, it is not recommended. Be sure to stick to a white background for your table. Some e-mail clients may not display background images, so ensure your e-mail creative is satisfactory with a white background in the event the image does not display properly.

- **You should explicitly state the colors, font styles, font sizes, etc in your HTML coding** — This is because some Web based e-mail programs may apply their own style sheets to your e-mail if you do not specify them. This may cause them to appear significantly different than you intended.

- **Do not use cascading style sheets in your e-mail** — They tend to cause multiple problems with a variety of e-mail clients. You should ensure that your final HTML creative will appear as you intended based solely on the HTML coding you used, not on external style sheets.

- **Use the <BR> tag instead of the <P> tag in your HTML.**

- **Do not embed forms in your e-mail creative** — Direct recipients to a form on your Web server. There are some Web based e-mail clients which do not properly support forms. Hyper-links work great in all Web based e-mail clients (and all other e-mail applications), plus they provide you with a great way to track what how your recipients are responding to your e-mail blast by tracking activity on each hyperlink.

- **Follow the basic rules of spam complianc**e — Include an unsubscribe link, and I also recommend a link to your Web administrator in the event there is a problem with the auto-unsubscribe so e-mail recipients can contact your for a manual removal.

- **Test each e-mail blast with a variety of e-mail clients** — This is to ensure it is displayed properly. Also, it may be a good idea to include a link at the top of your e-mail which states, "If this e-mail is not displayed properly, please click here."

- **Use HTML templates to provide you with a professional feel** — There are many companies which sell e-mail marketing templates online, and you can also find many free ones. I recommend **templatezone.com** which features several feature rich programs which will guide you through the e-mail creation process and are loaded with professionally designed templates. One word of caution, templates are comprised of many images, make sure you put those images on your Web servers and use absolute URLs in your e-mail creative, and as always, test before you blast.

- **Keep the e-mails concise, short, and to the point** — If you want someone to read your e-mails, you need to get to the point quickly and grab his or her attention. No one will read a novel, and you will more than likely fail to achieve any measurable success if your e-mail is long. If your message is long, you may opt to provide a captivating brief introduction and provide a link back to your Web site with full detailed information. Your communications should be inspiring or compelling. Use strong action words which communicate your message quickly and clearly. Rule of thumb is two to three paragraphs maximum, use keywords, and if your message is primarily text based, put the information in bullets to make it easy to read and digest.

- **Use a strong subject and introduction** — I will cover the subject line in the next chapter, and you need to need to use a strong introduction to grab the attention of your recipients. You need to quickly convey a message that will make the recipient want to read on instead of hitting the delete key.

- **Include contact information and be clear on what you want the recipient to do** — If you want them to call you, make sure you have full contact information and it is clear. Nothing is more frustrating than getting an e-mail with no contact information (well, I guess there are more frustrating things, but this is one of them). If you want recipients to buy products, be clear and be sure that the forms and other contact methods function properly.

- **Create a Web Page** — If you are providing or seeking specific information, a Web page is the perfect resource to allow customers to choose what information they want to read. Do not direct them to your home page and expect them to hunt through your site to navigate to the right page, though. Give them the right page and lead them to it.

- **Interject your business name into your e-mail** — You want them to learn you company name, so put it in the e-mail early.

- **Give some thought to the from address you will be using** — I recommend using a from e-mail address which is first and foremost a valid e-mail address, and one that represents your company. Using personal e-mails such as **bruce@mysite.com** is not advised because they cannot associate your e-mail address to your company. My recommendation is to be straightforward and use your full company name. You want them to recognize your company as legitimate and that your e-mail is also legitimate, not spam. Do not use ridiculous sounding e-mail addresses such as freestuff@, bestdeals@, nospam@.

- **Personalize your e-mail blasts where possible.**

- **Do not be intimidated** — Creating an HTML e-mail is not difficult, but takes some patience and skill. Track results. If they are not what you anticipated, tweak your campaigns and try again at a future date. If you do not get any significant responses, do not continue to send the same e-mail over and over again.

- **If you need professional assistance, ask** — Many all-in-one service providers walk you through the process and provide you with pre-built templates. They dramatically reduce the learning curve and simplify the process. **Topica.com** pricing, for example, is based on e-mail volume. If you sign up for a year of service, you get a good discount and have a monthly allotment of e-mail you can send. When you exceed that limit you will pay overage charges, which can add up quickly. However, the support, free templates, and other features are all included with your subscription, so you might as well take advantage of them unless you want to create your own custom HTML e-mail blasts.

HOW TO DESIGN A TEXT BASED E-MAIL

I think it is important to use text based e-mails where possible with your HTML e-mail blasts; however, they are not critical. If you do not want to invest the time in converting graphic-rich HTML content into basic text formatting, then do not do it. The use of text e-mails is completely optional. The fact is that a majority of spam e-mails are text based.

If there is no un-subscribe link on the e-mail, I do not hesitate before it heads to the trash bin. The only reason for using text based e-mails is so you can provide a non-HTML, non-graphical e-mail for those whose e-mail clients cannot read HTML format or display it properly. If you want to be 100 percent sure that your e-mail will be received and displayed properly, text is the answer. All e-mail clients can properly read text based e-mails, and you can use hyperlinks in your text e-mails as well.

Here are some general guidelines for creating text based e-mails:

- **Software tools for creating an HTML e-mail** — Notepad (Windows) or TextEdit (Mac). Do not use Microsoft Word or any other program. Notepad is perfect for text based e-mail creation and comes with all versions of Windows so you already own it. TextEdit is the Macintosh equivalent to Notepad.

- **Limit your line length to no more than 80 characters.**

- **Limit your e-mail to two to three paragraphs** — Use bullets to get across critical points to recipients.

- **As with an HTML e-mail, shorter is better.**

- **You can use hyperlinks, but you must use the absolute link in proper HTML formatting** — Examples include: Click Here to Register: http://www.atlantic-pub.com. Likewise, you must use a mailto: in front of any e-mail addresses, such as mailto:bruce@atlantic-pub.com.

- **Use hard character returns** — This will force line wraps where you want them.

- **Do not use ASCII graphics** — You may get other advice on this subject, but personally, I hate ASCII graphics and will not use them. ASCII graphics are graphics created by using ASCII key symbols, such as the carot symbol as a graphical symbol in your e-mails. Below is an example of an ASCII graphic depicting a rabbit.

```
((()))(())
 ( '.' )
(___)___)o
```

The following are some great reference sources for learning how to write the content of your e-mails. Unfortunately, I can only give you the best possible advice and industry proven techniques on how to properly design, test, and implement an e-mail marketing program. Ultimately, you must create your e-mail content. Do not be afraid to ask others to review your e-mail content. You will find that how others perceive your e-mail will help you to improve the content and ultimately improve your chance for e-mail marketing success:

- A beginner's guide to effective e-mail — **http://webfoot.com/advice/e-mail.top.html**

- Writing sensible e-mail messages — **http://www.43folders.com/2005/09/19/writing-sensible-email-messages/**

- E-mail: an author's guide — **http://www.blueflavor.com/ed/tips_tricks/email_an_authors_guide.php**

- Writing competitive e-mail — **http://www.powerhomebiz.com/vol8/Writing.htm**

- Six steps to selling by e-mail — **http://www.powerhomebiz.com/vol10/e-mail.htm**

- Business writing — **http://www.businesswritingblog.com/business_writing/e-mail/index.html**

AUTO-RESPONDERS

An auto-responder is simply a program which automatically responds to anyone that sends e-mail to it by sending a pre-formatted e-mail back to the recipient. An auto-responder is commonly used for a variety uses, and can be a valuable ally in your e-mail marketing campaign. The most common use today is for out of office notifications, where, upon receipt of an e-mail an auto-responder sends a reply back to the sender notifying that the recipient is currently not in the office, typically it includes contact information, when they will be back, etc. An auto-responder can be used in conjunction with your e-mail campaign. When someone responds to your e-mail campaign, such as filling out a Web form for additional information, your auto-responder can automatically send them a wealth of information about your products or services. By automating this process, you are freed from manually responding to each potential customer. The primary benefits of using an auto-responder is time savings and timely responses to inquiries. There are dozens of auto-responder programs available for purchase, and most all-in-one solution providers include this service as part of their offered services.

In the e-mail above, notice that the absolute URL's are used for each graphic. In this example the image in the creative was sliced into 3 x 3 rows and columns, each "piece" of the image is placed in the appropriate cell in the HTML table to ensure exact positioning. Since each image is unique, each has its own hyperlink associated with it.

The HTML view below is what will be received by the user when the e-mail blast is sent and received by the HTML compatible e-mail client.

Case Study: Christopher Knight

Ezine Article Ideas — 15 to Spur Your Creative Writing Spark

Are you ever sitting at your computer with your eyes in a blank stare and your fingers ready at the keyboard, but you're stumped for ideas on what your next e-mail newsletter article should be about? Below are my top 15 ideas to help spark your creative writing imagination to crank out your next ezine article.

For this article, I'm going to use my favorite sport of Racquetball to illustrate article TITLE examples for each of my ezine article ideas below. You can just replace the topic of "Racquetball" with your niche expertise.

#1 Ezine Article Idea: Give Tips

Most people love to eat small "info-snacks" so feed them what they want. Give them quick tips or small bytes of a strategy to solve a problem or create an opportunity.

Example Titles:

5 Tips on How To Perfect Your Backhanded Kill Shot

Own The Center Court - 3 Mental Tips

17 Tips I Learned From Watching Sudsy Monchik, World Racquetball Champ

#2 Ezine Article Idea: How To Articles

When in doubt, return to "How To" articles as there are always an endless list of things you could teach your target audience.

Examples Titles:

Case Study: Christopher Knight

How To Pass Your Racquetball Opponent Before He Knew What Hit Him

How To String Your Head Racquetball Racquet

How To Prepare For A Racquetball Tournament

#3 Ezine Article Idea: Do an Interview

Become the "Reporter" and you will never run out of quality content ideas. Find someone with an expertise that your niche audience would value and setup an interview. You can do this via telephone, e-mail, live chat or in person.

Example Titles:

Interview With Superstar Racquetball Coach Fran Davis

Cliff Swain, Racquetball Champ Interview

Jason Mannino, Racquetball Champ Tells All In Exclusive Interview

#4 Ezine Article Idea: Make a List

Lists are easy and fun to do. For a great example, check out what I'm doing today for Ezine-Tips. I ran out of ideas so I decided to make a list of ideas for you. Pretty creative, no? : Your lists can be numbered or bullet points of information.

Example Titles:

72 Racquetball Serves You Can Learn Too

14 Ways To Hit A Church Shot in Racquetball

5 Reasons Why Racquetball Can Help You Burn 800 Calories An Hour

#5 Ezine Article Idea: Product Reviews

You can review your products and give examples of how people use your products or get more out of them. Anything that adds value to your current clients may also be valued by prospective clients. These can get cheesy if you sell too hard, so better to just give strategies and techniques on how to leverage your products value.

Example Titles:

Head's Liquid Metal Racquet Review- Accelerate Your Game

Penn Green Racquetballs - Why They Are The Fastest

Head Safety Racquetball Glasses - Helps Improve Vision Under Stress

Case Study: Christopher Knight

#6 Ezine Article Idea: Other People's Product Reviews

If you an affiliate marketer, this is a perfect strategy for you. Give a comprehensive review of other people's products and show the pro's and the con's of the product and its application.

Example Titles:

Wilson Racquetball Shoes - Are They Worth The Price?

ProKennex Racquetball Gear Makes You Look Smart... Why?

Ektelon Racquetball Head Band Reviews

#7 Ezine Article Idea: Use Humor or Comedy to Entertain Your Audience

Tell a joke or a humor thing that happened recently. Share funny things that have happened when people used your products in the wrong way. Make fun at how absurd your business can be at times or under heavy stress. Your readers will be entertained and relate to the human side of you.

Example Titles:

Things You Shouldn't Do In A Racquetball Court

Top 10 Racquetball Jokes To Tell Your Opponent

How You Know If Your Racquetball Opponent Has Been Drinking

#8 Ezine Article Idea: Tell a Story or Spin a Tale

I recommend telling a "SHORT" story. Ezine readers do not have time to read 7 page stories any more. Keep it short, get to the point, interject some fun in your story and spin your tale.

Example Titles:

How I Won My First Racquetball Tournament and You Can Too!

Why Racquetball Is A Great Sport For Singles of Both Genders

How I Scored A Point Against A Racquetball Legend

#9 Ezine Article Idea: News Excerpts As a Lead In

Grab a news byte of information to lead into your article or story. Fair use doctrines

Case Study: Christopher Knight

allow you to copy a short handful of sentences provided you give proper credit and don't alter the excerpt. Give your analysis or comments about the story.

Example Titles:

Mexico Takes World Racquetball Champ Title

Wisconsin Junior State Racquetball Champ is 15 And He Can Beat You

Clothing Optional Racquetball is Never a Good Idea - Here's Why

#10 Ezine Article Idea: Get Visual

Include charts, graphs, powerpoint presentations, check lists, short video clips or anything to visually add value to your article.

Example Titles:

Knight's Racquetball Z Lob Serve Video Clip

Racquetball Winning Percentage System

Racquetball Tour Checklist - Don't Leave Home Without It

#11 Ezine Article Idea: Get Other Experts To Contribute Articles

There are plenty of other experts in your niche that are more than willing to give you articles for free in exchange for a resource box below their article that promotes their Web site address. EzineArticles.com can help you find a perfect match.

Example Titles:

Racquetball Genius In You, By: Someone Other Than You.

Racquetball Rules, By: Someone Other Than You.

Racquetball Camp on a Hot Island in Winter, By: Someone Other Than You

#12 Ezine Article Idea: Recycle Old Articles

Articles can become outdated but base concepts are often timeless by nature. Go back into your archive of articles and refresh them with new and updated information.

Case Study: Christopher Knight

Example Titles:

Racquetball Legend Marty Hoag is Not Retired Yet

Pro Racquetball Ruben Gonzalez Teaches Youngsters Our Favorite Sport

What You Need To Do To Get In The Racquetball Hall of Fame

#13 Ezine Article Idea: Hire An Ezine Writer

There are plenty of ghost writers willing to work for a penny to a buck per word. Often times the lower cost ghost writers can pen excellent articles but you should do the TITLE for the articles or generate the theme for them to work with.

Example Titles:

Racquetball Nutrition, By: Your Ghost Writer

Weight Lifting For Racquetball Players, By: Your Ghost Writer

Supplements & Vitamins For Racquetball Players, By Your Ghost Writer

#14 Ezine Article Idea: Word or Phrase For The Day

There is always a new word to learn. Share a common term from your niche and define it well giving examples of its use.

Example Titles:

Passing Shot Defined - Your Racquetball Cornerstone Winning Strategy

Intentional Hinder Defined - When and What is a Racquetball Hinder?

Skip Ball Defined - What a "Skipped" Racquetball Sounds Like

#15 Ezine Article Idea: Use A Holiday

Holiday's or "On This Day In History" are great idea generators for new article content possibilities. Chase's Calendar of Events is quite popular for defining holidays and events.

Example Titles:

Racquetball League Begins This Month-How To Prepare

Winter Blues Got You Down? Racquetball Camp in Aruba Reviewed

Racquetball Safety Awareness Day - 10 Tips To Protect Yourself

Case Study: Christopher Knight

Conclusion:

Can you believe that I've never written a single article about racquetball and yet with today's Ezine-Tips article, I now have 45 excellent Racquetball titles ready for me to produce the body of the articles. You can do the same exercise with your niche expertise or core focus. Print this page out and refer to it whenever you need your creative writing genius to be sparked a little. :-)

Christopher M. Knight is an E-mail List Marketing Expert, author and entrepreneur. You can get a weekly dose of e-mail newsletter publishing, marketing, promotion, management, email-etiquette, e-mail usability and deliverability tips by joining his free Ezine-Tips newsletter: **http://www.emailuniverse.com/subscribe/**

Case Study: Christopher Knight

Increase Your Ezine Frequency via Smarter E-mail Segmentation

One way to raise sales, conversions and web traffic is to increase the frequency of your ezine deliveries... but, how do you do that without losing your members who didn't sign up for that frequency (misrepresentation issue) and without alienating the positive relationship you built with the other members who don't mind the frequency increase but don't find every e-mail relevant to their needs?

Solution: Segment your ezine into a handful of narrower segments of members of similar interests or members who respond to your ezine offers by opening or clicking on anything within your past 3-9 months of issues.

The Ezine Frequency/Relevancy Truth: The greater the relevance your ezine is to your readers, the more they will allow you to increase the frequency of your issues without bailing out.

An Example to Illustrate This Principle:

You've got 10,000 list members for your racquetball tips ezine that you send weekly. In the last 6 months, 2,500 of your members have clicked on links for racquetball equipment interests, 2,500 members have clicked on articles or offers relating to wanting more racquetball training, and 4,000 members have opened any of your e-mails (assuming you track open rate) of which 2,000 of your members have opened every single e-mail you sent in this time period.

Case Study: Christopher Knight

If you didn't do any e-mail segmentation, in a typical month, you would mail out 4 times to your 10,000 members and achieve 40,000 deliveries. You bring in an average of $2500 per issue in sales for your business via infoproducts, web traffic delivered to your shopping cart or pay per click ad revenue profit center.

But, this month is different as you've implemented Chris Knight's suggestion and have segmented your ezine. In addition to the normal mailing to your 10,000 members 4 times a month, you also sent a bonus issue aimed at offering additional reviews of the latest racquetball gear that was just released (2,500 members), another bonus issue to the 2,500 members who have clicked on previous offers for racquetball training where you interview or reviewed the newest racquetball training DVD, and for the 2000 folks who open ever single e-mail, you sent a Sunday morning bonus issue that is either more personal than your typical issue and offers some racquetball tips or tournament insights that have really worked for you and could work for them as well.

Net result is an increase by 7,000 deliveries or 17.5% over the previous month…and annually you're delivering an additional 84,000 e-mails (assuming no list growth or list growth meets attrition). You'll never know without testing, but I can assure you that your segmented lists will out-perform your non-segmented lists in terms of revenue per list member. If these 7,000 extra deliveries bring you an extra $2,000 per month in increased sales, you just found a way to increase your sales by $24,000 annually without alienating your existing list members who are happy with the normal distribution schedule.

The increased cost to deliver the extra e-mails is negligible but there would be an increased labor cost to setup the segmentation and invest the time studying your ezine analytics (stats).

How To Overcome The Frequency Representation Issue:

I'm not advocating throwing the e-mail frequency you represented to your list members out the window, but perhaps you might find some value in making it a bit vaguer than you have in the past. Some of my ezines say the delivery schedule is: Periodic whenever I have quality information or tips to share whereas others might say: Weekly with periodic bonus issues.

Another way to keep your word and increase the e-mail frequency: Create offers that have a 'name squeeze' attached to them forcing your members who want the offer to sign up to get access. You then send them either a 7 part e-mail course (via an e-mail autoresponder) or send them bi-weekly additional mailings related to the topic they signed up for.

Case Study: Christopher Knight

I've done this strategy to pack my teleseminars, increase sales and increase the speed of the typical sales cycle. You can too! :-)

Ezine Segmentation Conclusion: You can push the envelope on your ezine frequency if you up the relevancy of your e-mails to address the needs of your list members as they have represented by their prior actions (clicking or opening your e-mails).

Christopher M. Knight is an E-mail List Marketing Expert, author and entrepreneur. You can get a weekly dose of e-mail newsletter publishing, marketing, promotion, management, email-etiquette, e-mail usability and deliverability tips by joining his free Ezine-Tips newsletter: **http://www.emailuniverse.com/subscribe/.**

10

THE SUBJECT LINE

The importance of the subject line cannot be stressed enough. This is the first thing your e-mail recipient will see, and it can be the single determining factor in whether they will open your e-mail or delete it. Additionally, it is one of the primary flags for spam filtering software; therefore, you need to avoid certain words which tend to trigger spam filters, also preventing your e-mail from reaching the recipient.

You should put as much thought and analysis into the subject line, as you do for your actual e-mail creative. Take a quick look through your junk folder or trash bin in your e-mail application — chances are you will find a variety of subjects which immediately trigger you to add the sender to your spam list and send the e-mail to the junk folder without giving it a second thought. I spent 60 seconds scanning the e-mail I have received today (including my junk folder), and found some of the typical suspect subject lines:

- Your $10,000 line of credit has been approved

- Get Slim For 100,000.00 & A New Car

- Need a Date? Find one now!

- Best prices for u

- Exclusive Site for Single Women and Men

- Thank you for your loan request

- This is your big opportunity to double your investment for short period

- This is not Spam!

- Participate and Receive $1,200 to Pay Credit Cards for One Year

- Add 1000++ global TV channels into your PC

The list is seemingly endless; I could write an entire book of bad subject lines. Luckily all of these e-mails found their way to my junk folder, and if the had actually gotten into my inbox, I would have happily sent them on their way. However, you do need to consider that the potential exists where many of your well intended, spam-free e-mails may suffer the same fate, and never find their way into the inbox of your desired recipient. Even if they do make it into the inbox, most people simply scan the subject line and determine if it is spam or junk mail without ever even opening or reading it. If they decide that there is a chance this is a legitimate e-mail they may look at the sender name, which I discussed last chapter, and why it is important that you use your company name or some other recognizable e-mail address to help associate your e-mail with your company, and gain trust in the recipient.

I mentioned it earlier, but the subject line is one of the primary methods that anti-spam software use to identify spam e-mails. America Online (**www.aol.com**) released its AOL's 2005 Top 10 Global Spam Subject Lines:

- Donald Trump Wants You — Please Respond

- Double Standards New Product — Penis Patch

- Body Wrap: Lose 6-20 inches in one hour

- Get an Apple iPod Nano, PS3 or Xbox 360 for Free

- It's Lisa, I must have sent you to the wrong site

- Breaking Stock News** Small Cap Issue Poised to Triple

- Thank you for your business. Shipment notification

- [IMPORTANT] Your Mortgage Application is Ready

- Thank you: Your $199 Rolex Special Included

- Online Prescriptions Made Easy

BASIC RULES FOR WRITING SUBJECT LINES

Let us go over some basic rules when writing subject lines. Obviously, the content of your e-mail will drive the construction of your e-mail subject line. There is a fairly simple formula to follow when creating an e-mail subject line, depending on your e-mail content. However, no matter what your subject, it definitely needs to describe the subject of your e-mail content. If your e-mail subject is entirely different than your e-mail creative content, your e-mail will be heading to the junk bin quickly, as with any chance of establishing a positive relationship with the recipient. Your e-mail subject line should fall into one of the following categories:

- Be an announcement, newsletter, publication, or article — Typically the subject line is the title of the article, publication, newsletter, or the month/issue of a publication, for example:

  o The Food Service Professional E-zine Issue #124

  o Developer Shed Weekly News for 2007-01-04

- Entice the recipient with an intriguing offer or something which would make them want to open and read your e-mail, for example:

  o DEALNEWS ALERT: 2 new deals including Dell 20" Widescreen LCD Display for $279

  o Southwest Airlines: Special Offers and News You Can Use

- Entice the recipient with something that may benefit them by reading your e-mail:

  o E-mail Marketer Monthly News: "How to write an effective e-mail"

  o Jogging Daily: "How to choose the best Running Shoes"

Put it in perspective — you read e-mails everyday, what e-mail subjects entice you, make you curious, sounds like a great deal, have new or information which may benefit you personally or professionally? Write your e-mail subjects professionally and to the point. Subject lines which emphasize and promote cost-savings, opportunities for learning, new products, or services which may improve their business or personal lives or other benefits are the most likely to succeed. Keep your subject short, and get your message delivered clearly.

Personalization of e-mails is a topic we have already discussed. I like personalizing e-mails, but I am not a big fan of including personalization in the e-mail subject. The theory is that a personalized e-mail subject will make the recipient think it is from someone who knows them and they are more likely to open it. Statistics actually support this, but I believe this trend is reversing. In my experience 90 percent of the e-mail I get with my name included in the subject line is either spam or unsolicited e-mails. Again, there are contradictory opinions on this, and ultimately you need to decide if you want to personalize your subject lines.

If you are producing newsletters or other recurring e-mail blasts, it is important that your maintain consistency in both your subject and your from e-mail address. As I have already said, I recommend you stick to your company name, newsletter title, or other standardized from e-mail address. If you publish a series of e-mail newsletters you should use a consistent format for the subject so you recipient recognized it, such as: "The Food Service Professional E-zine Issue #124."

DO'S AND DON'TS WHEN CREATING YOUR SUBJECT LINE

Let us discuss some do's and don'ts in regards to e-mail subjects:

- Do not use subject lines that shout. All caps is considered to be the same as shouting. You will have much better success with, "Improve your E-mail Marketing Campaign," than with, "IMPROVE YOUR E-MAIL MARKETING CAMPAIGN." Same message, but perceived entirely differently.

- Do not overuse the word "free." It is okay to use it if you are truly promoting something that is free, but do not make it the first word in the subject or spam filters will file it away quickly.

- Do not mislead your recipients with false claims, offers, or misinformation. Make sure your e-mail subject matches the content.

- Do not get carried away with punctuation, and avoid the "!" in your subject lines.

- Do not forget to spell check. Yes, it sounds very obvious, but for there are plenty of poor spellers out there. Do not be one of them.

- Do emphasize urgency in an e-mail. If you have a deadline or some other form of compelling action sooner rather than later you will achieve better results (i.e. 50 percent off all orders placed by midnight).

- Keep the subject short, simple and to the point.

- Incorporate your brand name or company name where possible. This increases brand recognition and builds trust and confidence with recipients. If they recognize your brand name, they are more likely to open the e-mail (i.e. which would you open first — an e-mail from Dell Computer Corporation or Acme Computers?).

- Avoid using the $ symbol in the subject line. This is a commonly used by and associated with spammers.

Case Study: Eddie Machaalani

Increase Your E-mail Open Rate By Improving Your Subject Lines

Eddie uses his diverse range of internet, marketing and management skills to help create great PHP products for web masters, web designers and their clients.

Just like a direct sales letter, the subject line of your e-mail can make or break your campaign. If you don't have a compelling subject line the chance of your e-mail even getting read is slim.

According to a recent **MarketingSherpa.com** survey, 40 percent of e-mail marketers said testing changes to just their subject line had a high impact on their return on investment (ROI). 45 percent said subject line changes accounted for a medium ROI and only 15 percent said that testing changes to their subject line results in a low ROI.

Case Study: Eddie Machaalani

For every e-mail you send you have got room for no more than 50 characters in your subject line, and today I am going to share with you ten tips that we use to increase the open rates of our e-mail campaigns.

Test the subject line — Take a look at e-mail campaigns you have sent in the past. Which subject lines worked the best and gave you the highest open and conversion rates? You might find that for a particular topic there's a general trend or subject style that resulted in higher open rates.

The subject of importance — Try and put as much important and relevant information into your subject lines as possible. For example, if you are sending out an e-mail about a special offer make sure the product name and details on the offer appear in the subject line in a clear and concise format such as "$40 off ACME Widget Until - Today Only."

Personalize the subject line — If you have details about your subscribers then use them in your subject line to get their attention. A subject line containing the subscribers first name ALWAYS out pulls one that does not.

Avoid spam keywords — Most e-mail servers automatically filter out any e-mails that contain spam keywords in their subject line — Words such as free, stock, e-bay, password, mortgage, etc all trigger spam detection software so keep them out of your subject lines at all times.

Trigger curiosity — The best way to improve your open rates is to pique the interest of your subscribers. A compelling headline that entices them to open and read the contents of your e-mail can do wonders for your conversion rate. I have been thinking about headlines that trigger curiosity, and if you can work this one into your e-mail campaign I would like to hear the response rate: "Hi [First Name] — I have a question for you."

Make the offer clear — If you are making a special offer to your subscriber then be upfront and include it as part of your subject line. People love bargains and special offers so let them know about it before anything else.

Emphasize the benefits — We use this technique for our newsletters. We always use the format of "Interspire Newsletter – [Benefit]." In our case, benefit is always the title of an article contained in the newsletter, such as "Interspire Newsletter — 10 Tips for Better Subject Lines." It works every time.

Case Study: Eddie Machaalani

Copy what works — Mitch recently wrote an article on the top 12 headlines of all time. Why not take some of these and use them in the subject line of your next e-mail campaign?

Easy identification — Make sure your subscribers know the e-mail is coming from you. Deceptive subject lines can confuse people so always try and including your company name in the subject line. Also, make sure you set the "From" attribute of your e-mail to include your name and your companies name, such as "From: John Smith ".

Exclaim nothing — Avoid using excessive punctuation at the end of your subject lines. Google bans punctuation from AdWords ad's for a reason – too much hype can annoy and confuse people.

Interspire is a private company and was officially founded in 2002 by Eddie Machaalani and Mitchell Harper. Our one and only goal from the start has been to create amazing PHP software that web designers can use to empower their clients -- and we're still hard at work on our goal some 4 years since we started.

Due to our fast paced growth and our now diverse product range, we have 2 company offices. The first is our support and development office in Sydney, Australia, where the majority of development and big important meetings take place. The second is our sales and first level support office in Nashville, Tennessee.

Back when we started Interspire the concept of web-based applications was still new. Today, however, they're everywhere and thanks to huge leaps in technology over the last few years it's now quite amazing what you can do with just a web browser and an Internet connection.

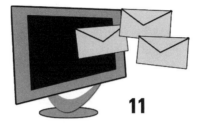

11

WHEN TO E-MAIL, HOW OFTEN, AND WHAT TIME

Now that you have created your e-mail masterpiece, you must address the issue of when to send it, how often should you send it, and what time of the day is best to send out your e-mail blast. There is no cut and dry answer to any of these questions, so I will give you the best advice possible and you will have to determine what works best for you based on the type of e-mails you are sending.

WHAT DAY OF THE WEEK IS BEST TO E-MAIL

The answers may surprise you. Traditionally, Mondays and Fridays have been the worst days to e-mail. The reasons are fairly obvious — Monday is the traditional first day back to work after the weekend and typically a busy day for meetings, catching up from the previous week, planning the week ahead and clearing out e-mails from the weekend. Your e-mail's may fall to victim of overload and although on any other given day your e-mail might be given the proper attention, it may find its way to the deleted e-mail folder simply due to the fact that the recipient is task saturated with other issues. Fridays have long been considered the worst day to e-mail simply because it is the end of the work week, people are looking forward to the weekend, cleaning out their e-mails and may be less inclined to review new, incoming e-mails.

Tuesdays and Wednesdays are evenly split for the title of busiest day for e-mail marketing. More are sent and received on Tuesdays and Wednesdays than on any other day of the week. In fact more than 95 percent of all e-mail marketing campaigns are sent Tuesday through Friday. Research also reveals that e-mails sent out Wednesday through Friday will yield the highest open rates. Surprisingly, the highest click rates are obtained on e-mails delivered on weekends. The truth is the best day to send e-mails is a constantly moving target, and you will have to test the waters to determine what works best for your type of business or e-mail marketing campaign.

My advice is to start your e-mail campaigns on a Tuesday or Thursday and then test the waters from there. Once your campaign is established, try a weekend, and compare it to your other results. Try a Friday, check your open rates and compare them to your averages on Thursdays. Depending on your target audience, you may have better luck on Mondays or weekends. Do not discount the weekends. I spend more time on e-mail on the weekends than during the week, and this is becoming common in the workplace as traditional working hours are replaced by flex schedules, telecommuting, and remote access. You should definitely avoid scheduling e-mail blasts on holidays and holiday weekends.

WHAT TIME OF THE DAY IS THE BEST TO SEND E-MAIL CAMPAIGNS

There is no golden rule to follow. Research supports the best time to send an e-mail blast is between 7 a.m. and 10:30 a.m. Keep in mind that time zones may play havoc on an e-mail campaign unless you segment the delivery schedule by zones. A 7 a.m. delivery on the East coast is a 4 a.m. delivery on the West coast. Be aware that e-mails may take seconds to hours to deliver to all of your recipients — they will not all receive it at the exact same time. If you are delivering articles or newsletters you may want to ask your subscribers what day of the week and time they prefer to receive your e-mail blasts. By making the time the most convenient for them, you will increase the likelihood of achieving positive open rates.

HOW TO DETERMINE THE FREQUENCY FOR E-MAIL CAMPAIGNS

You guessed it! There is no golden rule for e-mail frequency. Some of the issues regarding e-mail frequency may be established by the type e-mail you are sending. For example, if you are generating newsletters, articles, and other items on a recurring basis, you need to establish the frequency up front, and make it clear in your e-mail creative so you can establish a positive relationship and set the expectations of your subscribers.

Timing is everything, and the best advice to follow is to not overload your list subscribers with e-mails. Once as week is a good general rule to follow as a maximum frequency of e-mails to send. Exceed that and you will quickly annoy your subscribers and find them removing themselves from your list. Use segmentation to avoid saturating your list with off-content or e-mails, which are not relevant to the recipients.

The bottom line with frequency is to establish what works best for you and your customers. Creating e-mail campaigns can be time consuming, do not commit to sending weekly e-mails if you do not have the time and resources to produce them. As with when to send your e-mails, you will have to experiment and test your e-mail frequency to balance optimal results with workload to ensure that the return on investment is maximized. Depending on the type of e-mail campaigns you are sending, different rules may apply. Again, you can ask your subscribers what they prefer, and cater to their desire to improve effectiveness. I recommend a maximum of once per week, and would average two to three times per month for any e-mail campaign that does not have a pre-prescribed frequency, such as weekly newsletters or monthly articles.

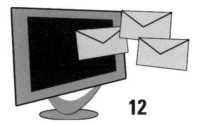

12

THE FUTURE OF E-MAIL MARKETING

In 2002, GartnerG2 (**www.gartner.com**) released a report which stated entitled *E-Mail Marketing Campaigns Threaten Traditional Direct Mail Promotions*. They predicted that companies would have to build cost-effective, permission-based e-mail campaigns to remain competitive and that permission based e-mail marketing is the biggest threat to the $196.8 billion direct mail marketing business. It is five years later, and while direct mail marketing has not vanished, it has certainly taken a definitive hit from e-mail marketing.

One thing is clear: e-mail marketing is here to stay for the long term and will grow in both frequency and volume. Although there are challenges to developing successful e-mail campaigns, they have carved out a significant portion from direct mail business lines. Here are some of the issues, in my opinion, which will affect the future of e-mail marketing:

- Anti-Spam Laws — They will only get tougher and more restrictive on e-mail marketers. Anti-spam technology will improve and many well-intentioned, spam-free e-mail will get clogged in spam filters.

- The cost for developing and sending e-mail campaigns will increase. While it will never rival the costs of direct mail, it may not be a truly low-cost option.

- E-mail clients will become smarter, more spam savvy, and may integrate with other technology, significantly changing how we communicate and how effective e-mail marketing may be.

- Relationship-based e-mail marketing will become reality, where a one-on-one relationship exists between e-mail marketers and their subscribers dictating frequency, timing, and content.

- Permission-based e-mail marketing will cease to exist and be replaced by a system which eliminates or blocks all e-mails from e-mail marketers who are not specifically subscribed to, eliminating the questionable practices of selling lists or signing up for one list and finding yourself on a dozen others you never wanted to be on.

13

SEARCH ENGINE OPTIMIZATION

You need to incorporate proper search engine optimization on your Web site and in your e-mail campaigns. There are over two billion Web pages on the Internet, and this means that there are many Web sites that are directly competing with yours for potential customers — often your competitors are selling identical products to yours. You need to take realistic and time-proven measures to ensure that your online business gets noticed and obtains the rankings within search engines that will deliver the results you desire. We already discussed how placing your e-mail campaigns on your Web site as individual Web pages, in particular articles and newsletters, and how they can help you improve overall Web site visibility in search engines. This chapter provides you basic search engine optimization guidance.

We are going to concentrate on some of the most popular search engine optimization techniques, which can be easily implemented on your Web sites and within your e-mail campaigns. They include:

- Basic search engine optimization

- Proper meta tag formatting and inclusion

- Proper use of ALT tags

- Search engine registration and submission

- Search engine services

- Privacy policies

- About and feedback pages to improve search engine visibility

- Copyright pages

- Other proven Web site marketing techniques

Search engine optimization (SEO) consists of a variety of proven techniques which you can use to push up the ranking of your Web site within your target market on the Internet by using keywords that are relevant and appropriate to the product or services that you are selling on your Web site.

When you implement a SEO plan, you use a methodology that allows you to make sure that your Web site is visible in search engines and is subsequently found by potential customers. SEO accomplishes this by taking the keywords that people may use to search for your products or services on the Internet using a search engine and placing these keywords in title pages, meta tags, and into the content of your Web site.

When you properly use SEO and optimize your Web site based on sound Web site design principles, you know that your Web site is ready to be submitted to search engines and that you will significantly increase the visibility and ranking within the search engines, driving potential customers to your Web site and obtaining the hits you need to increase your profits and the success of your business. Focus on the content on each Web page, and be sure to strive to include at least 200 or more content related words on the pages of your site. Integrate your keywords into the content you place on each page, but be cautious of keyword stuffing, which is where you overload the pages with keywords, which may result in you being blacklisted from major search engines.

SUCCESSFUL SEARCH ENGINE OPTIMIZATION

Understanding the concepts and actions necessary for successful SEO can sometimes be confusing and hard to grasp when you're first starting out using SEO techniques. There are several steps that you need make sure are followed so that you ensure you are getting the most out of your SEO. Some of these steps include:

- Making sure that your Web site is designed correctly and set up for optimal SEO.

- Choosing the right keywords that are going to bring you the most hits to your Web site.

- Using the right title tags to identify you within search engines.

- Ensuring appropriate content writing on your Web site.

- Using properly formatted meta tags on your Web site.

- Choosing the right search engines to which you submit your Web site and understanding the free and paid listing service options available.

Once you know on which areas to focus when it comes to successful SEO, you will discover your ranking in search engines will increase dramatically.

The main problem with SEO and the number one reason most site builders fail to properly ensure a site is optimized is that it requires significant time and patience to obtain high rankings in search engines. SEO will not get you immediate visibility in search engines, where pay-per-click advertising will. You need to be realistic in your expectations and expect it to take months to see tangible results.

META TAG DEFINITION AND IMPLEMENTATION

Meta tags are a key part of the overall SEO program that you need to implement for your Web site. There is some controversy surrounding the use of meta-tags and whether or not their inclusion on Web sites truly impacts your search engine rankings; however, I am convinced they can be an integral part of a sound SEO plan, and some search engines do utilize these tags in their indexing process. You do need to be aware that you are competing against potentially thousands (or more) other Web sites often promoting similar products, using similar keywords, and employing other SEO techniques to achieve a top search engine ranking. Meta tags have never guaranteed top rankings on crawler-based search engines; however, they do offer a degree of control and the ability for you, as the Web site or business owner, to impact how your Web pages are indexed within the search engines.

When it comes to using keywords and key phrases in your meta keywords tag, you want to use only those keywords and phrases that you have actually included within the Web content on each of your Web pages. It is also important that you use the plural form of keywords so that both the singular and the plural will end up in any search that people do in search engines using specific keywords and key phrases. Other keywords that you should include in your meta keyword tags are any words that are the misspelling of your keywords and phrases since many people commonly misspell certain words, and you want to make sure that search engines can still find you despite these misspellings.

Do not repeat your most important keywords and key phrases more than four to five times in a meta keyword tag. Another thing to keep in mind is that if your product or service is specific to a certain location geographically, you should mention this geographical location (i.e. Washington DC, District of Columbia) in your meta keyword tag.

Meta tags comprise formatted information that is inserted into the head section of each page on your Web site. To view the head of a Web page, you must view it in HTML mode rather than in the browser view. In Internet Explorer you can click on the toolbar on the view menu and then click on source to view the source of any individual Web page. If you are using a design tool such as Microsoft Frontpage, Microsoft Expression Web, Adobe Dreamweaver, Microsoft SharePoint Designer 2007, or Microsoft Expression Web Designer, you will need to use the HTML view to edit the source code of your Web pages. You can also use Notepad to edit your HTML source code.

This is a simple basic layout of a standard HTML Web page:

```
<!DOCTYPE HTML PUBLIC "-//W3C//DTD HTML 4.01//EN"
<HTML>
<HEAD>
<TITLE>This is the Title of My Web Page</TITLE>
</HEAD>
<BODY>
<P>This is my Web page!
</BODY>
</HTML>
```

Every Web page conforms to this basic page layout, and all contain the opening <HEAD> and closing </HEAD> tags. Meta tags will be inserted between the opening and closing head tags. Other than the page title tag, which is shown above, no other information in the head section of your Web pages is viewed by Web site visitors as they browse your Web pages. The title tag is displayed across the top of the browser window and is used to provide a description of the contents of the Web paged displayed. We will discuss each meta tag that may be contained within the head tags in depth.

THE TITLE TAG

Whatever text you place in the title tag (between the <TITLE> and </TITLE>) will appear in the reverse bar of an individual's browser when they view your Web page. In the example above the title of the Web page to the page visitor would read as "This is the Title of My Web Page."

The title tag is also used as the words to describe your page when someone adds it to their favorites list or bookmarks list in popular browsers such as Microsoft Internet Explorer or Mozilla Firefox. The title tag is the single most important tag in regards to search engine rankings. The title tag should be limited to 40–60 characters of text between the opening and closing HTML tags. All major Web crawlers will use the text of your title tag as the text they use for the title of your page in your listings as displayed in search engine results. Since the title and description tags typically appear in the search results page after completing a keyword search in the Web browser, it is critical that they be clearly and concisely written to attract the attention of site visitors. Not all search engines are alike: some will display the title and description tags in search results but use page content alone for ranking.

THE DESCRIPTION TAG

The description tag enables you to control the description of your individual Web pages when the search engine crawlers, which support the description tag, index and spider the Web site. The description tag should be no more than 250 characters.

Take a look at the head tag from the Web site **www.crystalriverhouse.com**, which is a site designed to promote the rental of a Florida Gulf Coast vacation house on a secluded canal located in Crystal River, Florida. The tag that says "name=description" is the description tag. The text you want to be shown as your description goes between the quotation marks after the "content=" portion of the tag (typically up to 250 characters is allowed for search engine indexing, however, the full description tag may not be displayed in search results:

```
<head>
<meta http-equiv= "Content-Type" content= "text/html; charset=windows-1252">
<title>Beautiful Crystal River Vacation Rental Home</title>
<meta name= "keywords" content= "Crystal River rental, Florida, Citrus County,Gro
uper,Fishing,vacation home,Gulf Coast rental,florida vacation, florida gulf coast">
<meta name= "description" content= "Casa Dos Crystal River vacation rental resort.
Located on beautiful canal off Crystal River.  Crystal River, Florida is famous for its
manatee watching, diving, grouper and other worldclass fishing trips, world class
golfing and many more activities.">
<meta name= "robots" content= "ALL">
<meta name= "rating" content= "SAFE FOR KIDS">
<meta name= "distribution" content= "GLOBAL">
<meta name= "classification" content="">
<meta name= "copyright" content= "(c) 2007 APC Group, Inc.">
<meta name= "revisit-after" content= "30 Days">
<meta http-equiv= "reply-to" content= "info@crystalriverhouse.com">
<style>
<!--
.sitecredits { color: #FFFFFF}
-->
</style>
</head>
```

It is important to understand that search engines are not all the same, and that they index, spider, and display different search results for the same Web site. For example, Google ignores the description tag and generates its own description based on the content of the Web page. Although some major engines may disregard your description tags, it is highly recommended that you include the tag on each Web page since some search engines rely on the tag to index your site.

THE KEYWORDS TAG

A keyword is simply defined as a word that may be used by Internet users when searching for information on the Internet, and is also a critical component to developing your pay-per-click campaign, which we will discuss in great detail in later chapters of this book. Using the best keywords to describe your Web site helps get those searchers to find your site in search engines. The keywords tag allows you to provide relevant text words or word combinations for crawler-based search engines to index. Again, although we maintain that the keyword tag is vitally important and should be included on every page, many crawler-based engines may use your page content for indexing instead of the contents of the keywords tag. In truth, the keywords tag is only supported by a few Web crawlers. Since most Web crawlers are content based (in other words, they index your site based on the actual page contents, not your meta tags), you need to incorporate as many keywords as possible into the actual content of your Web pages. For the engines that support the description tag, it is beneficial to repeat keywords within the description tag with keywords which appear on your actual Web pages — this increases the value of each keyword in relevance to your Web site page content. You need to use some caution with the keywords tag for the few search engines which support it since repeating a particular keyword too many times within a keyword tag may actually hurt your Web site rankings.

If you look at the example earlier, you will notice that the keywords tag is the one that says <meta name= "keywords" content= "">. The keywords you want to use should go between the quotation marks after the content= portion of the tag. It is generally suggested that you include up to 25 words or phrases, with each word or phrase separated by a comma.

To help you determine which keywords are the best to use on your site, visit **www.wordtracker.com**, which is a paid service that will walk you through this process. Wordtracker's suggestions are based on over 300 million keywords and phrases that people have used over the previous 130 days. A free alternative to determining which keywords are best is Google Rankings (**http://googlerankings. com/dbkindex.phs**).

THE ROBOTS TAG

The robots tag lets you specify that a particular page within your site should or should not be indexed by a search engine. To keep search engine spiders out, add the following text between your tags: <META NAME= "ROBOTS" CONTENT= "NOINDEX">. You do not need to use variations of the robots tag to get your pages indexed since your pages will be spidered and indexed by default; however, some Web designers include the following robots tag on all Web pages:

<meta name= "robots" content= "ALL">

OTHER META TAGS

There are many other meta tags that exist; however, most provide amplifying information about a Web site and its owner and do not have any impact on search engine rankings. Some of these tags may be utilized by internal corporate divisions. In our example earlier you can see some examples of other meta tags which can be incorporated (note that this is not a complete list of all possible meta tags).

You may also use the "comment" tag, which is primarily used by Web designers as a place to list comments relative to the overall Web site design, primarily to assist other Web developers who may work on the site in the future. A comment tag looks like this:

<!-begin body section for Crystal River Vacation House>

ALT TAGS

The ALT tag is an HTML tag that provides alternative text when non-textual elements, typically images, cannot be displayed. The ALT tag is not part of the "head" of a Web page, but proper use of the ALT tag is critically important in Search Engine Optimization. ALT tags are often left off Web pages; however, they can be extremely useful for a variety of reasons, including:

- They provide detail or text description for an image or destination of a hyperlinked image.

- They enable and improve access for people with disabilities.

- They provide information for individuals who have graphics turned off when they surf the Internet.

- They improve navigation when a graphics-laden site is being viewed over a slow connection, enabling visitors to make navigation choices before graphics are fully rendered in the browser.

Text-based Web content is not the only thing that increases your ranking in the search engines. Images are just as important because these images can also include keywords and key phrases that relate to your business. If any visitors to your Web site should happen to have the image option off when hitting your site, they will still be able to see the text that is associated with your images. ALT tags should be placed anywhere there is an image on your Web site. It is key to remember not to use too lengthy of descriptions when describing your images, but that you do include accurate keywords within the ALT tag. The keywords and key phrases that you use in the ALT tag should be the same keywords and phrases that you used in meta description tags, meta keyword tags, title tags, and in the Web content on your Web pages. A brief description of the image, along with one or two accurate keywords and key phrases, is all you need to optimize the images on your Web pages for search engines. Do not use ALT tags within your e-mail campaigns, instead establish them after you place you e-mail blast on your Web site.

Most major Web design applications include tools to simplify the process of creating ALT tags. For example, in Microsoft Frontpage 2003, right click on the image, choose properties and the general tab, and you can enter ALT tag text information. To enter ALT tag information directly into a Web page, go to the HTML view and enter them after the IMG tags.

HOW TO USE THE CORRECT KEYWORDS

When it comes to keywords, you need to choose the words or word combinations for which your potential customers are searching when they look for products or services using a search engine on the Internet. If you start to optimize keywords that are incorrect, you may be wasting your time as your potential customers search using keywords that don't put you up there in the top rankings of search engines. You will need to do some market research to find out what keywords are being used by people in search engines to find similar products or services to what you are selling. There are software tools on the market that you can use to find out just what these keywords are so that you can implement them into your Web content and into your meta tags. As we stated earlier, the importance of the keyword meta tag has faded over the years; however, using keywords within the content of your individual Web pages is critical and is the key to high Web site rankings.

Search engine optimization means that every page of your Web site will be optimized to the greatest extent possible for search engines. Keywords will vary based on the individual Web page content. By using the wrong keywords, you risk sending your potential customers in an entirely different direction than to your Web site. Always keep in mind that if you are not listed in the top rankings of search engines, your customers may have difficulty finding you, and your competition will have an edge over you. Unfortunately, there is no magic formula to developing search-engine-optimized and effective search phrases.

As I mentioned previously, you will have to have a different list of keywords and key phrases for each Web page that you are optimizing for the Internet based on the content of that individual page. Keywords that work for some of your Web pages may not work for others. This is why you need to constantly assess how your SEO campaign is progressing and be prepared to make changes along the way.

A good way to keep on top of top keywords is to keep an eye on your competition. Use a search engine yourself and use some of the keywords and key phrases that you know target your type of product or service. Take a look at the top-ranking Web sites and view the source HTML code as well as the keywords that they have used in their meta tags. The HTML code will show you the keywords that the site's creator used. You will not only be able to come up with more keyword ideas, but you will also be able to keep up with your competition so that you rank at the top of search engines as well.

OPTIMIZATION OF WEB PAGE CONTENT

Web page content is by far the single most important factor that will affect and determine your eventual Web site ranking in search engines. It is extremely important that you have relevant content on your Web pages that is going to increase the ranking of your Web site in search engine rankings. The content on your Web page is what visitors to your Web site are going to read when they find your site and start to read and browse your Web pages, whether you browse to a page directly or via a search engine. You need to optimize your Web site with all the right keywords within the content of each web page so that you can maximize your rankings within search engines. You can use software tools to find out what keywords people are using when they search for certain products and services on the Internet, and we will provide some of those to you throughout this book.

Not only are the visitors to your Web site reading the content on these pages, but search engine spiders and Web crawlers are reading this same content and using it to index your Web site among your competitors. This is why it is important that you have the right content so that search engines are able to find you and rank you near the top of the listings for similar products that people want to buy. Search engines are looking for keywords and key phrases to categorize and rank your site; therefore, it is important that you focus on just as many key phrases as you do keywords.

The placement of text content within a Web page can make a significant difference in your eventual search engine rankings. Some search engines will only analyze a limited number of text characters on each page and will not read the rest of the page, regardless of length; therefore, the keywords and phrases you may have loaded into your page may not be read at all by the search engines. Some search engines do index the entire content of Web pages; however, they typically give more value or weight to the content which appears closer to the top of the Web page.

OPTIMIZE YOUR WEB SITE

If you want to get the best results from search engines, here are some tips that you should follow to optimize your Web site.

- Make sure that you have at least 200 words of content on each page. Although you may have some Web pages where it may be difficult to put even close to 200 words, you should try to come as close as you can since search engines will give better results to pages with more content.

- Make sure that the text content that you have on your Web pages contains those important keywords and key phrases that you have researched and know will get you competitive rankings and are the most common phrases potential customers might use to search for your products or services.

- No matter how much content you have after incorporating keywords and key phrases, make sure that the content that you have is still understandable and readable in plain language. A common mistake is to stack a Web site full of so many keywords and key phrases that the page is no longer understandable or readable to the Web site visitor — a sure bet to lose potential customers quickly.

- The keywords and key phrases that you use in the content of your Web site should also be included in the tags of your Web site, such as meta tags, ALT tags, head tags, and title tags.

- Add extra pages to your Web site, even if they may not at first seem directly relevant. The more Web pages that you have, the more pages search engines will have to be able to find you and link to. Extra pages can include tips, tutorials, product information, resource information, and any other information or data that is pertinent to the product or service that you're selling.

Optimizing your Web content and Web pages is one of the most important tips that you can use to ensure the success of your Web site. If you are unable to optimize your Web site yourself, you should hire an expert so that you get the most out of the Web content that you have on your Web site.

WEB SITE OPTIMIZATION TIPS, HINTS, AND SECRETS

It is critically important that you explore and implement the wide range of tips, suggestions, and best practices we have provided in this book to give your Web site the most competitive edge, obtain the highest possible rankings with search engines, and ultimately, in conjunction with your pay-per-click advertising campaigns. The following pages contain various best practices, tips, and secrets:

- It is important to use your keywords heavily on your Web pages. Use key phrases numerous times, placing them close to the top of the page. Place key phrases between head tags in the first two paragraphs of your page. Place key phrases in bold type at least once on each page. Repeat keyword and key phrases often to increase density on your pages.

- Design pages so they are easily navigated by search engine spiders and Web crawlers. Search engines prefer text over graphics and also prefer HTML over other page formats. You must make your page easy to navigate by the search engines.

- Do not use frames. Search engines have difficulty following them, and so will your site visitors. The best advice we can give on frames is to NEVER use them.

- Limit the use of Macromedia Flash and other high-end design applications as most search engines have trouble reading and following them, hurting you in search engine listings.

- Consider creating a site map of all pages within your Web site. While not necessarily the most useful tool to site visitors, it does greatly improve the search engine's capacity to property index all of your Web site pages.

- Many Web sites use a left-hand navigational bar. This is standard on many sites; however, the algorithm that many spiders and Web crawlers use will have this read before the main content of your Web site. Make sure you use keywords within the navigation, and if using images for your navigational buttons, ensure you use the ALT tags loaded with appropriate keywords.

- Ensure that all Web pages have links back to the home page.

- Use copyright and "about us" pages.

- Do not try to trick the search engines with hidden or invisible text or other techniques. If you do, the search engine will likely penalize you.

- Do not list keywords in order within the content of your Web page. It is perfectly fine to incorporate keywords into the content of your Web pages, but do not cut and past your keywords from your meta tag into the content of your Web pages. This will be viewed as spam by the search engine and you will be penalized.

- Do not use text on your Web page as the page's background color (i.e., white text on a white background). This is a technique known as keyword stuffing, and all search engines will detect it and penalize you.

- Do not replicate meta tags. In other words, you should only have one meta tag for each type of tag. Using multiple tags (such as more than one title tag) will cause search engines to penalize you.

- Do not submit identical pages with identical content with a different Web page file name.

- Makes sure that every Web page is reachable from at least one static text link.

- Make sure that your title and ALT tags are descriptive and accurate.

- Check for broken links and correct HTML.

- Try using a text browser such as Lynx to examine your site. Features such as JavaScript, cookies, session IDs, frames, DHTML, or Flash keep search engine spiders from properly crawling your entire Web site.

- Implement the use of the robots.txt file on your Web server. This file tells crawlers which directories can or cannot be crawled. You can find out more information on the robots.txt file by visiting **http://www. robotstxt.org/wc/faq.html**.

- Have other relevant sites link to yours. We will cover the use of cross linking your Web site with others later in this chapter; however, this is an often overlooked but extremely important way of increasing your search engine rankings. This is also known as back-linking, and is critically important to gain search engine visibility.

- Design Web pages for site visitors, not search engines.

- Avoid tricks intended to improve search engine rankings. A good rule of thumb is whether you would feel comfortable explaining what you have done to a Web site that competes with you. Another useful test is to ask, "Does this help my users? Would I do this if search engines didn't exist?"

- Do not participate in link schemes designed to increase your site's ranking. Do not link to Web spammers as your own ranking will be negatively affected by those links.

- Do not create multiple pages, sub-domains, or domains with substantially duplicate content.

- Do not use "doorway" pages created for search engines.

- Consider implementing cascading style sheets into your Web site to control site layout and design. Search engines prefer CSS-based sites and typically score them higher in the search rankings.

WEB DESIGN & OPTIMIZATION SUGGESTIONS

Shelley Lowery, author of the acclaimed Web design course *Web Design Mastery* and *Ebook Starter — Give Your Ebooks the Look and Feel of a REAL Book*, offers valuable tips and suggestions for Web design and Web site optimization. You can visit **www.Web-Source.net** to sign up for a complimentary subscription to Etips and receive a copy of the acclaimed ebook, *Killer Internet Marketing Strategies*.

Establish Links with Reputable Web Sites

You should try to find quality sites that are compatible and relevant to your Web site's topic, and approach the Webmaster of that site for a link exchange. (Note: do not link to your competitors.) This will give you highly targeted traffic and will improve your score with the search engines. Your goal is to identify relevant pages that will link to your site, effectively yielding you quality, inbound links. You need to be wary of developing or creating a "link farm" or "spam link Web site," which offers massive quantities of link exchanges but with little or no relevant content for your site visitors or the search engines.

How to Establish a Reciprocal Link Program (backlinks)

Begin your link exchange program by developing a title or theme that you will use as part of your link request invitations. Your title or theme should be directly relevant to your site's content. Since most sites use your provided title or theme in the link to your Web site, be sure you include relevant keywords, which will improve your Web site optimization and search engine rankings. Keep track of your inbound and outbound link requests. Begin your search for link exchange partners by searching a popular engine such as Google and entering key phrases such as link with us, add site, suggest a site, add your link, etc. If these sites are relevant, they are ideal to being your reciprocal link program since they too are actively seeking link partners. Make sure that the Web master of other sites actually links back to your site as it is common that reciprocal links are not completed. If they do not link back to you in a reasonable time, remove your link to them as you are only helping them with their search engine rankings.

You may want to use **www.linkpopularity.com** as a free Web source for evaluating the total number of Web sites that link to your site.

Free Link Popularity Report for Atlantic Publishing Company (www.atlantic-pub.com)

Google	981 links
MSN	680 link
Yahoo!	661 links

Establish a Web Site Privacy Policy

Internet users are becoming more and more concerned with their privacy. You should establish a privacy Web page and let your visitors know exactly how you will be using the information you collect from them. This page should include the following:

- For what do you plan on using their information?

- Will their information be sold or shared with a third party?

- Why do you collect their e-mail address?

- Do you track their IP address?

- You should notify site visitors that you are not responsible for the privacy issues of any Web sites you may be linked to.

- Notify them that you have security measures in place to protect the misuse of their private or personal information.

- Provide site visitors with contact information in the event that they have any questions about your privacy statement.

Establish an "About Us" Page

An "about" page is an essential part of a professional Web site for a variety of reasons. One reason is that your potential customers may want to know exactly who you are, and secondly, it is a great opportunity to create a text-laden page for search engine visibility. An about page should include the following:

- A personal or professional biography

- Photograph of yourself or your business

- Description of you or your company

- Company objectives or mission statement

- Contact information, including your e-mail address

Establish a Testimonials Page

Another way to develop creditability and confidence among your potential customers is to include previous customer testimonials. You do need to make sure your testimonials are supportable, so include your customer's name and e-mail address for validation purposes.

Establish a Money-Back Guarantee

Depending on the type of Web site you are operating, you may wish to consider implementing a money-back guarantee to completely eliminate any potential risk to customers in purchasing your products. By providing them with a solid, no-risk guarantee, you build confidence in your company and your products with potential clients.

Establish a Feedback Page

There are many reasons to incorporate a feedback page into your Web site. There are times when potential customers will have questions about your products and services or may encounter problems with your Web site, and the feedback page is an easy way for them to contact you. Additionally, it allows you to collect data from the site visitor such as name, e-mail address, or phone number. A timely response to feedback is critical to ensure customers that there is a living person on the other end of the Web site, and this personal service helps increase the likelihood they will continue to do business with you.

Establish a copyright page

You should always display your copyright information at the bottom of each page.

You should include both the word Copyright and the © symbol. Your copyright should look similar to this:

Copyright © 2007 Profit Strategies & Solutions, Inc.

HOW DO SEARCH ENGINES WORK?

There are several different types of search engines including: crawler-based, human-powered, and mixed. We will discuss how each one works so you can optimize your Web site in preparation for your pay-per-click advertising campaign.

Crawler-Based Search Engines

Crawler-based search engines, such as Google, create their listings automatically. They crawl or spider the Web and index the data, which is then searchable through **Google.com**. Crawler-based search engines will eventually revisit your Web site; therefore,, as your content is changed (as well as those of your competitors), your search engine ranking may change. A Web site is added to the search engine database when the search engine spider or crawler visits a Web page, reads it, and then follows links to other pages within the site. The spider returns to the site on a regular basis, typically once every month, to search for changes. Often, it may take several months for a page that has been spidered to be indexed. Until a Web site is indexed, the results of the spider are not available through the search engines. The search engine then sorts through the millions of indexed pages to find matches to a particular search and rank them in order based on a formula of how it believes the results to be most relevant.

Human-Powered Search Directories

Human-powered directories, like the Open Directory, depend on humans for its listings. You must submit a short description to the directory for your entire site. The search directory then looks at your site for matches from your page content to the descriptions you submitted.

USING A SEARCH ENGINE OPTIMIZATION COMPANY

If you are not up to the challenge of tackling your Web site search engine optimization needs, it may be to your benefit to hire a SEO company so that the optimization techniques that you use are properly implemented and monitored; however, you can certainly do this for your e-mail campaigns. There are many SEO companies on the Internet that can ensure that your rankings in search engines will increase when you hire them. One word of caution is to be wary of claims of anyone who can guarantee you top ten ranking in all major search engines: these claims are baseless. If you have the budget to hire a SEO company, it may be extremely beneficial for you since (a) you will know that the experts at the SEO company are taking care of you and (b) you can focus your energies on other important marketing aspects of your business. To find a SEO company, follow these basic rules:

- Look at the business reputation of the SEO companies that you are thinking about hiring. Ask the company for customer references that you can check out on your own. You can also contact the Better Business Bureau in their local city or state to confirm their reputation at **www.bbb.org**.

- Do a search engine check on each company to see where they fall into the rankings of major search engines such as AOL, MSN, and Google. If the company that you are thinking about hiring to manage your own search engine optimization doesn't rank high in these search engines, how can you expect them to launch you and your business to the top of the ranks?

- You want to choose a SEO company that actually has people working for them and not just computers. While computers are great for generating the algorithms that are needed to use search engine programs, they cannot replace people when it comes to doing the market research that is needed to ensure that the company uses the right keywords and key phrases for your business.

- You need to make sure that the SEO company uses ethical ranking procedures. There are some ranking procedures that are considered to be unethical, and some search engines will ban or penalize your business Web site from their engines if they find out that you, or the

SEO company that you've hired, are using these methods. Some of these unethical ranking procedures include doorway pages, cloaking, or hidden text, as we have discussed previously.

- The SEO company that you decide to hire should be available to you at all times by phone or by e-mail. You want to be able to contact someone when you have a question or a problem to which you need a solution.

Once you have decided to hire a SEO company, it is important that you work with the company instead of just handing over all the responsibility to them. How much control of your Web site you should allow your SEO company is an area of debate; however, since you will be controlling your pay-per-click advertising campaign, you must have control over your SEO efforts. Use these tips to work effectively with your SEO provider:

- Listen carefully to the advice of the SEO account manager. They should have the expertise for which you hired them and typically can provide factual and supportable recommendations. SEO companies are expected to know what to do to increase your ranking in the search engines; if they fail to deliver, you need to choose another company.

- If you are going to be making any changes to your Web site design, ensure you let your SEO account manager know. This is because many times any changes that you make can have an effect on the already optimized Web pages. Your rankings in search engines may start to plummet unless you work with your search engine optimization account manager to optimize any changes to your Web site design that you feel are necessary to make.

- Keep in mind that SEO companies can only work with the data and information that you have on your Web pages. This means that if your Web site has little information, it will be difficult for any SEO company to pull your business up in the search engine rankings. Search engine optimization relies on keywords and key phrases that are contained on Web pages that are filled with as much Web content as possible. This may mean adding two or three pages of Web content that contain tips, resources, or other useful information that is relevant to your product or service.

- Never change any of your meta tags once they have been optimized without the knowledge or advice of your SEO account manager. Your SEO company is the professional when it comes to making sure that your meta tags are optimized with the right keywords and key phrases needed to increase your search engine ranking. You will not want to change meta tags that have already proven successful.

- Be patient when it comes to seeing the results of SEO. It can take anywhere from 30 to 60 days before you start to see yourself pushed up into the upper ranks of search engines.

- Keep a close eye on your ranking in search engines, even after you have reached the top ranks. Information on the Internet changes at a moment's notice, and this includes where your position is in your target market in search engines.

SEARCH ENGINE REGISTRATION

It is possible to submit your Web site for free to search engines; however, when you use paid search engine programs, you will find that the process of listing will be faster and will bring more Web traffic to your Web site more quickly. Other than pay-per-click and other advertising programs, such as Google Adwords, it is not necessary to pay for search engine rankings if you follow the optimization and design tips contained in this book and have patience while the search engine Web crawling and indexing process takes place. At the end of this chapter we have provided a wealth of tools and methods to submit your Web site to search engines for fee. If you do decide to hire a third-party company to register you with search engines, we have provided some basic guidance to ensure you get the most value for your investment.

Submitting to Human-Powered Search Directories

If you have a limited advertising budget, you will want to make sure that you have at least enough to cover the price of submitting to the directory at Yahoo! (called a directory search engine because it uses a compiled directory), which is assembled by human hands and not a computer. For a one-time yearly fee of approximately $300 you'll be able ensure that search engines that are crawlers (a search engine that goes out onto the Internet looking for new Web sites by following links) will be able to find your Web site in the Yahoo! directory. It may seem like a waste of money to be in a directory-based search engine, but the opposite is true. Crawlers consistently use directory search engines to add to their search listings. If you have a large budget put aside for search engine submissions, you might want to list with both directory search engines and crawler search engines, such as Google. When you first launch your Web site, you may want it to show up immediately in search engines and don't want to wait the allotted time for your listing to appear. If this is the case, you might want to consider using what is called a paid placement program. Remember that your pay-per-click advertising campaigns will show up with the top search engine rankings, based your keyword bidding.

Submitting to Crawler Search Engines

Submitting to search engines that are crawlers — search engines that look throughout the Internet to seek out Web sites through links and meta tags — means that you will likely have several Web pages listed within the search engine. The more optimized your Web site is, as discussed previously in this chapter, the higher you will rank within the search engine listings.

One of the top Internet crawler search engines is Google. Google is extremely popular because it is not only a search engine, it also is the main source of power and information behind other search engines, such as AOL. The best thing that you can do when getting your Web site listed at Google is to make sure that you have links within your Web site. When you have accurate links on your Web site, you ensure that crawler search engines are able to find you. One thing to keep in mind is that if you have good links and you listed your Web site with a successful directory search engine, such as Yahoo!, you may find that crawlers are easily able to find you, thus eliminating your need to list with Google in the first place. However, do not let this stop you from building good links into your Web site and constantly updating them.

Using Search Engine Submission Software

There are dozens of software applications which can submit your Web site automatically to major and other search engines. We have reviewed most of these products extensively and recommend Dynamic Submission (**www. dynamicsubmission.com**). Dynamic Submission, currently in version 7.0, is a search engine submission software product which proclaims to be "multi-award winning, Web promotions software package, the best on the market today."

Dynamic Submission search engine submission software was developed to offer Web site owners the ability to promote their Web sites to the ever-increasing number of search engines on the Internet without any hassles or complications. Dynamic Submission search engine submission software helps you submit your Web site to hundreds of major search engines with just a few button clicks and drive traffic to your Web site. To use Dynamic Submission, you simply enter your Web site details into the application as you follow a wizard-based system, which culminates in the automatic submission to hundreds of search engines.

Since nearly 85 percent of Internet traffic is generated by search engines, submitting your Web site to all the major search engines and getting them to be seen on the search engine list is extremely important, especially in concert with your pay-per-click advertising campaign. It is essential to regularly submit your Web site details to these Web directories and engines. Some search engines de-list you over time, while others automatically re-spider your site. Dynamic Submission is available in four editions (including a trial edition, which we highly encourage you to try) to fit every need and budget. Here are the major features of Dynamic Submission 7.0:

- Automatic search engine submission

- Supports pay-per-click (PPC) and pay-per-inclusion (PPI) engines

- Support for manual submission

- Keyword library and keyword builder

- Link popularity check

- Meta tag generator

- Web site optimizer

- Incorporated site statistics service

Paying for Search Engine Submissions

You can may choose to use a fee service to have your web site listed in popular ranking directories. Also be sure to manually submit your site to the Open Directory at **www.dmoz.org**, which is free.

SEARCH ENGINE OPTIMIZATION CHECKLIST

There are many aspects to search engine optimization that you need to consider to make sure that it works. We have covered each of these in depth earlier in this chapter, but the following checklist can serve as a helpful reminder to ensure that you have not forgotten any important details along the way.

- *Title tag* — Make sure that your title tag includes keywords and key phrases that are relevant to your product or service.

- *Meta tag* — Make sure that your tags are optimized to ensure a high ranking in search engine lists. This includes meta description tags and meta keyword tags. Your meta description tag should have an accurate description so that people browsing the Internet are interested enough to visit your Web site. Do not forget to use misspelled and plural words in your meta tags.

- *ALT tags* — Add ALT tags to all the images that you use on your Web pages.

- *Web content* — Use accurate and rich keywords and key phrases throughout the Web content of all your Web pages.

- *Density of keywords* — Use a high ratio of keywords and key phrases throughout your Web pages.

- *Links and affiliates* — Make sure that you have used links, and affiliates if you're using them, effectively for your Web site.

- *Web design* — Make sure that your Web site is fast to load and easy to navigate for visitors. You want to encourage people to stay and read your Web site by making sure that it is clean and looks good.

- *Avoid spamming* — Double check to make sure that you are not using any spamming offenses on your Web site or in your e-mail campaigns. Some spamming offences include cloaking, hidden text, doorway pages, obvious repeated keywords and key phrases, link farms, or mirror pages.

Always be prepared to update and change the look, feel, and design of your Web pages to make sure that you are using search engine optimization techniques wherever and whenever possible.

FREE WEB SITE SEARCH ENGINE SUBMISSION SITES

http://dmoz.org/ Open Directory Project

http://tools.addme.com/servlet/s0new

http://www.submitexpress.com/submit.html

http://www.ineedhits.com/free-tools/submit-free.aspx

http://www.submitcorner.com/Tools/Submit/

http://www.college-scholarships.com/free_search_engine_submission.htm

http://www.quickregister.net/

http://www.global.gr/mtools/linkstation/se/engnew.htm

http://www.scrubtheweb.com/

http://www.submitaWeb site.com/free_submission_top_engines.htm

http://www.nexcomp.com/weblaunch/urlsubmission.html

http://www.submitshop.com/freesubmit/freesubmit.html

http://www.buildtraffic.com/submit_url.shtml

http://www.mikes-marketing-tools.com/ranking-reports/

http://selfpromotion.com/?CF=google.aws.add.piyw

http://www.addpro.com/submit30.htm

http://www.Web site-submission.com/select.htm

Note: There are many other free services available on the Internet, and we make no guarantee as to the quality of any of these free services. We do recommend you create and use a new e-mail account just for search engine submissions (i.e., **search@yourwebsite.com**).

ADDITIONAL FREE WEB SITE OPTIMIZATION TOOLS

- **www.hisoftware.com/accmonitorsitetest**
  A Web site to test your Web site against accessibility and usability: Section 508, Complete WCAG, CLF, XAG standards.

- **www.wordtracker.com**
  The Leading Keyword Research Tool. It is not free, although there is a limited free trial.

- **https://adwords.Google.co.uk/select/KeywordSandbox**
  Gives ideas for new keywords associated with your target phrase but does not indicate relevance or give details of number or frequency of searches.

- **http://inventory.overture.com/d/searchinventory/suggestion**
  Returns details of how many searches have been carried out in the Overture engine over the period of a month and allows a drill down into associated keywords containing your keyword phrase as well.

- **www.nichebot.com**
  This site and Overture-based tools as well as a nice keyword analysis tool, which focuses on Google™'s results.

- **www.digitalpoint.com/tools/suggestion**
  Gives search numbers on keywords from Wordtracker and Overture sources.

WEB SITE DESIGN AND OPTIMIZATION TOOLS

- **www.Webmarketingtoolscentral.com**
  A large variety of tools, guides, and other services for Web design and optimization.

- **www.htmlbasix.com/META.shtml**
  Free site that automatically creates properly formatted HTML META tags for insertion into your Web pages.

- **www.coffeecup.com**
    - ◊ **HTML Editor** The CoffeeCup HTML Editor 2005 is two editors in one!
    - ◊ **Direct FTP** The only drag and drop FTP client that edits HTML, previews images, and more!
    - ◊ **VisualSite Designer** Now anyone can make a Web site . . . no experience needed!
    - ◊ **Flash Firestarter** The fastest and easiest way to make killer Flash effects for your Web site.
    - ◊ **Flash Form Builder** Create Flash e-mail forms without using HTML or scripts!
    - ◊ **Live Chat** Live chat with users on your Web site.
    - ◊ **Flash Web site Search** Add customized search to your Web site in a flash!
    - ◊ **Google™ SiteMapper** Create powerful Google™ site maps in seconds!
    - ◊ **RSS News Flash** Add headlines and news to your Web site fast!
    - ◊ **Flash Blogger** Easily create and modify your own online journal!
    - ◊ **Password Wizard** Password-protect your site quickly and easily with Flash.
    - ◊ **PixConverter** Easily re-size your digital pictures for Web sites, e-mail, CDs, and more.
    - ◊ **MP3 Ripper and Burner** Easily rip MP3s or burn music CDs now!
    - ◊ **Image Mapper** Often imitated—never duplicated—the original image mapper!
    - ◊ **StyleSheet Maker** Create advanced Web sites using cascading style sheets.
    - ◊ **Button Factory** The most popular button software on the Net now makes Flash!
    - ◊ **GIF Animator** The coolest animation software on the planet now does Flash!
    - ◊ **WebCam** Putting live WebCam images on your Web site has never been easier.
    - ◊ **PhotoObjects 10,000** More than 10,000 ready to use graphics that are perfect for Web design.

14

SUMMARY

When I sat down to write this book, I wanted to produce a cut to the chase, fact filled reference book that had relevant material for the small business to begin designing and implementing an effective e-mail campaign. I concentrated on providing specific advice and proven techniques specifically targeted for the small business to develop and implement a successful e-mail marketing campaign on a minimal budget, with little to no experience in e-mail marketing or Web site design. In addition I sought out the advice of industry leaders to fill this book with case studies, tips and tricks, advice, and secrets for success from the industry experts who do e-mail marketing every day. My hope is that you will find this guide an invaluable addition to your reference library and refer to it often as you design and implement your e-mail marketing campaign.

As I researched this book I found a wide variety of opinions and advice on how to properly design and implement successful e-mail marketing campaign. Often times, the material was conflicting and out of date.

TOP REASONS TO FOLLOW THE GUIDELINES IN THIS BOOK

- E-mail marketing is a proven, successful method for advertising, giving you the potential to exponentially increase your Web site traffic and sales performance.

- You can quickly (almost instantly) reach thousands of potential customers every day.

- E-mail marketing is highly cost-effective.

- As your business becomes more prominent and established you gain enormous credibility in the eyes of competitors and most importantly potential customers by turning those potential customers into repeat customers.

- E-mail marketing is significantly less costly than a traditional marketing campaign, and significantly more effective.

- If you believe that your e-mail marketing campaign is not, you have full control over your content, delivery schedule, frequency, and campaign management.

- The Internet is becoming more and more expandable when it comes to the types and methods of advertising that can take place on the Web.

- With e-mail marketing, you can use highly targeted marketing campaigns to get your message to the most relevant recipients.

15

E-MAIL MARKETING
CASE STUDIES

Help The American Society of Curriculum Development Add Hundreds of New Members With eLoop's Member-Get-A-Member Referral Module

Over the past several years, it has become customary for many individual member based organizations to ask their current members to refer their colleagues and co-workers for membership. When association marketers saw the opportunity to channel these efforts more systematically, the member-get-a-member campaign was born. This type of viral marketing has traditionally been facilitated with a letter sent via the US Postal Service telling association members how important it is to recruit new members accompanied by a referral form and a return envelope.

Several years ago, when this unique system was first implemented, it was highly successful, yielding healthy results by turning professional acquaintances and friends into paying members. However, as postal rates increase, and the natural decline of campaign responses sets in, the ineffectiveness of continuing to use this system becomes evident forcing association marketers to seek alternative mediums for their member-get-a-member campaigns.

Case Challenge

When the Association for Supervision and Curriculum Development (ASCD) approached Marketing General to design, develop, and execute their quarterly member-get-a-member campaign, Marketing General knew it that it had to deliver something different. Their campaign proposal needed to follow the traditional

Case Study: Gold Lasso

member-get-a-member style, yet speed the process of gathering and soliciting referrals in a cost effective way.

The idea of using e-mail to replace direct mail campaigns came up at an accounts executive meeting. At first, this seemed like an easy task since many e-mail marketing services offer a "Refer A Friend" feature that forwards the e-mail received with a message from the original recipient. After further research, MGI realized that this type of feature offered limited customization and proved difficult to implement for their proposed campaign strategy.

As Marketing General's primary e-mail marketing service provider, Gold Lasso offered to review the proposed technical specifications for ASCD's member-get-a-member campaign to decide if building a separate module in its eLoop system was an option. During the due diligence process, Gold Lasso discovered that other association clients were also seeking a more efficient way of planning and executing their member-get-a-member campaigns and building an additional module into eLoop made sense from both a technical and business standpoint. Marketing General developed the initial specifications for the project and Gold Lasso refined them to not only be used for member-based organizations, but for companies that need to communicate with a critical mass of customers.

The Solution

After a thorough review of the campaign specifications provided by MGI, Gold Lasso concluded that multiple e-mail actions needed to occur to create the speed and data processing efficiencies for the project's success – hence eLoop's referral module was born. The idea behind the module is simple, but to ensure flawless execution, selecting and writing the correct business logic proved to be challenging. After much debate and testing, the following was decided:

- To provide an association with a platform to send a personalized e-mail requesting their members to make membership referrals

- To provide the members with an easy to use referral form that can be incorporated into the initial message or accessed by clicking a link

- Capture and create relationships between the referral data and members

- To provide an association with a platform to send a personalized e-mail requesting their members to make membership referrals

- To provide the members with an easy to use referral form that can be incorporated into the initial message or accessed by clicking a link

Case Study: Gold Lasso

- Capture and create relationships between the referral data and members

- Simultaneously send two personalized e-mails based on the referral data collected; one to the member thanking them for their referrals and the other to the prospective member informing them that their colleague and co-worker referred them for membership and would they like to join the association

- Provide a secure Web form where prospective members can join the association by providing their personal and payment information (this last step for the ASCD campaign was provided by MGI at **www.joinup.org**)

Once a technical solution was approved, MGI wanted to ensure that this campaign would experience more than an average success rate. But the challenge of inspiring busy professionals to leverage their rolodex for a greater cause can sometimes be a daunting task. As a twist, MGI suggested to ASCD that they make the referral process fun by creating a competitive spirit. It was decided that ASCD would offer a prize (what is the prize?) to the member who provided the most referrals. This strategy proved to be very successful.

Deploying the campaign through eLoop provided both MGI and ASCD real-time results. Almost immediately ASCD members stepped up to the challenge providing hundreds of referrals. Within the week it was clear the campaign was a winner netting over 350 new memberships to its success. The large return on the campaigns investment can be attributed to the following:

- The campaign strategy of encouraging members to act on behalf of the association

- The immediacy of the e-mail responses providing instantaneous communication between members, member prospects and the association

- The personalization of each e-mail executed from the system listing members and referrals in their respective parts of the e-mail

*Gold Lasso, LLC, located in Gaithersburg, MD, is an interactive technology marketing firm that started operations in 2001. The company primarily services the association, publishing, retail, education and hospitality industries. For more information, visit the Gold Lasso Web site at **http://www.goldlasso.com** or call 301-990-9857.*

Case Study: XM Satellite Radio

XM Satellite Radio, America's No. 1 satellite radio service, transmits over 120 radio channels to nearly 2.5 million subscribers throughout the continental U.S. in crisp digital sound, representing the first technological advance in radio since the popularization of FM in the 1970s. XM radios are available at consumer electronics stores stores nationwide and in many new vehicles made by General Motors, Honda and Toyota.

The service offered by XM hints of a new "permission marketing" radio format, where paid subscribers enjoy expanded programming which includes 68 channels of uninterrupted music each month.

Challenge: Updates needed for 120 channels

"A major challenge for the customer service side of XM Satellite Radio", said Systems and Reporting Analyst Lars Unhjem, "is keeping up-to-date with all the happenings for the vast number of music and talk radio channels the service offers."

XM uses Campaign Enterprise to compose its information newsletter, XM Signal. Hundreds of thousands of XM subscribers and potential customers receive this newsletter each week, with recipients signing on to the e-mail list via XM's Web site at **www.XMRadio.com.**

"Even though we are a relatively new company, when you take what would be happening with one new company, and multiply it by 1 00— because we have a more than a hundred different channels — there's a lot going on in any given week," Unhjem said.

Campaign to inform and excite

The XM Signal e-mail newsletter is used primarily to keep current subscribers informed and excited about the content coming across the radio. "It's almost a 'TV Guide'-like way to get people familiar with what's happening on a week-to-week basis," Unhjem said. XM Signal highlights popular programming, major events, on-air artist visits, and more.

For potential customers, Unhjem said the e-mail service communicates not only the latest happenings, but it also espouses the benefits of being an XM subscriber. Digital sound quality from your radio, coast-to-coast uninterrupted service coverage, and comprehensive, commercial-free programming are but a few of the perks touted by the company each week using Campaign Enterprise software.

Case Study: XM Satellite Radio

Solution: Meeting future growth needs

Unhjem said XM was looking for proven software that would deliver a proven, commercial-level e-mail program. "We initially gauged the software by the quantity and quality of its current customer base," he said. "This made us feel more confident that it was going to do the things it said it could, such as the personalization of e-mail."

"Another strong aspect of Campaign", Unhjem said," is its ability to handle not only the current e-mail campaign load, but the loads of future growth of the company. XM, with approximately 692,000 subscribers, is on pace to having one million subscribers before the end of the year. "

XM Satellite Radio also applies Campaign to maintain communication with its subscriber base on the sensitive topic of billing issues, using e-mail to discretely update customers on the status of their accounts. This communication might include e-mail updates on service payments or as e-mail reminders if credit cards expire.

"There are business benefits to the software other than the marketing side," Unhjem said.

Results

XM currently uses Campaign Enterprise Team Edition and cites the program's ease of use, reliability and scalability as its leading featured capabilities.

Unhjem said the firm is in the process of taking advantage of the multipart features of Campaign software, but for now is sending out the XM Signal newsletter in html and text formats separately.

"Campaign has been great. It's helped us stay in communication with our subscribers, which keeps them engaged with what XM is offering," Unhjem said.

Despite having such a huge selection of channels, Unhjem said each of the channels offered have their own listenership, just like favorite television channels. "Being able to use Campaign to help us communicate what's airing each week helps engage subscribers with what makes us different over traditional radio."

Unhjem said the current key mission for the company is to track and understand the results of its varying marketing activities over time. "The more insight into how well the newsletter is being received — which people are really opening it, reading it, and following the links to learn more about the programming we're featuring — the better our understanding of how well people are responding to our marketing

Case Study: XM Satellite Radio

activities," he said. "Being able to understand the changes in behavior that take place each week, and as we change our messaging, is extremely valuable."

About XM Satellite Radio

XM Satellite Radio is America's No. 1 satellite radio service. Whether in the car, home, office, or on the go, XM offers 68 commercial-free music channels, 33 channels of news, sports, talk and entertainment, 16 dedicated channels of XM instant traffic and weather, and the industry's smallest and lightest radios and antennas. More information can be found at **www.XMRadio.com**.

About Arial Software

Founded in 1993, Arial Software is widely considered the industry leader in comprehensive software designed exclusively for relationship marketing through personalized e-mail messaging. Arial's mission is to be a universal provider of software tools to automate, personalize and measure meaningful e-mail communications. **www.arialsoftware.com.**

Case Study: Dirt Devil

DirtDevil.com optimizes transactional e-mails with Campaign

Royal Appliance Manufacturing Co. introduced Dirt Devil hand-vacuums in 1984 and has since grown the brand to become Royal's signature product line, enjoying approximately 98 percent brand name awareness.

Dirt Devil builds brand loyalty for its line of floor care products and powerful vacuums with strong consumer satisfaction, assisted by its Web site at **DirtDevil.com** using a unique, product-based e-mail marketing strategy driven in part by Campaign Enterprise e-mail marketing software.

DirtDevil.com e-mails are sent automatically to people who have signed up on the Web site — customers who have registered product warranties or who have bought Dirt Devil products or accessories and are notified via e-mail confirmation when their items are outbound. "We also use Campaign to drive the 'tell-a-friend' function of the Web site, to e-mail reminders for things like new sweepstakes, or when we run a 'send an e-card feature,'" said Michael Crowdes, the interactive marketing and e-commerce manager for **DirtDevil.com.**

Campaign Enterprise runs these automated functions as well as drives the response e-mails sent out when shoppers register at the Web site. It is all consumer-based, but a unique mix of e-marketing and transactional e-mails, Crowdes said.

Case Study: Dirt Devil

Challenge: Daily automated e-mailing from existing database

Campaign is used for transactional e-mails because those are a daily occurrence, Crowdes said. **DirtDevil.com** has several hundred people registering on the Web site each week, all which require responses, and has occasional outbound e-mail campaigns going to opt-in customers, usually numbering over 120,000.

Dirt Devil's automated transactional e-mails are an easy set up — including message scheduling and establishing recurring e-mails — using Campaign Enterprise. "Being able to schedule recurring e-mails was probably the second most important thing we were looking for in an e-mail software solution," Crowdes said.

The most important feature for **DirtDevil.com** was the software interacting directly with the existing Dirt Devil customer database, without requiring a complete importation of customer data into the program. "One thing I don't have time for is reconciling two separate lists for things like opt-outs and other tracking," Crowdes said. "It would be impossible to do anything else if users from the site were registering product and we had to answer each one with e-mails by hand."

"I'd have to do that through JavaScript if the e-mail software were not able to directly interact with the database," he said. "It was good fortune to find Campaign online… our criteria is such that the e-mail solution is something we own, because we're not big fans of ASP solutions in general, particularly for something like this."

Solution: Confirming customer trends

Campaign's automation and its ability to integrate with not one but two of Dirt Devil's customer databases — customer information is stored in a SQL database and certain shipping notifications use Oracle — allows Crowdes to focus on other aspects of the interactive customer experience without having to constantly monitor customer transactional e-mail.

"I do look at a couple of top-line metrics," Crowdes said. "If those are off — say nobody has confirmed a product registration all afternoon — then I will wonder if something has happened… but that's never happened, and I just don't think about these things in general because of the software's automation."

Direct interaction with Dirt Devil's customer databases mean automated scheduling of e-mail product offers can be set in tandem with print campaigns such as circulars in Sunday papers. Near real time updates of unsubscribes and e-mail bounces keep customer data clean and the online interaction positive.

Case Study: Dirt Devil

The value of tracking e-mail from Campaign Enterprise is really in understanding the customer list better, Crowdes said, sometimes more than the recorded results.

Dirt Devil looks at analytical data, like the propensity for someone to open an e-mail based on the amount of time they have been on their list. "The people who've engaged you most recently are the ones who are most likely going to engage you again. The people who've been on our list for a year or two years, their open rate is way down." Additionally, e-mail open rates from specific states may fluctuate in strange ways, or open rates tracked by individual ISPs can tell Crowdes and his team if there are any spam issues.

It's nice to have these trends confirmed with Campaign, Crowdes said.

Results: Campaign for sharp analytics

DirtDevil.com gauges the success of an e-mail campaign from the analytics side, using a robust program called WebTrends and setting it up to specifically track the web traffic coming in from an e-mail campaign. Analytical measurement ability is then already in place to track the e-mail campaign — including the resulting sales, which Crowdes calls the 'gold standard.'

"You're limiting yourself as an interactive marketer if you have no understanding of the technology that's driving all your communications," Crowdes said. "For some folks that means understanding print, for some that means understanding broadcast… for us, it means understanding databases, protocols and all of those things."

About Royal Appliance Manufacturing

Royal Appliance Manufacturing Co., headquartered in Glenwillow, Ohio, develops, assembles and markets a full line of floor care products for home and commercial use under the Dirt Devil and Royal brand names. Company information can be found at **http://www.royalappliance. com** *and product information is at* **http://www.dirtdevil.com.**

About Arial Software

Founded in 1993, Arial Software LLC is widely considered the industry leader in comprehensive software designed exclusively for relationship marketing through personalized e-mail messaging. Arial's mission is to be a universal provider of software tools to automate, personalize and measure meaningful e-mail communications.

Case Study: Terra Lycos

The Terra Lycos global network compliments its marketing plan with interactive customer e-mails

With some 111 million unique visitors per month to its network of Web sites, Terra Lycos is one of the leading Internet companies in the world. Its significant global presence and clear focus on profitability and growth has generated over 4 million access subscribers to date, averaging 500 million page views a day featuring products and services from more than 3,000 advertising customers. The group's network of Web sites includes Wired News (**Wired.com**), **Quote.com, HotBot.com, Gamesville.com, Angelfire.com, Matchmaker.com** and more.

Terra Lycos' goal of profitable growth is achieved by efficiently managing resources and generating recurrent revenue from paying subscribers. Part of this efficiency is to compliment existing and future marketing strategy with cost-effective e-mail marketing.

Challenge: Remove the outbound e-mail choke factor

The marketing department at Terra Lycos had a problem. Their e-mail software would choke each time they would send an outbound e-mail marketing campaign involving more than 250,000 e-mails. Terra Lycos' Terra.com division has over one million subscribers in its Oracle 9i database, and issues e-mail newsletters to the entire database every two weeks.

Campaign Enterprise's Bulletproof Mailer technology solves outbound e-mail choking problems by using technology which monitors SMTP server performance and adjusts accordingly. If the SMTP server is slow, the program slows the mail delivery and waits for the server to catch its breath; if the server disconnects, the program will pause before retrying the connection.

Alex Karamanoglou, direct marketing manager at Terra Lycos' Terra.com division office in Miami, Fla., also said the company's previous e-mail application didn't have the capacity to provide enough information on the response level of individual campaigns. "It would just send e-mails without accounting for any bounces or tracking," he said. "We felt lost as to the effectiveness of our e-mail campaigns."

One of the specific goals of Terra Lycos' e-mail campaigns is to compliment current marketing strategies — results almost impossible to measure without the instantaneous write-back features of Campaign Enterprise. "We want to gain as much insight as possible as to the efficacy of our campaigns, and to react appropriately to any trends," Karamanoglou said.

Case Study: Terra Lycos

Terra.com subscribers are segmented by age, location (state), and opt-in status. "We are thrilled to have a very active user base that is very responsive to our e-mails... and who don't mind giving us information about their likes and dislikes," Karamanoglou said. "We try to listen as much as we can, to provide them with the best experience possible when visiting our portal."

Solution: Campaign Found

Karamanoglou initially found Campaign Enterprise through a search using **Google.com**. "I was desperate for a better solution, and (a competing application) was completely outside what our budget would allow... I was very surprised to find that Arial Software offered an application that was just as flexible at a much more affordable price," he said.

Karamanoglou cites speed, flexibility, dependability and reporting capabilities as the most important components of e-mail marketing software that his department needs. "Click thru and e-mail open tracking are paramount for us," he said. "Also, knowing immediately which e-mails have bounced — so we can immediately remove them from our e-mail list — is also critical," Karamanoglou said.

The marketing division of Terra Lycos is currently in the process of completely integrating Campaign Enterprise into its Oracle database, where, once complete, e-mail campaigns issued by the company will be fully customized, including first and last name e-mail fields, as well as tracking opened e-mails and click thrus. The company will also move the subscribe/unsubscribe functions of its e-mail to its Campaign software, versus sending its users to a separate Web page, where they must first log in before changing their user preferences.

"We want to make it as convenient as possible for our user base to interact with us and be able to change settings at their leisure," Karamanoglou said. "The flexibility that Campaign offers us with using stored procedures will allow us to perform many other functions that were not possible with previous applications."

Besides the marketing department, Terra Lycos' client services and Web traffic departments also use Campaign Enterprise.

Results and Customer Oriented

Terra Lycos has an ongoing commitment to customer satisfaction, now further enhanced with personalized e-mail messages using Campaign Enterprise permission e-mail marketing software. The result of this customer-oriented approach is an increased number of paying subscribers to the network.

Case Study: Terra Lycos

Since Campaign was integrated, Terra Lycos has seen a significant increase in subscribers and open rates. "The write-back reports we created allow us to see what our users are responding to, and lets us change with them," he said.

"Campaign Enterprise has had a huge positive impact on our business," Karamanoglou said. "It's dependable, predictable, flexible, fast, and comes with fantastic tech support... I would recommend this software to any companies looking for an internal e-mail marketing solution, without reservation."

About Terra Lycos

Terra Lycos is a global Internet group which resulted from Terra Networks, S.A's acquisition of Lycos, Inc. in October 2000. It operates some of the most widely visited Web sites in the U.S., Europe, Asia, and Latin America, and is the largest access provider in Spain and Latin America. Terra Lycos' network of Web sites includes Terra in 18 countries, Lycos in 22 countries.

About Arial Software

Founded in 1993, Arial Software LLC is widely considered the industry leader in comprehensive software designed exclusively for relationship marketing through personalized e-mail messaging. Arial's mission is to be a universal provider of software tools to automate, personalize and measure meaningful e-mail communications.

Case Study: The Children's Place

The Children's Place gains from in-house e-mail marketing

New Jersey-based The Children's Place Retail Stores is a leading retailer of high quality, value-priced apparel and accessories for children. The company sells products under its own label and has 693 retail stores in the United States and Canada. The company also sells its merchandise through its online store at **www.ChildrensPlace.com.**

The Children's Place sends outbound e-mail campaigns to its customers featuring store information and product promotions for both its retail locations and its online store. Coupons, news about the latest line, and different sales alerts are all part of the active, ongoing messaging between the retailer and its customers. The coupons contain an online code which drives traffic to the Web site. "There's always a spike in the number of orders when we are using e-mail messages to drive online traffic," said James Diee, e-marketing analyst for The Children's Place. And because the

Case Study: The Children's Place

e-mail coupons are also printable, the e-mail campaigns become important for driving traffic to the retail stores as well, Diee said.

E-mail campaigns are coordinated directly with the marketing department and are often sent in tandem with print advertising campaigns. E-mail customers receive the same promotion, with links back to the Web site directing consumers to the same items online that they can find in the stores.

The challenge: improve e-mail turnaround time and delivery

The initial challenge for The Children's Place was to improve its delivery, open, and click-thru rates for its e-mail messaging at a competitive cost. The retailer also wanted to improve the turnaround time for its marketing e-mails. Outbound e-mail marketing campaigns are sent by the company between two and four times a month, and each of them is critical to the levels of traffic at both its online store and its retail locations.

Prior to Campaign Enterprise, e-mailing was outsourced, and coordination of the message between the marketing department and service provider was an extra and sometimes lengthy step in the process. Also, because the service provider charges per e-mail, the cost of e-mailing was directly associated with the size of the campaign.

"The cost of sending e-mails was probably the most attractive aspect for management in making the decision to bring its e-mail campaigns in-house," Diee said.

The solution: in-source the e-mail

"We chose Campaign Enterprise because it is very powerful and easy to use," Diee said. "Campaign Enterprise offered everything other outsource vendors did, at a much more competitive price.... we were looking for a product that would give us the ability to bring all of the aspects of sending mass e-mail campaigns in-house." Diee said.

Besides meeting standard Children's Place vendor requirements like best price and ease of use, Diee said Campaign Enterprise's ability to handle e-mail bounces, unsubscribes, expired addresses, and other automatic database cleansing features — all performed in near real time reporting — made it a clear leader as a comprehensive e-mail marketing solution. Diee also said vendor companies for The Children's Place must typically have five years minimum experience in the field. "Arial Software's been in business for over 10 years, and they have a strong client list," he said.

Case Study: The Children's Place

Results: E-mail helps gain sales

Sending campaigns at a lower cost than using a service provider, shorting e-mail turnaround times and improving coordination between the marketing and IT departments led to immediate management endorsement for bringing the e-mail campaigns in-house. "They love the fact we were able to streamline the process at a lower cost," Diee said.

The company's online business made big gains in 2003 thanks in part to ongoing in-house e-mail marketing campaigns: The Children's Place e-commerce saw a 120 percent sales gain on top of an 80 percent increase over its sales numbers in 2002. Company officials attributed these results in part to increased marketing exposure resulting from its new in-house e-mail capability.

Even more e-mail marketing plans scheduled for the future means The Children's Place will look to do even stronger sales for 2004.

"Campaign Enterprise has had an extremely positive effect on our business," Diee said.

About The Children's Place

The Children's Place Retail Stores, Inc. is a leading specialty retailer of high quality, value-priced apparel and accessories for children, newborn to age 10. The Company designs, contracts to manufacture and sells its products under the "The Children's Place" brand name and it operates stores in the United States and Canada. Its virtual store is at **www.ChildrensPlace.com***.*

About Arial Software

Founded in 1993, Arial Software LLC is widely considered the industry leader in comprehensive software designed exclusively for relationship marketing through personalized e-mail messaging. Arial's mission is to be a universal provider of software tools to automate, personalize and measure meaningful e-mail communications.

Case Study: Geeks.com

Campaign Enterprise is Geeks.com favorite for delivering deals

Geeks.com is a popular discount online retailer that specializes in all things computer hardware: full systems, computer peripherals, and most anything that plugs into a computer.

Case Study: Geeks.com

Geeks.com buyers scout the planet for great deals on computer supplies for their customers, obtaining merchandise from such far away places as Taiwan and Hong Kong. "We'll look for deals wherever we can find them, even when they're not exactly computer related but still an electronic that's a great deal," says Peter Green, marketing specialist for **Geeks.com**. These deals might include cordless drills, in-dash auto DVD and CD players, and other consumer electronics.

Green says the e-mail offers **Geeks.com** would send to their customers at the start of their business would sell inventory, but after a while staff began to wonder if they were leaving money on the table by sending e-mails without knowing anything about specific subscriber activity. Could they be selling more?

"We'd start out with 500 products in stock, send an e-mail blast, sell the 500 products, and then we would say 'Great!'" Green says. "But then we would ask: Did we have the potential to sell more? Did only 500 subscribers open the letter? Is there something else that they might really want?"

It was soon realized that in order to take their discount computer supply Web site to the next level, **Geeks.com** needed reliable activity data from their e-mail campaigns to determine what subscribers really want.

Solution: Campaign Enterprise delivers campaign data

Geeks.com began using Campaign Enterprise to deliver e-mail campaigns a little over two years ago. Prior to Campaign Enterprise they used SMTP software that had the ability to bounce e-mail addresses and determine good addresses, but lacked the technology to capture any campaign effectiveness data. "We could scrub our list, but we couldn't gauge campaigns in any way," Green says of the SMTP tool. "We upgraded our e-mail system specifically so we could have some open data from our campaigns. And Campaign Enterprise gave us an effective means to do that."

The **Geeks.com** crew were immediately impressed with the ease of setup and integration of Campaign Enterprise to their custom database, in addition to the speed which the software could send campaigns out the door. "It was a welcome change. It saved us a lot of time," he said.

Geeks.com uses Campaign Enterprise to deliver campaigns and track e-mail open information, and Coremetrics to analyze the performance data. Their daily e-mail marketing campaigns are in the 200k-to-220k size range.

Using Campaign Enterprise, **Geeks.com** sends out three types of e-mail: Daily Geekmail, which offers a highlighted deal of the day, usually a discounted item or

Case Study: Geeks.com

an item new to the Web site and available only to Geekmail subscribers; TechTips, an information-only e-mail newsletter which covers geek specialty talents like how to install a video card or how to convert old media to new media; and "new arrivals" e-mails, usually sent on Fridays and featuring new products or upcoming sales events.

"Our main goal is sales, but by offering Tech Tips e-mails to our customers, we want to be seen as a knowledge base for the industry," Green says. "We try to make it easy for our customers. If customers want to repost a Tech Tip on their own Web site as content, we're happy to let them do it, as long as they cite us as the source."

Results: Gauging promotions and expanding business

The Geeks originally acquired Campaign Enterprise to get a handle on their consumer-based computer supply e-mail environment, but once they implemented the software and saw how well it was working, it was decided to use Campaign Enterprise with their business-to-business side as well, so they purchased a second copy.

"We wanted to have the software registered under each domain, with separated campaign information," Green says. "We like to run each business as separate entities. We even have two separate mail servers."

Evertek.com sells computer hardware just like **Geeks.com**, but in a wholesale-only pricing environment. It runs a smaller customer e-mail list — approximately 25k — and because of the resellers certificate and tax ID required to shop there, the Web site caters to a more specialized audience. **Evertek.com** e-mail subscribers receive e-mails twice a day: Daily computer supply specials in the morning, and new arrivals to the Web site in the afternoon. The Evertek e-mail open rate is a consistent 25-27 percent, Green says.

"Campaign Enterprise gave us a level of visibility that we never had previously," said Green. "It really gave us more confidence on what we could put out there in terms of e-mail promotions, including gauging the receptiveness of our e-mails by measuring open rates. Today we have a solid 30-to-32 percent open rate, which we are very proud of."

About Geeks.com

Geeks.com, *headquartered in Oceanside, Calif., is a leading direct-to-consumer e-commerce site specializing in providing computer-related excess inventory, manufacturer-closeouts, high-demand and unusual computer components and*

Case Study: Geeks.com

peripherals at highly-discounted prices to tech-savvy consumers. Their deals can be found at **http://www.Geeks.com**.

About Arial Software

Founded in 1993, Arial Software is widely considered the leading developer of permission-based e-mail marketing software used for delivering e-mail newsletters, customer specials, automatic responses, exclusive offers and more. Arial Software products are used by corporations, retailers, universities and other organizations to deliver personalized messages directly to subscribers, customers, prospects and members. More information can be found at **http://www.arialsoftware.com.**

Case Study: Kobold Watch Company

Kobold Watches Reach New Heights with E-mail Marketing Director

Kobold Watch Company manufactures high-quality, extremely durable wrist instruments designed for use by polar explorers and other extreme professionals requiring accuracy and reliability in a wristwatch. Made from high caliber materials including surgical stainless steel, aerospace-grade titanium, and virtually scratch proof sapphire crystal, each Kobold watch is powered by mechanical movement and is rugged enough to survive the most punishing conditions.

While Kobold watches reach new heights on the wrists of their owners, Kobold Watch Company uses e-mail newsletters composed and sent by E-mail Marketing Director software to reach clients and tell them about their specialized products. Kobold's e-mail marketing campaigns — organized by Marketing Director Nicole Amato — focus primarily on new products the company launches, but also include assorted messages covering the high profile charity events the company participates in.

Challenge: Boost visual appeal of e-mail newsletter

Kobold's Marketing Department faced a major challenge: they needed to make their e-mail newsletters more visually appealing. Kobold's subscriber list consists of customers who have already purchased a product from the company and provided an e-mail address.

As their subscriber list grew, Amato felt it was important to have a more eye-catching newsletter. To do this, she needed an e-mail software solution that included

Case Study: Kobold Watch Company

professionally-designed HTML templates as a feature. Amato felt that by making the e-mail newsletter more visually appealing, interest in receiving the newsletter would increase, which eventually would lead to a direct increase in sales.

Solution: E-mail Marketing Director to create buzz

E-mail Marketing Director's built-in database allows Amato to reach more clients in less time via e-mail to announce their new products directly. "We want to create a buzz, because the more people talk, the more likely there are sales," she explains. An additional bonus: when Kobold's newsletters drive customer traffic back to the Web site to review product information, they are also increasing the Web site's natural search results.

E-mail Marketing Director's database filtering also makes it easier for Amato to segment her customer lists, to get the right new product information to the right clients.

Results: Products in front of the right audience

Using e-mail newsletters, Kobold is getting their new products in front of the right people: already proven customers of the company. And their e-mail newsletters make it easier for existing clients to learn about new Kobold products without having to remember to check the Web site regularly themselves, Amato says.

E-mail newsletters sent with E-mail Marketing Director gives Kobold high expectations for creating exiting product buzz. "We hope it will get people talking," Amato says. "It just takes one or two clients to read our e-mail newsletter, or discuss the new information on our company's message board, for us to get results," she says.

About Kobold Watch Company

Kobold Watch Company is the manufacturer of high-quality and extremely durable wrist instruments. Kobold uses components made and assembled in factories in Switzerland and Germany, where highly skilled watchmakers spend up to two months assembling and testing each individual watch. More company information can be found at **http://koboldwatch.com.**

About Arial Software

Founded in 1993, Arial Software, LLC is widely considered the industry leader in comprehensive software designed exclusively for relationship marketing through personalized e-mail messaging. Arial Software products include Campaign Enterprise

Case Study: Kobold Watch Company

e-mail marketing software and E-mail Marketing Director easy-to-use desktop software.

More information on E-mail Marketing Director can be found at **http://www. arialsoftware.com/EmailMarketingDirector.htm.**

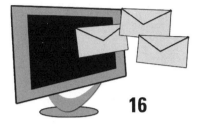

16

INDUSTRY HINTS, TIPS, & SECRETS

I have sought out the best advice, tips and secretes from the experts who do it every day, and compiled them in one Chapter. The individuals and companies profiled in this chapter are industry leaders, recognized for their excellence in e-mail marketing. I hope you learn from them as much as I have.

Tip: Gold Lasso

Spam filters, phishing detectors and the sheer e-mail volume flooding inboxes has critically devalued e-mail as a marketing medium. Marketers who fail to follow best practices are wasting 30 percent of their e-mail marketing budget and time before they even hit the send button. If your e-mail service provider does not offer the following features you are not following best practices and you will eventually experience decreased deliverability, list attrition, and sub-par results.

Why You Need It:

Unique IP Address — An IP address physically identifies a computer or server on the Internet. It is similar to a social security number in that no two IP addresses are the same and each IP address carries a reputation. Black lists, Internet Service Providers (ISPs), and corporate network administrators routinely fight spam or unwanted mail by blocking IP addresses. E-mail Service Providers (ESPs) that group multiple clients per IP address are cheating them out of building a good reputation. Just as you would never blindly share your social security number, there is no reason why you would want to share your IP address with other marketers who are less scrupulous than you. Based on an independent study by Jupiter Research, Marketing Sherpa and Return Path, almost 30 percent of all bulk e-mail gets blocked.

Tip: Gold Lasso

It is fact that marketers who send e-mail using a shared IP address experience lower deliverability rates than marketers who send using a unique IP address.

DNS Configuration — DNS Configuration, as it relates to e-mail marketing, allows you to send e-mail from your domain name instead of your ESP's domain. This is important for both branding and credibility. In addition, many anti-phishing filters will block your e-mail or warn e-mail recipients not to click on a link if a link in your e-mail does not match the domain from where the e-mail is sent. A credible e-mail service provider will help you with the DNS setup process so you can send e-mail from yourdomain.com instead of youremailserviceprovider.com.

Database Segmentation — Upon successfully sending a campaign that reaches your recipients' inbox instead of their spam folder you will be inundated with open and click statistics. A good ESP will have reports that show which recipients clicked on which links. A great ESP will not only give you a report, but the ability to automatically send follow-up e-mail to recipients who clicked on a specific link so timely opportunities are not missed. Automated database segmentation based on recipient behavior is the key to understanding how to generate additional interest using e-mail.

Sophisticated Personalization — Henry Ford, referring to the Model-T, the first mass produced car, once said that customers can have any color [car] they want as long as it is black. Take this attitude with your e-mail recipients and quickly watch your opt-out rate increase. Instead of mass produced e-mail, a quality ESP will give you the ability to create mass personalized e-mail. This ability goes beyond basic merge fields to create mass personalized automatically tailored based on interests and recipient behavior.

Data Collection — E-mail marketing is not a one way street. Your recipients want to respond to your e-mail and without providing them a systematic way of doing so, you lose the ability to capture valuable data. From surveys to landing pages, an ESP should have integrated forms to help you maximize your feedback collection. The information you collect should serve as a guide not only for future e-mail campaigns but other marketing efforts as well.

What Kind of Deliverability Should You Expect Once You Start Using Your New IP Address

Opening an account with a new e-mail service provider (ESP) that assigns you a unique IP address is just like trying to establish credit without any credit history. A new IP address is not a "shoe-in" for ensured deliverability.

When establishing credit, you need to confirm your identity, the same goes for your

Tip: Gold Lasso

new IP address. This is done by configuring reverse DNS with your new IP address and implementing a Sender Policy Framework (SPF) (**http://www.openspf.org**). Once your identity is established, it takes time for other mail servers to recognize your IP address as a valid source of e-mail. This is done in a number of ways; 1) Your recipients place your domain and/or your IP address on their "safe sender" list or e-mail address book; 2) Corporate Network Admins and ISP's place your domain and/or IP address on their white lists. The latter is often done automatically by checking your reverse DNS and SPF. This can sometimes take a while — all a process of building a reputation. Once your IP and domain are recognized as legitimate e-mail senders, you will notice an increase in your deliverability rates. However, the process does not stop here. You will need to maintain your reputation by keeping your spam complaints low and e-mail volume to a tolerable level.

Below is a list of the major ESPs and how they determine deliverability of bulk e-mail. As you can see, reputation is the most important.

Aldephia	CompuServe	Mail.com	USA.net
Reputation 44%	Reptuation 100%	Reputation 100%	Reputation 78%
Content 56%	Content 0%	Content 0%	Content 22%
AOL	Cox	MSN	Verizon
Reputation 100%	Reputation 50%	Reputation 32%	Reputation 86%
Content 0%	Content 50%	Content 68%	Content 14%
ATT	Earthlink	Netscape	Yahoo!
Reputation 90%	Reputation 77%	Reputation 88%	Reputation 80%
Content 10%	Content 23%	Content 12%	Content 20%
Bell South	Gmail	NetZero	
Reputation 97%	Reputation 100%	Reputation 90%	
Content 3%	Content 0%	Content: 10%	
Cablevision	Hotmail	RoadRunner	
Reputation 79%	Reputation 40%	Reputation 100%	
Content 21%	Content 60%	Content 0%	
Comcast	Mac.com	SBC	
Reputation 85%	Reputation 83%	Reputation 79%	
Content 15%	Content 17%	Content 21%	

Source: ReturnPath, Sender Reputation Causes E-mail Delivery Issues 83 percent of the Time, September 2006

Gold Lasso, LLC, located in Gaithersburg, MD, is an interactive technology marketing firm that started operations in 2001. The company primarily services the association, publishing, retail, education, and hospitality industries. For more information, visit the Gold Lasso Web site at **http://www.goldlasso.com** *or call 301-990-9857.*

Tip: Gold Lasso

What You Should Know About E-mail Marketing Deliverability

Successful delivery is the driving force behind an effective e-mail marketing campaign. Without it, the marketer wastes time, money, and resources and does not achieve the end goal. A variety of factors exist that can prevent successful delivery such as content that triggers spam filters, blacklisting and mail server configuration. The recipient's perception can also influence delivery — if they do not trust the source or recognize the message as relevant they may delete it before it is even read. How can marketers move past these potential barriers to increase their delivery rates? There are many easy-to-implement tips that can improve deliverability. Consulting with an e-mail service provider (ESP), more knowledgeable of the technical aspects of deliverability, helps marketers to develop tactics specifically designed for the organization's campaign scope and budget.

The purpose of this paper is to provide a summary of terms (or jargon) related to e-mail deliverability, increase general knowledge of the concept, discuss delivery barriers and provide tactics to overcome these issues.

WHY IS DELIVERY SO IMPORTANT?

Successful delivery of messages is not only a key metric for evaluating an e-mail marketing campaign; it has much further reaching implications for both the marketer and the e-mail marketing industry as a whole. The consequences of delivery issues unfold in a chain reaction. The individual organization risks losing money and wasting valuable staff time to develop messages that ultimately fail because they are not delivered or read. The campaign's response rate is lower because messages could not be delivered. The recipient does not respond to the message's call to action because it was not delivered.

Recipients that have not received the message are not able to build a relationship with the organization. The organization loses loyalty from its stakeholders and may lose the stakeholders all together. For the industry, the risks may be even greater. Without successful delivery, the medium loses its value and customers become skeptical of all e-mail marketing messages.

GLOSSARY OF COMMON TERMS RELATED TO E-MAIL DELIVERY

Understanding the jargon of e-mail marketing and specifically the concept of deliverability is an essential first step to handling any issues that arise. A summary of related terms is as follows:

Tip: Gold Lasso

- **Affirmative consent:** An active request by a reader or subscriber to receive advertising or promotional information, newsletters, etc. Generally affirmative consent does not included the following — failing to uncheck a pre-checked box on a Web form, entering a business relationship with an organization without being asked for separate permission to be sent specific types of e-mail, opt-out.

- **Authentication:** An automated process that verifies an e-mail sender's identity.

- **Bayesian filter:** An anti-spam program that evaluates header and content of incoming e-mail messages to determine the probability that it is spam. Bayesian filters assign point values to items that appear frequently in spam, such as the words "money-back guarantee" or "free." A message that accumulated too many points is either rejected as probable spam or delivered to a junkmail folder. (Also known as a content-based filter.)

- **Blacklists:** Lists of IP addresses that are being used by or belong to organizations or individuals that have been identified as sending spam. Blacklists are often used by organizations and Internet Service Providers as part of their filtering process to block all incoming mail form a particular IP address (or block of addresses).

- **Block:** An action by an Internet Service Provider to prevent e-mail messages from being forwarded to the end recipient.

- **Bounces:** E-mail messages that fail to reach their intended destination. "Hard" bounces are caused by invalid e-mail addresses, whereas "soft" bounces are due to temporary conditions, such as overloaded inboxes.

- **Bulk folder (also junk folder):** Where many e-mail clients send messages that appear to be from spammers or contain spam or are from any sender who's not in the recipient's address book or contact list. Some clients allow the recipient to override the system's settings and direct that mail from a suspect sender be sent directly to the inbox. E.g., Yahoo! Mail gives recipients a button marked "Not Spam" on every message in the bulk folder.

- **Challenge-Response:** An authentication method that requires a human to respond to an e-mail challenge message before the original e-mail that triggered the challenge is delivered to the recipient. This method is sometimes used to cut down on spam since it requires an action by a human sender.

- **DNS — Domain Name Server (or system):** An Internet service that translates domain names into IP addresses.

Tip: Gold Lasso

- **Domain Keys:** An anti-spam software application being developed by Yahoo! and using a combination of public and private "keys" to authenticate the sender's domain and reduce the chance that a spammer or hacker will fake the domain sending address.

- **E-mail harvesting:** The disreputable and often illegal practice of using an automated program to scan Web pages and collect e-mail addresses for use by spammers.

- **ESP (E-mail Service Provider):**The operator of the mail server whether it is the corporate IT department, a small independent domain with its own mail server, or an e-mail service provider that delivers on behalf of a client base.

- **False positive:** A legitimate e-mail message that is mistakenly rejected or filtered by a spam filter.

- **Firewall:** A program or set of programs designed to keep unauthorized users or messages from accessing a private network. The firewall usually has rules or protocols that authorize or prohibit outside users or messages. In e-mail, a firewall can be designed so that messages from domains or users listed as suspect because of spamming, hacking, or forging will not be delivered.

- **Footer:** An area at the end of an e-mail message or newsletter that contains information that doesn't change from one edition to the next, such as contact information, the company's postal address, or the e-mail address the recipient used to subscribe to mailings. Some software programs can be set to place this information automatically.

- **Hard bounces:** E-mail messages that cannot be delivered to the recipient because of a permanent error, such as an invalid or non-existing e-mail address.

- **Header:** Routing and program data at the start of an e-mail message, including the sender's name and e-mail address, originating e-mail server IP address, recipient IP address, and any transfers in the process.

- **IP address:** An IP address is a unique identifier for a computer on the Internet. It is written as four numbers separated by periods. Each number can range from 0 to 255. Before connecting to a computer over the Internet, a Domain Name Server translates the domain name into its corresponding IP address.

- **Joe job:** A spam-industry term for a forged e-mail, in which a spammer or hacker fakes a genuine e-mail address in order to hide his identity.

Tip: Gold Lasso

- **List hygiene:** The act of maintaining a list so that hard bounces and unsubscribed names are removed from mailings. Some list owners also use an e-mail change of address service to update old or abandoned e-mail addresses (hopefully with a permission step baked in) as part of this process.

- **Phishing:** An attempt to trick recipients into giving out personal information (i.e. credit card numbers or account passwords) by sending e-mail pretending to be from a legitimate source such as the user's bank, credit card company, or online Web vendor.

- **Reverse DNS:** The process in which an IP address is matched correctly to a domain name, instead of a domain name being matched to an IP address. Reverse DNS is a popular method for catching spammers who use invalid IP addresses. If a spam filter or program can't match the IP address to the domain name, it can reject the e-mail.

- **Soft bounces:** E-mail messages that cannot be delivered to the recipient because of a temporary error, such as a full mailbox.

- **Spam (also known as unsolicited commercial e-mail):** Unwanted, unsolicited junk e-mail sent to a large number of recipients.

- **Spoofing:** The disreputable and often illegal act of falsifying the sender e-mail address to make it appear as if an e-mail message came from somewhere else.

- **Whitelist:** A list of pre-authorized e-mail addresses from which e-mail messages can be delivered regardless of spam filters.

THE PROBLEM: BARRIERS TO E-MAIL DELIVERY

According to industry experts, spam and content filters erroneously block more than 20 percent of all opt-in commercial e-mail. Blocked messages that are legitimate mail are coined "false positives." Message delivery fails for different reasons. Most are blocked because the content triggers spam filters, configuration of mail servers, perception by the user that the message is spam, and ISP relationships.

Content

Messages that contain spam filter triggers in the content are typically not delivered. A trigger is a word, character, or image that is common to spam messages. It might be words such as "free" or "trial" in the subject line, excessive punctuation in the subject or body of the message, low resolution images, too many images, or themes common to spam messages such as mortgage offers or medications.

Tip: Gold Lasso

How do SPAM filters work?

Internet Service Providers (ISPs), corporations, and individuals use filters to reduce spam messages in their inboxes. Messages are filtered based on the sender's e-mail volume, the number of spam complaints lodged against the sender, sender's bounce rates, e-mail content, message formatting, and blacklists. Messages flagged as spam are blocked from delivery or sent to the "junk" (or bulk) folder of the inbox where they are usually deleted and never read.

Configuration of Mail Servers

Spam laws ban false or misleading header information. The e-mail's "From," "To," and routing information must be accurate in the header. This includes the originating domain name and e-mail address. If the information does not match, the message is not delivered. Sender ID programs are designed to verify that each e-mail message originates from the Internet domain from which it claims to come based on the sender's server IP address.

User Perception

User perception is essentially a "human" spam filter. If they do not recognize the sender, if the content has any triggers discussed above or if the content is not relevant and personalized, the delivery is in jeopardy. The consequence of negative user perception is blacklisting by ISPs from receiving excessive complaints. If the reader believes the message is spam they have the right to lodge a formal complaint against the sender through the CAN-SPAM Act of 2003. If complaints reach a benchmark, usually one in 1,000 messages, the ISP may blacklist the sender and block future messages.

ISP relationships

Without a good, working relationship with the ISP, the sender risks losing a spot on whitelists. It is also more difficult to rectify problems related to false positives.

THE SOLUTIONS: TIPS TO SUCCESSFULLY DELIVER MESSAGES

Recognizing the major challenges to e-mail delivery and working with an ESP to address them is the first step to developing successful campaigns. However, marketers can structure messages to increase their successful delivery rate.

Tips to Successfully Deliver Messages

- Include opt-in and double opt-in mechanisms to ensure recipients actually want to receive the messages.

Tip: Gold Lasso

- Request the user provide their "real" or primary account. For example, many recipients use Yahoo! and Hotmail accounts as throwaway accounts.

- Remove addresses that hard bounce or soft bounce two to three times within 30 days. The ISP may block future messages if messages are continually sent to an invalid address. Overall bounce rates should fall between six and eight percent.

- Always send a plain text version of the message. A 2004 study by **AWeber.com** shows that plain text messages are undeliverable 1.15 percent of the time and HTML-only messages were undeliverable 2.3 percent of the time.

- Check the blacklist status of advertisers or sponsor logos. If their URL is blocked due to spam complaints, the message could also be blocked just for having it in the content.

- Avoid using attachments that might spark a filter based on blocked viruses. It is better to provide a link to an online file.

- Have your ESP or legal counsel review your practices to ensure you are compliant with CAN-SPAM acts.

- Make the focus of your list building on quality not quantity.

- Investigate spikes in the bounce rate, which may signal e-mails are being filtered or blocked by one or more ISPs.

- Automate bounce filtering so that hard bounces are immediately suppressed and soft bounces are suppressed after a pre-determined number of attempts.

- Maintain a separate "bounce-out" suppression list versus putting bounced e-mails on the unsubscribe list.

- Review bounce-out lists to see if there is a particular problem with certain ISPs.

- Request subscribers add marketers to a "safe-list" or "add to the address book."

- Use a concise subject line (no more than 40 to 60 characters total so it shows up completely in the recipient's inbox).

- For e-newsletters or e-zines, start the subject line with the same prefix; i.e. myorg e-news.

Tip: Gold Lasso

- Do not use sensationalized headlines, overuse capitalization, or punctuation. It will tip off spam and human filters.

- Accurately portray your name/organization in the "From" field. Spam filters will also be tipped off by an individual's name.

- Consider common spam themes such as mortgage, medications, etc. and avoid language associated with them.

- Avoid overuse of images.

- Include prominent calls to action with multiple links (but no more than 10 to 20 links). An excessive ratio of links to content is typical of spam.

- Check the content with a spam checker (this can be provided by your ESP).

- Test the message not only in the primary e-mail account but with some of the biggest e-mail providers such as Yahoo!, AOL, Hotmail, GMAIL, etc. Most are free.

- Time e-mails to arrive in the morning before recipients typically start reading their mail. Sending e-mails earlier also avoids busier ISPs.

- Have consistency by using templates (provided by the ESP). Recipients are less likely to delete a message if they are expecting it or they recognize the look and feel of it.

- Stay alert to the changing landscape to achieve maximum deliverability.

- Respond to a challenge response. A growing trend in spam prevention is the challenge response message. If the ISP detects a new e-mail address it will send a response message to the "From" line requesting authentication. It is also a way to beat automation by requiring a human response.

- Check server configurations with the ESP.

WHAT STEPS IS THE INDUSTRY TAKING TO ENHANCE DELIVERABILITY

The mail marketing industry has taken steps to reduce spam and fraud and enhance delivery of legitimate messages by introducing e-mail authentication. Authentication is the process used to check and validate that the sending domain is authorized to send mail on the IP address's behalf. Industry leaders have developed tools to authenticate; the primary tools are the Sender ID Framework (SIDF) and DKIM which combines Yahoo! Domain Keys and Cisco's Identified Internet Mail programs.

Tip: Gold Lasso

SDIF is currently being implemented worldwide. The process can be broken down into the following steps:

(1) The domain administrator publishes SPF records in the Domain Name System (DNS). The SPF records identify authorized outbound e-mail servers by listing their IP addresses.

(2) The marketer sends an e-mail message to a receiver.

(3) The inbound mail server receives the message.

(4) The inbound mail server checks which domain claims to have sent the message and checks DNS for the SPF record of that domain.

(5) The inbound mail server determines if the sending server's IP address matches any of the IP addresses in the SPF record.

(6) The inbound mail server scores the e-mail. A positive score indicates that the IP addresses match and the mail is authenticated. A negative score indicates it does not match and it is not authenticated.

E-mail authentication is linked to user perception of the sender and message. According to Pews Research Center, 63 percent of consumers trust e-mail less. This is largely due to phishing scams. Authentication allows the recipient to verify the sender and determine if the message is legitimate.

WORKING WITH AN ESP

It is common for organizations to work with an e-mail service provider (ESP) to develop and execute the marketing campaign. The ESP should be an expert in the e-mail marketing field and have access to the technology available to effectively conduct an e-mail campaign — including enhancing delivery. Becoming well-versed in the challenges to delivery and solutions will help organizations communicate with the ESP and understand the tactics used. According to Chief Marketer, there are four common delivery problems organizations encounter when working with an ESP:

(1) **Using the ESP's default tracking links** — Many ESPs use default URLs to track and report on the campaign. If any ISP or corporate mail server administrator is blocking any part of these default links, their clients' campaigns may also be blocked. The solution to this is to define a DNS-based domain alias.

(2) **Using the ESP's default image tags** — Similar to the problems with default links, a campaign may also experience problems if references are made to default

Tip: Gold Lasso

image locations. Again, the use of a DNS-based domain alias in image tag references can combat this problem.

(3) **Relying on the ESP's white list status** — White list status can be revoked at any time at the sole discretion of the ISP due to a high number of abuse complaints. To stay on white lists maintain a low complaint level.

(4) **Not using a dedicated IP address** — Smart marketers request their ESP use a pool of IPs (maybe three) to spread your complaints per IP across different servers.

Another benefit of working with an ESP is the ability to receive detailed reports on key evaluation metrics such as open rates, click through, and bounce rates. Organizations should also request metrics on spam complaint ratios, scores within spam filters, and actual delivery rates (to a seeded list) for the top ISPs.

CONCLUSION

As marketers continue to use e-mail as a primary medium for communication, the importance of successful message delivery will increase. It is the organization's responsibility to understand the barriers to delivery and strategies available to break through them. They can accomplish this by staying educated on factors that impact the medium such as changes to spam laws and improvements in technology.

The organization should also consider contracting with a credible ESP to ensure they stay current with the industry. ESPs are expert e-marketers and their primary function is to achieve the goals outlined in this paper. By mastering a basic understanding of this ever-changing industry, the organization can evaluate and choose a quality e-mail vendor and evaluate their success as well as the success of the campaign.

In the end, the most effective way to ensure delivery is to send legitimate, relevant, and personalized messages.

Gold Lasso, LLC, located in Gaithersburg, MD, is an interactive technology marketing firm that started operations in 2001. The company primarily services the association, publishing, retail, education, and hospitality industries. For more information, visit the Gold Lasso Web site at **http://www.goldlasso.com** *or call 301-990-9857.*

Tip: Ross Kramer of Listrak, LLC.

Insiders Guide to Overcoming E-mail Deliverability Challenges at the Largest U.S. ISPs

What was true in the past will be true into the foreseeable future; deliverability will present itself as a challenge to anyone attempting to have their e-mail message reach the inboxes of their target recipients. At some point in time over the past several months almost all of us had a piece of e-mail falsely routed to a junk or bulk e-mail folder. Understanding and embracing the inefficiencies of the current deliverability landscape will help in overcoming the challenges of deliverability. Regardless if you are a marketing professional or technology provider you are reading this whitepaper because you are interested in enhancing your e-mail deliverability. The mission of this particular whitepaper is to magnify and examine the current challenges placed on permission-based e-mail marketers in relation to the eight largest ISPs in the United States.

This whitepaper is the culmination of several years of close analysis of how the largest ISPs filter e-mail. To our knowledge, there is no single resource that identifies the specific methods and technology used by these ISPs to filter e-mail. To that extent it should be noted that due to the ever changing nature of this topic, the information contained in this whitepaper could become outdated quite quickly. Additionally, the data presented in this whitepaper is based upon our specific Listrak findings. Your experiences with the ISPs presented in this whitepaper may differ from the data that we have collected.

One Overriding Premise: User Complaints

Even though the topic of e-mail deliverability is a moving target, there is one aspect that you can bet on: The more complaints generated by your e-mail activity, the greater the chance you will be blocked. I have had several conversations with top ranking e-mail administrators regarding e-mail deliverability and the tone is consistent across the board, "Send mail that my users want, mail that generates a low amount of complaints, and I'll deliver your mail to their inboxes." For anyone reading this whitepaper whose campaigns generate a substantial amount of complaints and are looking for a "silver bullet" within this text for how to get their mail delivered, please stop now, as you will not find your answer here or anywhere else. If your mail is unwanted, it will go undelivered. It is that simple.

For the rest of the permission-based e-mail marketers out there looking for their recipient anticipated mail to be delivered to the inboxes of the largest ISPs in the U.S., I am certain you will find the following information useful.

Tip: Ross Kramer of Listrak, LLC

AOL:

With over 22 million active subscribers, AOL is the largest ISP in the world. AOL offers customers access to their proprietary content and the Internet through both dialup and broadband access. Almost all AOL customers access their e-mail via the proprietary AOL software, the latest of which is 9.0.

If your lists are consumer-oriented, chances are good that they will contain a large percentage of AOL addresses. AOL receives billions of pieces of mail each day — a large portion of them (nearly 1.2 billion messages) in the form of unsolicited commercial e-mail (UCE), commonly referred to as spam. To curb this problem, AOL has taken a unique approach by allowing their users to simply click a button to report a message as spam. These reports are tabulated in real time and are analyzed by AOL to determine if action is warranted. Measures may include declining to accept e-mail transmissions from a particular sender.

Spam reports from AOL's members fell from a daily average of almost 11 million in November 2003 to a daily average of about 2.2 million in November 2004 and their e-mail filters handled 50 percent less e-mail traffic over that same time period. The company credits their anti-spam measures for the reduction in spam. What this means is that there is still a big window of opportunity for marketers to reach their AOL members with permission-based e-mail campaigns, but success will ride on the mailer's ability to maintain good-standing with AOL.

General guidelines for sending e-mail to America Online can be found at their Postmaster's Web site **http://postmaster.aol.com**.

One additional issue is that some messages get through to the AOL member but end up in their spam folder. Since each member's spam folder is controlled by their individual mail preferences, the postmaster team can neither view nor change the settings that control what mail is going to the spam folder. You will want to have your recipient check to make sure that isn't happening. If it is, the recipient will need to add the sending address of the e-mail to their address book.

Microsoft: (MSN / Hotmail)

While Microsoft does not publicly disclose the exact numbers of active MSN and Hotmail subscribers, for most e-mail senders the sum of their MSN and Hotmail addresses is usually secure at the number two spot, just behind AOL. MSN is a strictly pay-for dial-up and broadband Internet access service while Hotmail offers a mix of pay-for and free e-mail services available via the Web. E-mail for both MSN and Hotmail are filtered using the same technology and are listed together for that reason.

Tip: Ross Kramer of Listrak, LLC

MSN / Hotmail users receive more than one billion pieces of spam mail each day. Due to this fact, parent Microsoft has implemented a new content filtering technology called SmartScreen. This technology presents the most challenging content filter in use by any of the top ISPs. Listrak recommends changing text (that may trigger the SmartScreen filter) into images — .jpg or .gif graphics. Make sure that you maintain a balance of 50 percent text, 50 percent graphics in your message. Common words and phrases that are filtered include, but are not limited to: "unsubscribe," "privacy policy," "offers," and similar words and phrases. Another challenge with SmartScreen is that it discards messages that fail to pass its filter. No bounce reply is sent to the sender.

Additionally, Microsoft has integrated their SmartScreen technology into both their Outlook and Exchange Server products. Permission mailers sending B2B campaigns should be aware that this could lead to deliverability problems. Listrak recommends always testing your campaign by sending it to an e-mail account that uses Outlook and Exchange Server.

Yahoo!:

Through a partnership with SBC, Yahoo! has built a top ranking pay-for dial-up and broadband Internet access ISP in addition to their popular Web-based e-mail service.

Yahoo! maintains a top 5 position for most addresses on business-to-consumer lists. Although Yahoo! does not employ the same drastic filtering measures found at MSN / Hotmail, they do have some content filters in place via their SPAMGuard technology.

SPAMGuard automatically directs messages that are deemed as unsolicited bulk mail to a separate, "bulk mail" folder in the Yahoo! member's mail account. The challenge with the SPAMGuard technology is that it does not return a bounce so there is no way to tell if the mail is delivered into the bulk mail folder or the inbox. It is advised that you test your content using a test list containing at least one test Yahoo! Address. Use this address to check to make sure your message finds its way to the inbox and not the bulk mail folder.

Yahoo! Mail also provides two methods for its members to report spam that they receive in their inbox. They can manually report messages as spam to Yahoo! Mail without ever opening the message by simply clicking on the "spam" button located above the message. This will send the message to their bulk mail folder and send a spam report to the Yahoo! postmaster. Another option Yahoo! members have is that they can set up a blocker to match the address or domain of a particular sender. This blocker will prevent delivery of e-mail from that sender.

Tip: Ross Kramer of Listrak, LLC

It has been our experience that Yahoo! also limits accessibility to their mail server by time and quantity of mails but these thresholds are unknown and not published.

As with all ISPs to improve the chance of messages going to the inbox, instead of the bulk mail folder, it is important to get the subscriber to add your e-mail address to their Yahoo! Address Book. They can do this by opening the message and clicking the "Add to Address Book" link.

For more information on Yahoo!'s anti-bulk mail policies and procedures visit **http:// antiSPAM.Yahoo!.com.**

Outblaze Limited:

While not technically an ISP, Outblaze provides a mix of free and pay-for Web-based e-mail services for several thousand domains, the largest of which include Excite and **Mail.com**. Their total number of subscribers amounts to at least 30 million mailboxes.

Outblaze has made no secret of their belief that their mail services are for personal use — not commercial use. To this end, they are very aggressive in how they filter incoming mail. They have very little tolerance for commercial e-mail, regardless of permission level or relationship. Outblaze uses two main methods to conduct their anti-spam efforts.

They filter e-mail against external domain name block lists (listed below) and also run their own local block list of known / potential spam source IPs and net blocks, known as the OBSL (OutBlaze SPAMmers List).

United On-Line: (Juno / Net Zero / BlueLight)

United On-Line owns three leading discount ISPs that include Juno, NetZero, and BlueLight. All three ISPs offer dial-up only access.

The three ISPs share anti-spam measures and present similar challenges in deliverability. These providers use a combination of content filtering plus a fairly aggressive connection/quantity cap that will prevent delivery to mailboxes in these domains after a certain threshold is reached. To improve delivery rates to these providers it is suggested that you closely monitor your message content to avoid using words or phrases commonly associated with spam. The quantity caps are more difficult to circumvent. The best plan is to throttle the number of concurrent connections and proactively monitor the volume of bounces you receive.

United On-line is the second ISP behind AOL to publicly announce the availability of a feedback loop. This means that United On-line will alert you to the users who report

Tip: Ross Kramer of Listrak, LLC

your campaigns as spam. You can then unsubscribe those users who are contributing to your non-delivery.

Comcast

With over seven million broadband Internet customers, Comcast is the nation's leading provider of high-speed Internet access. In the past two years Comcast has led an aggressive strategy for acquiring new broadband cable modem subscribers. In 2004 Comcast acquired the AT&T Broadband which had previously acquired broadband provider Mediaone.

We have seen impressive response rates from Comcast.net subscribers. We attribute this to two factors: Comcast is a pay-for service (unlike free e-mail service providers like Yahoo! and Hotmail) and their ISP offering is fairly new. This means that there are fewer orphaned accounts — boosting your delivery percentage to this domain. Thus we have found their subscribers to be active Internet users and we feel that this ISP will see continued growth through customer and competitor acquisitions.

Comcast has been known to blacklist the IP addresses of high volume senders so if you feel that you are having problems getting messages delivered to this domain do not hesitate to contact Listrak support for assistance.

The bottom line is that each Comcast.net address that you have is valuable and it should perform well for you in terms of delivery, open/read, and conversion rates provided that you are playing by the rules of permission.

Earthlink:

Earthlink is a traditional ISP that offers Internet access in several different flavors including dialup, broadband, wireless, and satellite. Earthlink has grown their subscriber base through a series of over 100 acquisitions of smaller ISPs. For a complete list of all domains that Earthlink controls visit: **http://support.earthlink.net/mu/1/psc/img/walkthroughs/other/1694.psc.html**

Earthlink presents deliverability challenges on two fronts. First, they employ a service they call SPAMBlocker, which uses commercial blacklist provider, Brightmail, to filter all incoming messages. Brightmail is a multi-layer content filter that leverages over 17 different technologies, including spam signatures, heuristics, reputation filters, language identification, and many proprietary methods. The end result is that SPAMBlocker determines whether your messages reach the inbox or get routed to the "Suspect" e-mail folder (also known as a junk mail folder). We recommend keeping a keen eye on your content in order to avoid having your messages filtered by SPAMBlocker.

Tip: Ross Kramer of Listrak, LLC

The second challenge with sending e-mail to Earthlink members is their challenge-response system. There are several challenge-response systems in place today; however, Earthlink's is unique in that it never returns a response for commercial e-mail. If you are getting a low response rate from Earthlink you may want to ask your list members to add your e-mail address to their address book to get around the challenge-response issue. For more information regarding Earthlink's e-mail filtering please visit **http://www.earthlink.net/elink/issue24/focus_archive.html**.

Road Runner:

Road Runner, owned and operated by Time Warner Cable, is one of the nation's premier broadband service providers. The Road Runner service is available only in a broadband form to customers within the Time Warner Cable territory.

Road Runner has implemented its own set of spam filters, including a top layer of mail gateways whose primary function is to identify unsolicited messages coursing onto the network. Lately, they've been blocking about 40 percent of the messages coming in, most of them related to proxy servers, open hijackings, or other known spam source networks.

Cox Communications:

Cox Communications is the third-largest cable provider in the nation. Similar to Comcast and Road Runner, Cox Communications only offers their broadband service to customers within their territory.

Cox uses Brightmail's Anti-SPAM with BrightSig™ technology. Like other Brightmail implementations at other ISPs, the technology resides on the messaging gateway and filtering takes place before reaching Cox customers. The Brightmail Anti-SPAM solution is deployed by some of the world's largest Internet service providers and has helped Cox significantly reduce the amount of unwanted e-mail that reaches their customers' inboxes.

Based on their Brightmail implementation, Cox gives their customers two anti-spam choices. Cox customers can choose to either have their e-mail (that Brightmail has deemed as spam) blocked or flagged. If a Cox customer chooses to have their mail blocked, the Brightmail software will block the message at the gateway level and the message will never reach the recipient. If a Cox customer decides to have their mail flagged, the Brightmail software will place flagged mail in a bulk mail folder where the user can later review.

Tip: Ross Kramer of Listrak, LLC

In addition to Brightmail, Cox also currently offers the McAfee SPAMKiller product for an additional monthly charge.

Our research has also shown that some Cox Communications ISPs have implemented an artificial intelligence-based machine learning solution from Corvigo, an anti-spam vendor recently purchased by Tumbleweed Communications which may lead to some permission-based e-mail falsely filtered as spam.

Listrak is a leading provider of hosted e-mail marketing software that allows permission-based marketers to manage, send, track, and grow their e-mail marketing investment. Listrak services clients such as Daimler Chrysler, Motorola, L'Oreal, and the Islands of the Bahamas from its Lititz, PA headquarters. Listrak was named the 2006 Small Business Technological Excellence Award winner by the Philadelphia Chamber of Commerce, a Top Fifty Fastest Growing Company in 2006 and 2005 by the Central Penn Business Journal, and the 2005 Growth Company of the Year by the Technology Council of Central PA. Contact us at **www.listrak.com** to learn more.

HTML E-MAIL SPECIFICATIONS

To make sure that your HTML e-mail looks its best in all possible e-mail clients, here are the specifications to follow:

- Because many people keep their monitor resolution set to 800 x 600 or less, it is best to design HTML messages with a maximum width of 600 pixels. You want subscribers to see as much of your message body as possible without having to scroll right and left.

- Images must be in .gif or .jpg format and be stored on a Web server. You must use the full URL to pull any graphics in the e-mail. Ex: http:// www.mysite. com/ images/ picture.gif0.

- Links must point to a full URL. Ex: http: / / www.mysite.com/ page.htm.

- Image maps should not be used.

- Use tables in your HTML code for maximum control over placement of text and images, and the width of your message body. Cascading style sheets / layers should not be used.

- Use <p></ p> tags instead of <div></ div> tags for alignment purposes.

- Do not use java, JavaScript, frames, ActiveX, cache busters, or Dynamic HTML.

- Do not include meta tags.

Tip: Ross Kramer of Listrak, LLC

- HTML Code is sometimes interpreted differently by different e-mail applications. Test your message in as many applications and browsers as possible to ensure that it is formatted correctly for each.

- It is best to keep the message size, including images, to less than 40K to avoid long download times.

Listrak is a leading provider of hosted e-mail marketing software that allows permission-based marketers to manage, send, track, and grow their e-mail marketing investment. Listrak services clients such as Daimler Chrysler, Motorola, L'Oreal, and the Islands of the Bahamas from its Lititz, PA headquarters. Listrak was named the 2006 Small Business Technological Excellence Award winner by the Philadelphia Chamber of Commerce, a Top Fifty Fastest Growing Company in 2006 and 2005 by the Central Penn Business Journal, and the 2005 Growth Company of the Year by the Technology Council of Central PA. Contact us at **www.listrak.com** *to learn more.*

Tip: Nancy Houtz

Changing Times at Google

Remember the dot.com bust in the late 1990s when businesses thought all they needed to do was put up a Web site and customers would come in droves? They soon found out otherwise and numerous businesses went down under.

Next came pay-per-click search engine marketing in the early 2000s. Those who jumped aboard this type of marketing early found that using keywords to bring buyers to their Web sites could bring an amazing amount of business. Even more significant, they only paid if someone clicked to their sites. Quickly the popularity of pay-per-click marketing grew and businesses everywhere learned they must do likewise if they wanted to keep customers. Many new entrepreneurs began to set up Web sites to sell almost anything, since they could get people to their sites at relatively little cost. Single page sales letter-sites also became commonly used.

What is now happening during the last half of this decade is that Google has become so popular they are facing gridlock, not unlike freeways during rush hour traffic. Everyone wants to be on the first page on search results, but alas, when too many are competing for that space, some method must be established to give priority. At first, the bid prices made top positioning available; however, as bids amounts began increasing, there might be too many with the same high bids to prioritize for the first page. Cost factors also prevented bid amounts over a certain break-even point

Tip: Nancy Houtz

where it no longer pays to raise the price. No one wants to lose money for each order they receive.

Google needed to find a way to not only keep happy pay-per-click customers, but to have satisfied searchers as well. At first they gave quality scores for keywords that were most relevant to the ad. Still, gridlock prevailed. They made several changes the last half of 2006 that have had an impact on placement and results.

Google is now giving placement priority by screening the Web sites and landing pages for appropriate content for relevancy to the keywords and ads. Once I understood this, I can now easily see how important it is for a business to have a Web site that does not simply lock a searcher into one viewing choice. Web sites must attract searchers by offering what they are searching for. Sites must also encourage searchers to look around and check out information as well as buy a particular product or service if they are to receive high Google ratings and preferential ad positioning.

Business owners must begin to work more closely with their pay-per-click manager as well as Web technicians to achieve profitable results. It is no longer a matter of coming up with a bunch of search terms and hoping for the best. Every single step of this type of marketing must be carefully monitored and applications made that will get results with Google if there is to be continued success at affordable cost. Experienced pay-per-click managers can see at a glance which Web sites will maximize opportunities for success with Google. Business owners should listen carefully to suggestions made for changes and try to make them where appropriate.

Nancy Houtz

Google Advertising Professional

www.PayPerClick4uj.com

Tip: Tony Tateossian

E-mail marketing is one of the powerful effective marketing tools on the Web today. It is quick, offers immediate results, and delivers a high investment on return. A very important aspect is to start building a list on your site. In order to attract visitors you must give them something for free, whether it is a newsletter, software, eBook, or a tangible product, this will entice them to join your list and enable your e-mail marketing

Tip: Tony Tateossian

strategy. It is always good to have a complete software package or service that will drive your e-mail marketing campaigns. You want to be able to measure the performance of deliverable e-mails, as well as bounces and open rates, in order to maximize profits. Be honest in your e-mail, and provide a resource so readers will look forward to your next e-mail, rather then sending spam-like e-mails that will rarely be looked at. Make sure the software or service package has many features like list collection for opt-in registration. Never use spam related software to collect e-mail addresses from the Web, as this is considered a spam tactic and will get your site labeled for spam. Build a respectable and informative e-mail campaign and your product and service will grow. A patchy campaign will get you low results; therefore, be committed, and make sure you build an e-mail marketing campaign that will be informative and have users thinking of your product or service for days.

One of the primary segments of the search engine marketplace that is currently underserved is the need for Web sites to be able to generate Web traffic on a shoestring budget. Most search engines offer pay-per-click advertising campaigns and allow you to bid on keywords and drive visitors to your Web site for a cost per click. For many PPC advertising systems, the highest bid typically gets the highest position, and you'll be charged when someone clicks on your ad, whether it is a legitimate click or fraudulent. Cosmodex seeks to provide consumers and prosumers a viable alternative and solution to the high costs associated with online advertising and marketing.

Cosmodex provides marketing and advertising solutions for e-commerce sites, personal home pages, small businesses, and even bloggers with a number of unique programs that generate traffic at no cost, as well as a wide variety of additional economical premium advertising options. This is the new wave of the Internet and Cosmodex seeks to pave the way.

Join us as we award anyone and everyone with free Internet traffic, based on the amount of searches conducted within Cosmodex, the search engine that rewards. **http://www.cosmodex.com**.

Tip: Get Response

E-mail Marketing: 15 List Building Tips

E-mail marketing can be profitable for any business, no matter what kind of product or service you are selling. It is significantly cheaper than other advertising methods and it enables you to build credibility with your subscribers. As a result, you can generate more sales and profits.

Tip: Get Response

The foundation of e-mail marketing is a targeted, responsive, and permission-based e-mail list. If you have a list of subscribers that trust you and consider you to be an expert in the field of your interest, you are on the right track.

Below you will find several list building ideas that will help you make the most out of your e-mail marketing.

Provide useful, relevant, and unique content. Your visitors will not give you their e-mail address just because they can subscribe to your newsletter free of charge. You have to provide unique and valuable information that will be useful for your subscribers.

Add a subscription form to every page of your Web site. Make it elegant and accessible. Locate it at the top-left corner of your site, as that is where the human eye will initially travel.

Make the sign up process as easy as possible. You shouldn't ask for too much information upfront, because you will lose subscribers. Collecting just the name and e-mail address should be enough for most e-mail marketing campaigns.

Address your visitors' privacy concerns. Most people are worried that they will receive spam after giving out their e-mail address. Tell your potential subscribers that you respect their privacy and link this statement to a privacy policy page.

Show an example issue to your visitors. This lets your potential subscribers review your newsletter before they sign up and determine if it is something they would be interested in.

Create a Web based newsletter repository. By putting an archive of all of your newsletter issues online you can make it more appealing for your visitors to subscribe. You will also generate additional traffic from search engines.

Contact other newsletter publishers. Let them know that you'd be interested to announce their newsletter if they're up to do the same for you. This way, both of you can build your lists faster.

Give away useful free stuff. Write an e-book or a PDF report. Hire a programmer to create downloadable or Web based software. Then give it away to your visitors provided that they join your list.

Request that your subscribers pass it on. Word of mouth is a powerful viral technique that works great with e-mail marketing. If your subscribers find the content you share with them to be useful and informative, they will pass your newsletter on to their

Tip: Get Response

friends. This can be a good source of new subscribers.

Let others reprint your newsletter, as long as its content is unmodified. Many Web masters and newsletter publishers are actively looking for high quality content, and if they reprint your newsletter, you will get new subscribers, traffic, and links pointing to your site.

Include a "Sign Up" button in the newsletter. If you are using plain text instead of HTML, provide a text link to your subscription page. You may feel that this is not required, because the subscriber is already on your list, but remember that your readers will forward your newsletters to others, or reprint it online. You want to make it easy for them to subscribe.

Add a squeeze page. A squeeze page is typically designed only to build your list. It features a powerful headline and a couple of the most important benefits that should make your subscribers salivate to sign up to your list. Once created, use a service such as WordTracker to find hundreds of targeted keywords, and advertise on them using pay-per-click advertising on Google, MSN, and Yahoo!. Include testimonials in your squeeze page. This is crucial. Put one or two strong testimonials from satisfied subscribers on your squeeze page. This can be in any format, but you may find that multimedia (audio or video proof) is more "believable." People like to follow footsteps of other people.

Blog religiously. Blogging is a great way to communicate with your potential customers, and it creates a nice synergy with your e-mail marketing. Be sure to include your newsletter sign up form on each page of your blog.

Use a co-registration service to build your list. Co-registration is a great way to build your e-mail list. Your newsletter's ad appears on other Web sites and their visitors are able to check your subscription box and become added to your list. A good co-registration service can be found at **GetSubscribers.com**.

Simon Grabowski is an owner of the Web based GetResponse e-mail marketing software that makes it easy for thousands of marketers and small businesses to send their newsletters and build their e-mail lists. Try GetResponse free of charge at **http://www.getresponse.com**. Implix was established in 1998 by the online entrepreneur, Simon Grabowski: **http://www.implix.com/**.

GetResponse e-mail marketing service was Implix's first venture and today it remains the company's flagship product: **http://www.getresponse.com/** or **http://www.implix.com/product-getresponse-autoresponder.html**

Tip: Get Response

We offer an easy to use and set up auto-responder and newsletter hosting service that enables marketers to launch their e-mail marketing campaigns, deliver their newsletters, and maintain their lists' hygiene, all via an easy to use interface. Currently GetResponse has more than 500,000 active user accounts.

GetResponse prides itself on working closely with the anti-spam community and all the major ISPs/ESPs. We were the first auto-responder and newsletter hosting service that has joined the premier e-mail service provider organization E-mail Sender and Provider Coalition (ESPC): **http://www.espcoalition.org/member_news.php**

Tip: Matt Bacak

Reducing complaints and increasing list responsiveness

E-mail marketers have a huge impact on whether their messages will be considered spam and may escalate into complaints and accusations. With careful structuring of e-mail marketing campaigns, marketers can significantly lower their unsubscribes, minimize their complaints, and increase the responsiveness of their lists.

Below are several recommendations that I have found to be instrumental in achieving these goals.

1. Use the confirmed opt-in subscription model.

Confirmed opt-in requires your subscribers to confirm their intention to subscribe to your mailing list before you can deliver your information to them. Switching to the confirmed opt-in model is the single most important step you can take to prevent e-mail abuse complaints.

When you confirm your subscriptions, you are doing the best possible thing to shield yourself against spam accusations.

It is important that your e-mail marketing provider stores the important logs that can "prove your innocence," should you ever receive a complaint. Such proof may include: subscription method (i.e. e-mail subscription, Web form subscription, manual inclusion, list import), IP and time stamp of the original subscription request (i.e. a person who initially requested to be subscribed), IP and time stamp of the actual confirmation (i.e. a person who clicked on the confirmation link). A reputable e-mail marketing service provider will automatically archive the proof for you, and take care of the complaints on your behalf.

Tip: Matt Bacak

It should be noted that with the unconfirmed opt-in model you leave yourself vulnerable to attacks, joe-jobs, and spam accusations.

By confirming your subscriptions you will have cleaner, more responsive lists that are more targeted, generate significantly less complaints and unsubscribes, and contrary to what the urban myth is — do not negatively impact sales.

2. Identify yourself in your e-mail messages.

Many of the complaints are caused by the fact that the subscriber does not recognize the sender and automatically assume that the e-mail is spam.

You can combat this by adding clear information that identifies you and your company in the beginning of your message, and reminds your subscribers of who you are and what they signed up for.

When you do this, make sure that you do not say, "This e-mail is NOT spam" — people will assume it is.

Instead, you could try something like:

Hi Joe, You have signed up for my free e-mail course "How to make your parrots talk" a week ago at my site: **http://Make-Your-Parrot-Talk.com**. I was wondering…have you had a chance to review the first lesson and give it a shot?…

By identifying yourself clearly to your subscribers you are significantly reducing the chance that they will unsubscribe, complain, or click on the "This is Spam" button.

Another important aspect is to include your company name and address towards the end of your message.

This is necessary to comply with the CAN-SPAM legislation, but at the same time it provides important information to your subscriber and may result in lower complaints.

3. Ensure that your e-mails don't look like spam.

A lot of complaints and unsubscribes can be avoided if e-mail marketers structure their messages appropriately.

Here are a few tips:

Tip: Matt Bacak

a) Choose your subject line carefully. It is the first thing they will see. Make sure that the subject reflects the contents of your message and that it does not remind your subscribers of spam.

b) Do not write long e-mail copy. Go for "short and crisp," then point to your Web site for more information.

c) Do not repeat your Web site URL over and over again. You are more likely to get more complaints than more sales; once or twice is usually enough.

d) Write plain text messages instead of HTML enhanced messages.

e) Do not use "hash-busters" — i.e. special characters or punctuation entered in the attempt to fool the anti-spam systems (i.e. F'REE instead of FREE or v111agr^a instead of Viagra).

f) Run a spam-check on your messages before you send them out and fix any problems that it detects.

4. Provide an easy way to unsubscribe.

Every e-mail that you send out must contain an unsubscribe link at the bottom of your message.

The unsubscription process must be easy to follow and effortless, and must actually work. This may sound funny, but some of the unsubscribe systems I have seen had issues and some did not unsubscribe at all. Test your system thoroughly to make sure that it works.

You may use an outsourced e-mail marketing solution such as GetResponse to automate e-mail hygiene, handle unsubscribes, bounce-backs, complaints etc.

5. Be cautious of lead providers.

Purchasing leads is popular among many marketers who use them to increase the size of their lists.

Unfortunately, many lead generation companies resort to dirty tactics to increase their profitability at the expense of customers and their subscribers.

These include:

a) Sharing the same leads over and over again with multiple clients.

Tip: Matt Bacak

This not only significantly reduces the quality of the lead, but it also increases the chance that it will result in a spam complaint in the future. Quite simply, people who sign up for one publication, but start receiving e-mail from 15 similar campaigns are very likely to complain — and for a reason.

b) "Bribing" people to subscribe.

Another trick is "incentivizing" leads subscriptions by offering the subscribers some form of compensation for filling out the form, such as a coupon, a chance to win something etc. This produces leads of inferior quality, because most of the subscribers are not genuinely interested in your publication, but are signing up solely for the incentive.

c) Pre-selecting signup forms.

Some lead generating companies use lead generation forms with checkboxes that are pre-selected. This dilutes the list quality and results in spam complaints.

Purchasing leads carries a substantial risk for e-mail marketers. If you decide to purchase leads, here are a few questions that you may want to ask the supplier:

a) Are the leads generated specifically for me?

b) How are your leads generated? (ask for an example)

c) Is your lead generation process incentivized?

Remember — when it comes to lists it is always the quality that is important, and not the quantity. It is much better to have a small and responsive list than a large, diluted list that is much more likely to generate complaints, spam accusations, and customer support issues.

By outsourcing your e-mail marketing to a reputable provider you will have saved yourself the hassle of dealing with all the issues associated with e-mail hygiene.

GetResponse e-mail marketing service was Implix's first venture, and today, it remains the company's flagship product: **http://www.getresponse.com/** or **http://www.implix.com/product-getresponse-autoresponder.html.**

We offer an easy to use and set up auto-responder and newsletter hosting service that enables marketers to launch their e-mail marketing campaigns, deliver their newsletters, and maintain their lists' hygiene, all via an easy to use interface. Currently GetResponse has more than 500,000 active user accounts.

Tip: Matt Bacak

GetResponse prides itself on working closely with the anti-spam community and all the major ISPs/ESPs. We were the first auto-responder and newsletter hosting service that has joined the premier e-mail service provider organization E-mail Sender and Provider Coalition (ESPC): **http://www.espcoalition.org/member_news.php**

Tip: Michelle Howe

E-Mail is Transforming Customer Communication

E-mail is a wonderful communication tool for business. It is fast, cost-effective, and convenient. Employees commonly use e-mail to communicate with each other and e-mail is increasingly the method of communication with customers, thereby changing the way companies interact with their customers.

In 2006, about 54 percent of consumers used e-mail to contact organizations for help. Customers can use e-mail to ask questions, send referrals, complain, offer suggestions, or send compliments. For many people, e-mail is a more convenient and less intimidating way to communicate with a company.

Companies often offer an 800 phone number in order to open up the communication lines between themselves and their customers. Although the call is free, it still requires more personal interaction and less anonymity than using e-mail. Sometimes customers want to connect with a company, but making that phone call is just too personal. E-mail is a better solution.

Companies should consider using e-mail, in addition to an 800 phone number, as another effective tool in improving customer communication and satisfaction.

There are many ways a company can use e-mail to improve customer communication:

(1) Because e-mail is fast, a company can quickly respond to customer complaints via e-mail and find effective solutions. E-mail can also alert a company to a potential legal problem if it is receiving multiple complaints on a specific product. These warnings give the company a window of opportunity to fix the problem before it becomes a media nightmare.

(2) A communication program could be set up using e-mail for the test group to return online surveys and evaluations of the product. Existing customers might make an excellent test group for a new product.

Tip: Michelle Howe

(3) Existing customers could also be sent updated information about product upgrades, price changes, and new product lines.

(4) Customers can stay informed of the company's accomplishments through e-mail press releases.

Think of e-mail as another way to build customer loyalty. Respond to e-mails as soon as possible. Some companies have an auto-responder built into their Web site. Whenever an e-mail is received, the recipient is immediately sent a short e-mail telling them thank-you and that someone will be following up within 24 hours. This simple action shows concern for the customer by acknowledging that the message was received and that it will be quickly handled.

If you are a customer service representative responsible for communicating electronically with customers, you need to be especially careful when using e-mail:

(1) Be aware of the tone of your message. Try to use a pleasant, conversational tone. Be careful of the words you choose for your message and the way you phrase your answers. It is easy to accidentally be insulting to a customer just by using poor phrasing. Remember, everything you say represents the company.

(2) Try to understand the perspective of the customer. Although it may be quite clear to you what the problem is, it may not be clear to the customer. Take the time to patiently think things through and imagine what it must be like for the customer. It will give you a better understanding of the situation and more likely, a better answer for the customer.

(3) Be careful how you phrase bad news. Do not start the message off with the bad news. Start with a neutral statement and then give the reasons why you are going to say "no." Then, say no. For example, if a customer wanted to order a product that is no longer being manufactured, you would respond: "Your continuing business with BB3 is greatly appreciated. A company that is no longer in business manufactures the item you requested — Butterflies wallpaper by Pacer. Therefore, we do not have that item available for purchase. However, we do carry a butterfly wallpaper by Metzer, (item #678), that might meet your needs."

(4) Use the same formality and correct grammar in an e-mail as you would use in a letter to a customer. Use the customer's name in the salutation and be sure to have a polite close at the end.

(5) Be complete, but brief with your message. Get to the point right away and stick to the point. Stay focused on what you want to say and then be done. Do not try

Tip: Michelle Howe

to use your e-mail to sell products if the purpose of your e-mail was to answer a complaint.

E-mail is here to stay and companies can use this wonderful tool to dramatically improve their customer service. In fact, companies need to realize that online customer communication will continue to increase each year as customers become more and more comfortable using the computer to contact companies.

Internet writing expert Michelle Howe, MBA, understands the problems companies face. She consults with companies to assist them in effectively positioning their online marketing message. A former university professor, she is the author of Turn Browsers into Buyers **(http://www.turn-browsers-into-buyers. com)** *and* Persuasive Writing Made Easy **(http://www.saleswriting4you.com)**.

Her company, Internet Word Magic, specializes in improving online communication. The E-Mail Productivity System™ is a customized training program that covers the issues of business writing, e-mail etiquette, e-mail security, and the liabilities of e-mail.

Visit her Web site at **http://www.InternetWordMagic.com** *for the free report,* Five Easy Steps for Creating "I Wanna Read That" Articles. *For more information, please call (949) 733-1360 or contact Internet Word Magic at info@InternetWordMagic. com.*

Tip: Gold Lasso

Online Community for E-Marketers Is Open and Welcoming Visitors

Dotemail.com offers unlimited resources and tools for both novice marketers and sophisticated e-mail experts. Gold Lasso, LLC, a leading provider of on-demand e-mail marketing software and services, announced that it has launched Dot E-mail (**www.dotemail.com**), a new, free online community for e-mail marketers.

The Web site was built to serve the professional needs of today's e-marketers, and in keeping with Gold Lasso's open source roots, Dot E-mail was created entirely with open source software such as Joomla and related components. Dot E-mail features detailed resource links, message boards, links to industry news, blog commentaries, file sharing, and job and marketplace sections.

Tip: Gold Lasso

"E-mail marketing has become a billion dollar business, and those marketing professionals that count on e-mail as a valuable part of their marketing toolkits are able to apply innovative strategies and best practices to their work," said Elie Ashery, CEO and co-founder of Gold Lasso and the creator of **dotemail.com**. "This online community was built specifically for e-mail marketers as a forum to share their successful ideas, keep up with news, learn tricks of the trade, and just to comment or complain about some of the fun or vexing issues that serve to continually motivate them."

A sample of the issues already being discussed at Dot E-mail includes the potential impact of Internet video on marketers in 2007. A recent study by the media research firm Horowitz Associates reveals that Internet video content is grabbing more mobile device users all the time, with eight percent of all Internet users reporting they watch video content on a handheld device at least once a month. How will this growing trend impact e-mail marketers in 2007? Early users of Dot E-mail are already sharing opinions on the most successful methods for packaging an e-mail that is linked to video content in order to boost viewers.

Michael Weisel, Chief Technology Office of Gold Lasso, commented, "It is obvious that e-mail is helping to drive the growth of Internet videos and video podcasts, and in most instances, my team has found that by posting links to video in e-mails, you will get far more viewers than if you send video clips embedded in the e-mail."

Other issues that will surely impact the way marketers use e-mail in 2007 are e-mail deliverability and the continued growth of online ad spending.

"Not every marketing or sales professional has the time or resources to attend an expensive conference just to network and keep up with the latest electronic marketing trends," Ashery said. "But anyone can find the time to visit Dot E-mail each week in order to make new contacts, learn new marketing strategies, and keep up with the latest industry news. This free Web site represents our effort to give back to the marketing community, but like anything communal, you will get out of it what you put into it."

Gold Lasso, LLC, located in Gaithersburg, MD, is an interactive technology marketing firm that started operations in 2001. The company primarily services the association, publishing, retail, education, and hospitality industries. For more information, visit the Gold Lasso Web site at **http://www.goldlasso.com** *or call 301-990-9857.*

Tip: Christopher Knight

E-mail Segmentation 101 — Things to Segment Your E-mail Campaigns

Competition for the attention of your e-mail newsletter subscribers or permission-based e-mail marketing campaign members is rising. To increase the relevancy, deliver more value via e-mail, and increase your sales — now is the perfect time to begin doing more e-mail segmentation campaigns.

Here are (11) ideas for "what" to segment your e-mail list by:

Prospects that have become clients:

Once an e-mail list member has become a client, it's time to move them to a different level of list where they receive e-mails that are designed for clients and not prospects. There is nothing that can create more cognitive dissonance than for an existing client to receive an e-mail marketing to them as if they were a prospect offering them a better deal than they just received.

Product lines purchased:

If your firm has a wide line of distinct product lines, it is best to address your prospects and clients by product line. Give this segment specific offers or content relevant to the product line they are interested in or purchased.

Average ticket price:

Many times a client that gives you a sale in the $1,000+ average ticket price is worth far more than a client that purchased products from you in the less than $100 range.

Major clients:

VIP clients need to be acknowledged, remembered, and given better attention, gifts of exclusive information / content, and some of your best deals.

Most recent visit:

If you have transactional customers who only purchase your type of product once every three years (for example), do you think it would be wise to segment this type of buyer so that the moment you identify their recent visit or click of a specific campaign from your site, that they would be the perfect target for increased attention and offers vs. other times in this type of customer buying cycle?

Demographics:

Demographics might include age, race, gender, education levels, occupation,

Tip: Christopher Knight

location of residence, marital status, number of children, income, or other socio-economic factors, etc.

This is not to be confused with "Psychographics" or the identification of certain characteristics that your clients have that would influence their buying decisions. These could be factors that include measuring their attitudes, interests, opinions, cultural identity, etc.

Interest-based preferences:

If you have done surveys over the past year, then you know certain e-mail members have different interests that can help you classify their interest levels in various offerings related to your core product or service.

Open rate or CTR action rates:

Simply stated, e-mail list members that open your newsletter or click on something on a frequent basis are clearly more engaged than members who do not click on things; therefore, you can test sending a higher frequency to your most engaged members to increase conversion or response.

Sales Creates Sales: (Follow Up Campaigns)

As soon as you have segmented your clients from your prospects, now it is time to automate the sequence of e-mails that they will receive as a separate e-mail segment based on the types of products they purchased. Your goal is to reinforce the wise decision they made by purchasing from you and help them purchase the next level of product from you.

Acquisition Channels:

Where your e-mail members came from is known as an 'acquisition channel' and different acquisition channels have different characteristics. Example: Co-registration e-mail list members will always respond or convert differently than organically acquired e-mail members.

Geography:

Your prospects or clients in a foreign country really do not want to hear about your domestic holiday chit chat. Best to segment by the major countries you serve so that you can deliver geo-targeted messages that are more related to your members.

Do you see the e-mail segmentation pattern here?

Tip: Christopher Knight

This can be overwhelming if you are just starting out, so I recommend planning on at least segmenting by prospects vs. clients. Start there and as you begin to get improved results (better sales, conversions, etc), then continue narrowing your e-mail segments to improve list member loyalty, confidence, and improved purchasing likeliness. You can do it. Get started today.

Christopher M. Knight is an e-mail list marketing expert, author, and entrepreneur. You can get a weekly dose of e-mail newsletter publishing, marketing, promotion, management, e-mail etiquette, e-mail usability, and deliverability tips by joining his free E-zine-Tips newsletter: **http://www.emailuniverse.com/subscribe/.**

Tip: Christopher Knight

How Do I Make Any Money With An E-mail Newsletter?

While many non-profits use e-zine marketing as a strategy to grow contributions, the large majority of for-profit entrepreneurs and business professionals use e-mail newsletters to improve their bottom line.

Here's a 2006 look at ways to create cash on demand thanks to your e-zine.

NOTE: Making money is one of many reasons I publish e-mail newsletters, but it is only a single reason. The bigger picture is that e-mail newsletters build confidence, customer loyalty, market trust, and reduce the number of days in a typical sales cycle or they can even lower the cost of customer service labor because of educational training opportunities that can be presented via an e-zine.

Translation: Don't go after the fast buck with e-zines or you will have missed the point entirely of the truly incredible business-building power of your e-mail newsletter.

First, I will give you the transparent ways that I personally make money from my ezines:

Promoting My Products/Services Directly:

Because I give with every e-mail newsletter issue with very little expectation for needing anything in return, my audience is often warm to new relevant products that I create that can benefit them.

Affiliate Program Revenue:

Last year I brought in thousands of dollars each month from endorsements or mentions of products that I know, like, and trust will benefit my members.

Tip: Christopher Knight

Acquiring Affiliates to Promote My Products:

I have used my e-zines to acquire qualified affiliate partners who signed up to promote my products and services. While earning a buck directly is nice, making friends who will promote me for free on a commission basis is also a nice bonus thanks to the power of my consistently published e-zines.

Pay-Per-Click (PPC) Advertising on My Web Site.

I am able to monetize my newest E-zine Tips articles by using the traffic creation power of tens of thousands of list members who are alerted when I produce a new article. In addition, any of the 1,000+ old E-zine Tips articles are monetized thanks to our PPC partner.

The neat thing: The ads are so contextually related to my original quality articles, that they add value to my members and Web audience.

Advertising Revenue:

I'm not currently accepting new advertising clients at the moment, but the e-zine presents many opportunities for advertising revenue including ads within the e-zine, ads on the site, featured adverts, etc.

Acquiring Paid Speaking Gigs:

The majority if not all of the paid speaking gigs that I have received from all over the world have come thanks to the publicity power of my e-mail newsletters.

Ways That I Save Money Thanks To My E-zine:

Lower-cost and faster way to reach ideal prospects or clients than postal mail.

Use the e-zine to identify new partners, employees, or key business contacts needed from time to time.

Reduces administrative/customer support labor thanks to education give via the e-zine.

7 More Ways To Create Revenue From Your Ezine:

Sell qualified leads from your "thank you page" after each subscriber joins your list…give them access to related e-mail newsletters that you sell; each subscription-lead for $1 or more per subscriber.

Tip: Christopher Knight

The objective of segmenting your e-mail list members is to increase the relevancy of your messages so that they add more value to your members — ultimately, so that they buy more from you.

Use them to build another asset you can sell, such as an e-mail discussion list community, private membership site, any Web 2.0 mashup community, etc.

Create a private membership or premier list that you charge a premium for that includes secret or insider information never shared publicly via your free lead-generation e-zine.

Use your ezine to drive teleseminar/teleclass/telecourse revenues. Many are earning tens of thousands of dollars this way each year.

License your content: Create sub-topical e-zines that are co-branded and/or license your content out to companies who need to reach a target audience but don't have the expertise to write content for their e-mail newsletters.

Sell sponsored links. To keep yourself out of trouble, consider including the NOFOLLOW rel HTML tag so that your sponsored link sales are for traffic purposes and not SEO link-popularity reasons.

Segment your ezine to more narrowly target your members so that you can increase your level of offers to them that are the most relevant to their business lives or personal life.

E-zine Revenue Generation Conclusion:

Yes, earning more money from your ezine is often the end-destination point or reason for having an e-mail newsletter, but don't get caught up in trying to earn the fast buck when you should be building loyalty from your list of members that know, like, and trust you and what you have to say or offer them.

Christopher M. Knight is an e-mail list marketing expert, author, and entrepreneur. You can get a weekly dose of e-mail newsletter publishing, marketing, promotion, management, e-mail etiquette, e-mail usability, and deliverability tips by joining his free Ezine-Tips newsletter: **http://www.emailuniverse.com/subscribe/.**

Tip: Christopher Knight

Ezine Production - 4 Time Saving Tips to Reduce Your E-mail Newsletter Costs

How long does it take you and/or your team to produce your e-mail newsletter?

Interested in cutting that time in half? Whether you have an in-house e-mail newsletter production staff or you do the job yourself, being able to reduce the amount of time it takes to produce your e-mail newsletter can create a competitive advantage.

Let us explore some strategies to speed up your e-zine production capabilities:

#1: Use Templates

Whether you produce HTML or text newsletters, you should never be recreating the base look and feel for your e-zine. Never. You should create and store multiple templates for each style or type of e-zine that you send so that you can drop your new content into your template, test, and send.

#2: Automate what can be automated.

Anything that begins to become repetitive (such as typing HTML code by hand or a lot of copy and pasting) should have a script written to auto-assemble the core guts of your content. Scripts can be written in PHP and if you are not a programmer, hire one to produce this for you. It is not as deep or difficult as it seems and a few hundred dollars invested in programming could save you thousands of dollars in labor over the year.

Investments in a little programming behind the scenes can not only return itself from a cost standpoint, but it can become a competitive weapon.

#3: Do more than (1) issue at a time and schedule them.

If you've got 'evergreen' content that doesn't out date itself instantly, you can easily add an extra little bit of time to produce 2 or more newsletters at a time.

Release one and schedule the other for release in a week or two. This strategy can shave off of the time it takes to produce an ezine because you're increasing your efficiency.

If your content is time sensitive and outdated quickly, consider writing scripts or having them written for you that will automate the complete assembly of your ezine so all you have to do is write your personalization intro, test, and release to your list.

#4: Rest on your editorial calendar to produce on a set schedule.

Last minute labor time redirects are very expensive. Know in advance what topics

Tip: Christopher Knight

you will be covering in the future so that you can group together like-projects.

The more you create synergy and focus, the less time it will take to produce each issue.

Ezine Production Time Saver Summary:

Cost-savings might improve your profits, but speed can make or break the success of your e-zine. How many missed opportunities have you had because you could not get your e-zine out the door due to it taking longer than you expected? Focus a little more time on planning, and you will be able to up your e-zine frequency, increase your profits, decrease your e-zine production costs, and increase your competitive position. It is possible.

Today's E-zine Tips was produced in 50 minutes from start of concept of content, publishing on the Web site, updating the RSS feed, grabbing my template and pasting the content in it, testing, and releasing it to the 12k members of the Ezine-Tips list. Normally it takes me about 1-2 hours to get it done right, especially if there is a new call to action or new advertisement in the newsletter.

E-zine Action Step: Go find one tiny little action you can take to decrease an hour off your ezine assembly and production today. At the end of the year, you will find at least a thousand dollars in time savings...I guarantee it.

Christopher M. Knight is an e-mail list marketing expert, author, and entrepreneur. You can get a weekly dose of e-mail newsletter publishing, marketing, promotion, management, e-mail etiquette, e-mail usability, and deliverability tips by joining his free E-zine-Tips newsletter: **http://www.emailuniverse.com/subscribe/.**

Tip: Christopher Knight

How to Ensure Your E-zine Has Impact - 12 Tips

Every week, tens of thousands of e-zines are sent out the door to compete for the attention of the limited number of humans on this planet who get e-mail. What can you do to improve your ability to distance your e-zine from your competitors or all of the noise that reaches the inbox of your end recipients? It's a competition to make a positive impression with your newsletter for the precious 1-7 seconds that I would estimate you get once your members do open your e-mails.

Readability and Relevance Are Sisters in the Ezine Impact Department:

Tip: Christopher Knight

Did you ever read someone else's e-zine and think, "Damn! They really have it together" or better yet, it draws you in and creates a connection or warm fuzzy feeling…or better yet, influences you to take some kind of action that is in your and their best interest.

Amazingly, it is not that difficult to pull ahead of the inconsistency and slop that is in the marketplace as a high majority of e-zine publishers are still newbies…and the production of their e-zine shows it.

To separate yourself from everyone else, you must take action to do the extra ten percent that most competitor do not do.

Here is a quick 12 point idea check list for you to consider:

1.) Publish on a consistent schedule over a long period of time.

This is difficult for many folks, but if it were easy, we would all be doing it. Use an editorial calendar to support your consistency goals.

2.) Timelines: Get your e-zine delivered when it will be most relevant to your core audience.

It does not make much sense to send your newsletter when your audience is least expecting it.

3.) Add flash audio to your e-zines.

Having tested this myself, they do improve CTR (Click Through Rate) by 9-12% on average.

4.) Add simple, clean, and small graphics that are relevant to tell the tale within your e-zine if you publish in HTML.

You can also add graphs, charts, or other visuals that set the mood or communicate a point that is more fun to read than text.

5.) Have a professional header designed for your e-zine template so that it has the same brand look and feel of your Web site.

You are selling an image whether you intended to or not.

6.) If you do plain text for your format, consider indenting the first space on each line to create a unique look.

Tip: Christopher Knight

I give credit to Paul Meyers for this distinction as he uniquely separates his long running plain text e-zine from others that left justify all of their text. You do not have to do what Paul does, but you can do a lot with plain text newsletters other than the typical left justified 50-65 character hard line wrap that most folks do.

7.) Keep your articles brief and to the point.

Start with your main point in each paragraph and supporting the points with no more than 4-6 sentences thereafter.

8.) When you are all done with your newsletter tests and you are ready to send it out, ask yourself this question: If I invested just ten percent more time, how else could I create an easier to understand and higher value newsletter for my audience? Then do whatever comes to mind and test it.

Would it surprise you if I told you that I send about 9-16 tests of each of my own newsletters before I send them? Even with a template, I look to make small incremental improvements each week.

9.) Do content research via Google Suggest or one of the keyword tools or trade journals.

It is important that you stay on top of what your audience is buzzing about so that you can address the 'hot buttons' in your next newsletter issue. You can also survey your members on a quarterly, bi-annual, or annual basis. It is about relevancy.

10.) Subject line determines if your e-zine will be read or not.

There is nothing more important than making sure your subject line is benefit-driven.

11.) Writing articles for your e-zine also means being a keen copywriter.

This is where you leave the ego at the doorstep and lace up your "what's in it for me" benefit shoes to list what your audience can experience if they click on or take the action you want them to take.

12.) Personalize your e-zine.

It is not that difficult to put the first name of your member in the newsletter and every good e-mail list management software supports this technology.

Tip: Christopher Knight

You can take it even one step further and personalize your e-mail to be more relevant to each member of your list especially if you have a client database of your e-zine members and know their purchase history...but that is definitely an intermediate to advanced level discussion. For me, there is nothing sweeter than a favorite vendor that uses their database knowledge of me to deliver highly relevant e-mails rather than the useless "batch e-mail or mass e-mail" mentality trash that exists yet today.

E-zine Impact Conclusion:

Often times it only takes an additional ten percent of time and caring to create an enormous distance between your -ezine and that of your competitors in terms of end-user positive impact. I would encourage you to try some of today's suggestions and while it would be difficult to implement them all over-night — why not start out with the goal to make small incremental improvements in each issue. Within a year's time, you'll have made at least 52 improvements if your e-zine is weekly. Complacency is the enemy. Freshen up your e-zine with that little something extra and you will come out the winner.

Christopher M. Knight is an e-mail list marketing expert, author, and entrepreneur. You can get a weekly dose of e-mail newsletter publishing, marketing, promotion, management, e-mail etiquette, e-mail usability, and deliverability tips by joining his free Ezine-Tips newsletter: **http://www.emailuniverse.com/subscribe/.**

Tip: Abu Noaman of Elliance, Inc.

E-Mail Marketing Expert Tips

Obviously, e-mail provides a major cost-savings over communicating via paper. There are no printing costs, no postage cost. However, those who garner the most success from e-mail campaigns understand e-mail allows you to develop a deeper relationship with your recipient for two key reasons. First, it's a more personal form of communication. Second, it allows the recipient to take action immediately.

Abu Noaman is CEO of Elliance. His firm has won numerous awards for their online marketing toolkit, called ennect. Here, Mr. Noaman shares tips for getting the most out of an e-mail campaign.

Know Your Recipient

Tip: Abu Noaman of Elliance, Inc.

It is easy to send an e-mail to everyone on your list. And, at times that can be a bad thing. Just because it is easy to do, does not mean you should send everyone the same e-mail.

If the information you send is not relevant, it is sure to be deleted. On the other hand, if the information talks directly to the person, it has a greater chance of persuading the recipient to take action.

For example, a private university in Austin, Texas uses ennectMail to send permission-based e-mail to prospective students. When sending e-mails to international students in Central and Latin America, they included information promoting the multicultural events in and around Austin. Obviously this would be useless information if sent to prospective students who live in the Austin area.

Use Metrics

The true value of e-mail is the ability to see who actually reads your e-mails, how often, and what links they use. But what do you do with this information? Use it to make your content relevant.

One of our clients publishes a magazine and uses ennectMail to let subscribers know when a new issue is posted online. They could simply send out a two line message saying, "Our new issue is posted, click here to read the entire issue."

That would not enable them to utilize the data that is collected from their readers. So instead, they send an e-mail with short intro copy for the top articles. This intro copy is a link to the Web site with the actual article. As a link, it saves the recipient time. Instantly they can see what's in the issue and go directly to the article they are interested in reading. The publisher didn't supply this link simply as a time-savings benefit for their readers, but to collect real-time data on which articles are clicked on the most. By being able to precisely measure their readers' areas of interest, they can zero in on the topics that are most appealing. In addition, they use the metrics to tailor future content.

Follow up!

What happens after the e-mail blast can be an essential ingredient in your success. What is the reason you're sending the e-mail? Do you simply want to be nice and provide information? Or, do you want to motivate the recipient to take some type of action — enroll in your school, purchase your product, attend your event, provide information, etc?

Tip: Abu Noaman of Elliance, Inc.

Trade associations, universities, banks, publishers, and retail firms have all used ennectMail for different purposes. The common bond is that those who have been most successful have followed-up on the e-mail to reach their particular goal.

Here is what the world's largest non-traditional media company and the leading provider of retail marketing services does after they use ennectMail to distribute a monthly newsletter to 28,000 media and marketing professionals. Two days after they distribute their newsletter via e-mail, the sales team reviews the metrics.

Since ennectMail has a Hot Prospects tool which instantly ranks those who have interacted with the e-mail the most, the sales team knows which of their clients show the most interest in a particular mailing. With one glance, Hot Prospects tells the sales team where to focus their energies, making them more efficient and productive.

Tie Into Other Media

E-mail marketing rarely stands alone. Consider it another touch point with your customer and use it as part of a comprehensive marketing campaign. On a small scale, this means the e-mail should have a similar look and feel as your stationary and other marketing pieces. If you have a Web site, you should provide a place for people to sign up to receive your newsletter. If you use print advertisements, your Web address should always appear in the ad.

When integrated with other marketing efforts, e-mail can increase the overall success of a marketing campaign. One of our clients, an energy company, used e-mail, a CD-ROM, and print mail pieces to increase the sale of "non-electric" products and services to their electric companies.

First the customers received a welcome kit, which included the CD-ROM. Next came follow-up printed letters and e-mails. The tracking portion in ennectMail helped the client determine who should receive yet another mailing. The end result? The number of new customers taking an additional product was almost triple the original goal, and the average marketing cost per product was half of the expected cost. Would they have received the same results if they just used e-mail? Probably not.

Think Big

Using e-mail to communicate is very effective. But our most successful clients have combined e-mail with other electronic marketing tools to reach their goals.

Take for example a market research firm who had a client asking for a large amount of consumer preference data in a short period of time. Their client, a furniture

Tip: Abu Noaman of Elliance, Inc.

manufacturer, wanted to interview potential customers prior to finalizing the design considerations for new types and styles of furniture. They couldn't exactly send an e-mail to people if they don't have permission to contact them.

This marketing research firm took the innovative approach of holding a sweepstakes to gather research. They were able to have 200 people provide feedback on style preference, consideration for purchase, price elasticity, and other important details by using ennectSweeps. In exchange for answering this short survey, participants could win one of two $250 gift cards. Not only did this allow the market research firm to condense six weeks of research into a mere seven days but they now compiled a list of e-mail addresses that they can use for future mailings. It is common to use e-mail to send a newsletter. Brainstorming helps you realize different types of ways electronic communications can be used to help you reach your goals.

Use Online to Promote Offline

Having links from your e-mail to your Web site is a given. Web users have grown accustomed to moving back and forth between e-mails, Web sites, blogs, forums, etc. Remember, though, Web users are also people who live offline.

Shortly after 9/11, one of our clients had a booth at a trade show. The overall attendance at the tradeshow was down from previous years due to a nationwide fear of traveling.

Our client used ennectMail to send pre-show teasers to build interest in their exhibit. While the show's attendance was down approximately 30 percent, our client experienced a 50 percent increase in actual booth attendance. In previous years, this client never communicated with attendees prior to the show with e-mail. So, they attribute the large turnout at their booth solely to the use of e-mail.

Corporate Bio

Elliance is an eMarketing firm specializing in results-driven, Web site design, search marketing, and outbound eMarketing campaigns. The firm is the creator of the revolutionary ennect online marketing software toolkit. During its 12+ years of experience, Cisco, Dell, the eMarketing Association, and others have cited Elliance as one of the top innovators in the use of technology to deliver search engine optimization (SEO), e-commerce, and e-marketing solutions. For a free trial of their ennectMail product — the only marketing software that generates 'Hot Prospects' reports and combines four outbound eMarketing tools in a single toolkit — visit **www.ennect.com**.

Tip: TH UK Online Marketing, Ltd

When is the Best Time to Send Marketing E-Mails

There are many factors that contribute to a successful e-mail marketing campaign:

- Subject line

- Content

- Graphics

- Data

The list goes on, but one of the most common questions asked of our e-mail marketing department is, "When is the best time to send my e-mail?"

So let us take a look at some industry statistics.

Alchemy Worx, E-mail Metrics, Constant Contact have all said Tuesday to Thursday are the best days for broadcasting, with most agreeing that late morning to lunchtime is the optimum time.

Sundays and Mondays says Exact Target.

Mondays say ReturnPath and eRoi.

With industry figures disagreeing, how do we find the best time to send an e-mail campaign?

In our opinion, the answer is, it varies.

Imagine that you get into the office early; you may spend a few minutes reading your mail. Other times, you may read it at the close of play and if you have been particularly busy, you'll save it and read it at the weekend. However, if the e-mail is really relevant, you will normally open it straight away.

Still not getting an answer? That's because at TH UK we have learned that each of our clients' campaigns, with different approaches, different messages, all reach out to a different audience. The way to find out the best time to broadcast is to test.

Our in house newsletter is constantly monitored and we find the best time to send it is on a Wednesday. That doesn't mean that we recommend all of our clients send their campaigns on a Wednesday. We often break a client's database into four segments and compare the results, having sent the e-mail at different times. The following month we will do the same thing and on and on, until we have a broad range of days

Tip: TH UK Online Marketing, Ltd

and time to compare. Then, and only then, can we return to our client and highlight the optimum time to send their e-mail broadcast.

Do not wait around or you will never broadcast your campaign. Think about your target market, empathise with them, and then test. Do your best to pick a time when your clients will be most likely to respond, but do not worry too much, as figures show the difference is minimal.

TH UK Online Marketing Ltd is an online marketing agency, based in Bedford, Bedfordshire, UK. Our business has successfully developed in this fast moving industry, by mixing skill and experience, with the latest technologies available on the Internet. Our valued clients come in many shapes and sizes, from large global organizations to small and medium sized businesses — all with a common goal, to achieve results online.

As an online marketing agency, we are well positioned to provide integrated campaigns using different techniques, or to provide results with a single service.

TH UK is an online marketing company specializing in developing business on the Internet. Alan Spurgeon — Founding Director — is an expert in online marketing, having worked in the industry for 10 years.

www.thuk.co.uk

Tip: TH UK Online Marketing, Ltd

Building an In-House E-Mail List

Whether you intend to begin devising an e-mail marketing campaign, or you are already running an e-mail marketing strategy, there is one vital element which is key to your success…a good quality, in-house, e-mail list. **Data Quality**

You could have the most attractive and appealing creative campaign, coupled with a rock solid offer, but if you are sending it to the wrong people, or worse still, the e-mail is not being delivered at all, because the address is wrong, your campaign will not be successful.

Permission Based

It is extremely important that your list is permission based. There has been a lot

Tip: TH UK Online Marketing, Ltd

of media coverage regarding spam, and rightly so. The effect a nonpermission based list could have on your e-mail marketing campaign is one that should not be underestimated.

Therefore, it is very important that you use an opt-in process and preferably a double opt-in, when aggregating new subscribers.

Building Your In-House E-mail List

Fortunately, there are a number of different methods which you can use to help build a quality e-mail list. The following list, although by no means exhaustive, will certainly help you on your way to developing your in-house e-mail list.

Content Relevancy

Consider what would be of value to your recipients. If you operate in a specific industry, do you have access to up to date industry news? If not, how can you go about providing good quality news content? Although you may want to include your own company news items, this on its own may not be a big enough draw for your target audience.

The key here is in understanding your audience and reflecting this in the newsletter. The more targeted your list, the more appropriate you can make the content. For example if you are sending a newsletter which has a very generic subject, say travel, it is difficult to target the recipient with the correct type of content and offer. But, if you have a profiled list, you will know that I have a budget of £500 and like to take weekend city breaks; therefore, your content and offers should reflect this.

Statistics

Perhaps you have access to industry statistics. People love reading interesting statistics about their own areas of interest.

Polls

Online polls are very easy to create; you could include an online poll on your Web site, or in the newsletter itself. This is good for provoking interaction with your audience and you can publish the results in the following newsletter.

Profiling

Of course, when someone subscribes for the first time you may not have any information about this subscriber, other than an e-mail address and maybe a name. That is where e-mail marketing really comes in to its own.

Tip: TH UK Online Marketing, Ltd

Every newsletter you send out should help you to profile your recipients. Has the recipient opened the e-mail? What have they clicked on? Did they respond? etc. It is extremely important that this information is analyzed, then you can begin to segment your audience into groups of recipients by subject. When we have a profiled database, we can then set about sending far more relevant newsletters and the more relevant the newsletter, the more productive it will be for you.

Remember, content is very important. The content is why subscribers decide to want to receive your messages and what makes them want to continue receiving your messages. After all the hard work you have done to gain the subscription, you do not want them to unsubscribe because the information you send them is of no value.

Registration

The mechanism you use needs to be very easy to find and very easy to use. Your Web site should have an advertisement on many pages recommending that the visitor subscribes. At the same time you must do a good selling job. Outline exactly what the visitor will receive in exchange for providing their e-mail address.

Although it is nice to gather information about your subscribers, the point of subscription is not the place to ask too many questions. Keep the subscription process light. By light, start with the minimum requirements, for example the e-mail address. Then look at ways further down the line to build a profile. The lower the barriers to entry, the more subscribers you will receive.

3rd Party Lists

Using a 3rd party list, also known as a 'bought in list,' sometimes looks like a quick way to increase the size of your database. But, caution is required. As with all data lists, there is a range of quality available with e-mail data.

Beware of cheap lists, particularly those that offer millions of contacts for £300. Many lists are overused. E-mail lists need to be updated regularly and become out of date very quickly. Your reputation could be damaged by using an out of date, over used list.

Do your research on the list supplier: Do they advocate good practice, will they provide details of how the contacts opted in to receive e-mails, for example?

Telemarketing

Ensure that your staff or telesales company has an up to date script, which outlines the benefits your subscribers receive from the newsletter.

Tip: TH UK Online Marketing, Ltd

Then make sure that every client and prospect is asked the question, "You'd like to receive relevant information regarding X, wouldn't you?"

Document the date of the call and remember to offer the subscriber the opportunity to opt out of future mailings on each message.

Other Forms of Communication

Use every opportunity available to you. If it fits with your branding, why not draw attention to your e-mail list on your company stationery. Another great position to sell your e-mail subscription is on the signature of all of your e-mails. Make sure you create a hyperlinked description to make it very easy to locate the correct Web address and take the visitor directly to the subscription process whenever possible.

Summary

For the vast majority of companies, building an in house e-mail database should be as natural as keeping a list of prospect and customer telephone numbers.

Of course, you must be aware that certain methods and processes need to be considered first to make sure you achieve your objective. Building an e-mail list without meticulous preparation and possibly outside help, can result in creating more harm than good.

That said, once you have your strategy in place, e-mail marketing to a quality in house list is one of the most effective, low cost forms of marketing available.

TH UK is an online marketing company specializing in developing business on the Internet. Alan Spurgeon — Founding Director — is an expert in online marketing, having worked in the industry for 10 years.

www.thuk.co.uk

Tip: TH UK Online Marketing, Ltd

Increase Delivery Rates With Active Bounce Management

If an e-mail address in your list ceases to be valid, you remove it from the list. Simple enough, right? There are more subtle aspects of bounce management that you might not be acutely aware of, however. A bounce is a notification that your message, for whatever reason, did not make it to the recipient. Ideally, these bounces take the form of SMTP codes.

Tip: TH UK Online Marketing, Ltd

Using these codes, ISPs (Internet Service Providers) can communicate the reason for the bounce. Not everyone follows this standard, however, and accurate bounce handling may involve some keyword review of the replies.

Regardless of the bounce message's exact wording, there are two types of bounces: hard and soft. Depending on whom you talk to, they might have more technical definitions; but here is the gist of what they mean.

A hard bounce means either the receiving server purposely rejected the message or the receiving server does not exist.

Examples of hard bounces are:

- The user does not exist at the domain.

- The domain does not exist.

- The message was rejected.

A soft bounce typically denotes a temporary error with delivery and may be any response other than a hard bounce.

Examples of soft bounces are:

- The e-mail server is not responding.

- The user's mailbox is full.

Why Process Bounces?

It is important to properly process bounces for a couple reasons. You do not want to pay for e-mail messages sent to non-functioning addresses. If you do not process bounces correctly, a mailing list's natural churn will result in a large portion of dead addresses on the list.

Monitoring bounces can help show a potential delivery problem. Perhaps an e-mail domain that represents a significant portion of your list has stopped responding. Perhaps your messages are being rejected. By monitoring bounces after every campaign, you can quickly correct any irregularities.

Most important, ISPs look at bounce information when determining whether they are being targeted by a spammer. Spammers' e-mail lists are of very poor quality. If an ISP detects a large percentage of invalid e-mail coming from one IP, the mail stream may be identified as spam and blocked.

Tip: TH UK Online Marketing, Ltd

Bounces

Here are some tips to help effectively deal with or minimize e-mail bounces:

• ISPs recommend retrying hard bounces no more than three times. In our experience, retrying a hard bounce only once after a period of two to four days is sufficient.

• Remove hard-bounced addresses from the list either immediately or after the retry attempt fails. Remove soft-bounced addresses from the list if the address repeatedly generates bounces over a period of four to five e-mail campaigns.

• Scan keywords when processing bounces to help deal with non-standard bounce messages.

• Use a double or confirmed opt-in subscription process to minimize incorrect and false addresses from the start.

• Use an e-mail change of address service to help combat e-mail address churn in your mailing list.

• Add an e-mail address update link to your e-mail and a profile update form to your Web site, enabling subscribers to update their address and preferences.

• Consider contacting bounced subscribers via postal mail or phone (if you have contact information and permission) to obtain their new e-mail addresses.

• To ensure subscribers enter their e-mail addresses correctly, include a script that checks for syntax errors upon submission. Additionally, consider requiring subscribers re-enter their addresses in a second box.

• Monitor bounced messages (particularly from key ISPs and domains) for signs of e-mail rejection. The message may have been rejected due to blocking or filtering and you may need to contact the administrator of the receiving system.

• Monitor bounce rates continually, and establish a benchmark. Analyze the cause, and take appropriate action when a message lies outside of the norm. Though average bounce rates can vary dramatically, if your rate continually rises above five percent, you may have list input or hygiene issues.

• Pre-test messages for potential spam-oriented content to help minimize rejections by ISP and corporate spam filters.

Tip: TH UK Online Marketing, Ltd

TH UK is an online marketing company specializing in developing business on the Internet. Alan Spurgeon — Founding Director — is an expert in online marketing, having worked in the industry for 10 years. **www.thuk.co.uk**

Tip: Jennifer Myers Robb, President ebove & beyond

Building Customer Relationships with E-mail Preference Centers

Long gone are the days when a blast e-mail sent to everyone on your list will result in great response and strong sales. Today, in order to reach the inbox and engage customers with your brand, it is imperative to send e-mail when and how the customer prefers. An effective way to accomplish this is to let the customer control which e-mails they receive by offering an e-mail preference center.

What is an E-mail Preference Center?

An e-mail preference center is an area of your Web site designed for customers who sign up for your e-mail newsletters. This area allows customers to tell you what types of e-mails they want to receive by giving them the option of signing up for topics that interest them the most. E-mail preference centers help strengthen the relationship between your brand and your customers by allowing them to tell you what they wish to receive, and by allowing you to speak directly to them about their areas of interest.

Elements of an E-mail Preference Center

An e-mail preference center should of course be an integral part of your Web site; therefore, it should include your company name and logo, and be available as part of your Web site. In addition to these elements, there are several key pieces of information that should be included:

- E-mail Address Change — An easy way to minimize list churn is by offering customers to update their e-mail address. Rather than unsubscribing or letting your e-mails fall into an unused inbox, they can quickly let you know of their new address.

- Unsubscribe Option — E-mail preference centers will help to minimize unsubscribes. In addition to providing a way for customers to opt out of all e-mails, you can allow them to opt out "a la carte," and only unsubscribe to the e-mails that they no longer wish to receive.

Tip: Jennifer Myers Robb, President ebove & beyond

- Description of E-mail Types — Offer the customer information on the types of newsletters available, with an overview of what they can expect as well as the average frequency of the e-mails.

- E-mail Samples — Provide a sample of each newsletter so that customers will have a chance to decide whether the e-mails are of interest to them.

- Link to the Privacy Policy — Just as you always include a link to your company Privacy Policy in e-mails, it is important to reassure customers in the e-mail preference center that you will protect their privacy.

- Customer Service Information — Provide a way for customers to contact you with questions or concerns.

- Opt-In to Printed Mailings — In addition to providing e-mail sign up options, give customers the option of receiving your catalog or postal mailings.

What Types of E-mails Should You Offer?

Creating multiple newsletters is indeed more work, but this hard work will be rewarded with customers who are more engaged with your business and more likely to purchase. In general, there are promotional e-mails and content (non-promotional) e-mails. Here are some examples of each:

Promotional E-mails

- Special offers and discounts

- Sale announcements

- Sweepstakes

- Partner offers

Content E-mails

- Company newsletters

- Press releases

- Product updates

- Informative newsletters — tips, how-to articles

When deciding what types of e-mails to offer your subscribers, ask yourself these questions:

Tip: Jennifer Myers Robb, President ebove & beyond

- Would you want to receive the newsletter? If you personally have no interest in receiving messages about a certain topic, why would your customers?

- Is there unique and interesting content available for each e-mail category?

- What types of e-mails will contribute to sales, and which will not? The goal of course is to not only foster relationships with your customers, but to impact the bottom line by growing sales.

Remember that once you offer multiple e-mail categories, you must follow through and send unique and engaging content in each area. One approach is to start small and offer only a few options, and then grow as there is a need for a new e-mail category and there are resources to support it.

By offering customers the ability to control their e-mail content, you are increasing the value of that content in their mind. This in turn will lead to stronger brand loyalty, increased customer engagement with your brand, and more revenue from your e-mail program.

*ebove & beyond (***www.eboveandbeyond.com***) began in January 2003 with the goal of helping companies understand the growth opportunities available on the Internet and how to utilize specific online tools to effectively expand their business. The name "ebove & beyond" represents the extra effort we will go to in order to take your online business to the next level. The logo represents the upward and forward motion of our approach and the hands-on manner with which we work with our clients.*

Jennifer Myers Robb, President

Diane Burnett, Senior Consultant

3753 Carvette Court

High Point, NC 27265

954-778-0047

jennifer@eboveandbeyond.com

diane@eboveandbeyond.com

Tip: Jennifer Myers Robb, President ebove & beyond

Effective Ways to Grow Your E-mail List

Growing your e-mail list can seem like a difficult task, and increasing consumer concern about inbox overload and privacy make list growth even more challenging. Opportunities abound, however, to gain new subscribers. There are many ways to fill your list with customers that want to hear from you. The key is to leverage the customers already interacting with your business, and use e-mail to provide them with the relevant, unique content that they desire.

Take Advantage of Current Traffic — Make It Easy to Sign Up

To grow your e-mail subscriber list, start by touting the benefits of receiving e-mails to your current customers and site visitors. These customers in a sense are "pre-qualified;" they have either purchased from you already or are considering making a purchase. They are already interested, so offer them an easy way to hear from you.

A few ways to make subscribing easy are:

- Add an opt-in box at checkout, so that customers placing an order can easily choose to sign up to your mailing list.

- Offer an e-mail sign-up box on all pages of your Web site. People find your Web site in a variety of different ways (search engines, etc.) and do not always hit your homepage first. Make sure an e-mail sign-up is available regardless of which pages they view.

- Include a link to opt into your newsletter in all "transactional e-mails" such as order confirmations, order status e-mails, shipping confirmations, etc. Transactional e-mails are more likely to be opened and read than any other type of message.

You can further entice e-mail subscriptions through the use of special offers such as:

- Offer a special deal for signing up such as free shipping or a coupon towards their next purchase.

- Promote the benefits of receiving your e-mails. Show them what they will get. Offer examples of past campaigns and special offers available only for e-mail subscribers.

Tip: Jennifer Myers Robb, President ebove & beyond

• Mine your site for opportunities to communicate with your customers. Features such as asking if they would like to receive an e-mail when an item is back in stock, or a reminder that they left an item in their cart, can offer a chance to stay in touch.

Evangelize E-mail in All Customer Touch Points

The Web site is not the only way that customers interact with your brand, and it should not be the only way they hear about your e-mail newsletters. Reaching out to customers across all areas of your business offers a way to grow your e-mail list even further.

To capture e-mail subscribers across all customer touch points:

• Ask for e-mail addresses in the store. In-store e-mail sign-ups can be realized by sales associates asking for customer e-mail addresses at checkout, offering a place for customers to fill out an opt in form at the counter, or even including an e-mail opt in box on credit card receipts.

• Promote e-mail across the entire business. Stores and Web sites are not the only places to promote your newsletter. Offer information about your e-mails in catalogs, printed advertisements, direct mail, in package inserts, and the call center as well.

• Use current e-mail campaigns to encourage forwarding. Add a "Send to a Friend" link in the footer of every e-mail. A footer message such as "Did someone forward this message to you? Sign up here" with a subscription link will offer these recipients a chance to subscribe.

Get Creative! More Ideas to Grow Your List

Once you have started promoting e-mail across all areas of the business, there are a variety of creative ways to encourage continued e-mail subscriptions.

• Use "viral" e-mail campaigns to encourage e-mail subscribers to promote your newsletter for you. Special offers such as a Friends & Family Sale can prompt customers to forward your message to their address book. A clever, humorous e-card or game is also effective at encouraging forwards.

• Offer to send niche e-mails with information about a certain product or area of interest. Providing information separate from regular e-mails about a specific area will allow customers to choose what information is most important to them.

Tip: Jennifer Myers Robb, President ebove & beyond

• Create a sweepstakes and offer the option to subscribe to your e-mail list when entering. Care must be taken with sweepstakes, however, to ensure that the prize is extremely relevant and valuable to the customer base, otherwise you risk getting e-mail addresses of people who are not truly interested in your brand. For example, a book store might offer a chance to win a limited edition novel signed by the author.

• Offer online wish lists and gift reminder services. Wish lists that may be shared with friends and family, and gift reminder services around birthdays and holidays are a convenient service for your customers and allow you to send valuable, timely e-mail communications.

• Start a loyalty program that rewards your best customers and encourages frequent purchases. Loyalty programs offer yet another way to reach out to customers via e-mail.

Look Outside Your Business for List Growth

List growth is also possible by looking outside your business for opportunities. When approached with care and with utmost concern for customer privacy, services such as e-mail appending and co-registration offer ways to gain new subscribers.

A few of these types of opportunities for list growth are:

• Co-Registration is a way of purchasing leads for your e-mail newsletter. This is accomplished by giving visitors who are registering for a newsletter at a Web site the option of signing up for other newsletters as well. The customer simply needs to check the box of the additional newsletter he wants to sign up for. To ensure a responsive list from co-registration:

o Partner with sites that are closely aligned with your brand without being a direct competitor. For instance, a company selling baby supplies might want to run a co-registration campaign on a site that offers advice to stay-at-home moms.

o Always review the site and placement of your offer to ensure that your brand is represented in the way you intended.

o Keep e-mails acquired through co-registration separate from your house file, and test what types of campaigns work best for this group.

• E-mail Appending is when a company that does not have an e-mail address for a customer attempts to match back existing information (name, address, etc.)

Tip: Jennifer Myers Robb, President ebove & beyond

against a third party's database in order to find and purchase the customer's e-mail address. Care must be taken to adhere to all CAN-SPAM requirements:

o E-mail append is legal only if the customer has an existing relationship with your company, for example the customer has purchased from you in the past.

o E-mail addresses acquired in this way are typically not as responsive as those who opted in.

o The best approach when sending an e-mail to addresses acquired through an append is to first send an opt-in message. This means asking the customer to click a link within the e-mail if they wish to give the company permission to continue sending e-mails. This approach ensures a more responsive list, as these customers have indicated that they are interested in hearing from you via e-mail.

These are some of the ways to grow one of the most valuable assets in your business—your e-mail list. By taking advantage of all available opportunities to let your customers know why they should sign up, and then providing them with timely and relevant information, you will realize a stronger relationship with your customers and a larger, healthier e-mail file.

*ebove & beyond (***www.eboveandbeyond.com***) began in January 2003 with the goal of helping companies understand the growth opportunities available on the Internet and how to utilize specific online tools to effectively expand their business. The name "ebove & beyond" represents the extra effort we will go to in order to take your online business to the next level. The logo represents the upward and forward motion of our approach and the hands-on manner with which we work with our clients.*

Jennifer Myers Robb, President

Diane Burnett, Senior Consultant

3753 Carvette Court

High Point, NC 27265

954-778-0047

jennifer@eboveandbeyond.com

diane@eboveandbeyond.com

Tip: Rick Whittington, Rick Whittington Consulting

HTML E-mail Marketing — Where Do Customers Click?

A lot of companies use Web analytics to track how many people open their e-mails, how many customers click, and how much revenue they generate from e-mail marketing campaigns. But how many companies track creative performance of their e-mails? What in e-mail marketing campaigns do customers click on?

I recently created and sent out an e-mail marketing campaign for an e-commerce client, and we sought to measure this like I do with most of my e-mail marketing service clients. This time, I have decided to share the results since it is generally indicative of the kind of customer behavior we normally see.

Below, I have broken down the HTML version of the e-mail marketing campaign into common segments to show you how the clicks were distributed:

Branding / Header **9% of total clicks**	
Left Navigation 57% of total clicks	**Greetings / General Call-to-Action** **14% of total clicks**
	Product Images and Names **15% of total clicks**
	Product Category Links **5% of total clicks**

As you can see, over half of all clicks resulting from this HTML e-mail marketing campaign came from the left navigation containing product category links. I have seen this for years.

This may be a stretch, but I would correlate the willingness for customers to click simple left navigation with recent research that indicates that e-mail campaigns with fewer choices get better results. While products and offers contained in e-mail marketing campaigns often litter most retailers' e-mail creatives, the left category navigation remains the most-clicked area of the e-mail campaign.

Tip: Rick Whittington, Rick Whittington Consulting

Rick Whittington runs Rick Whittington Consulting LLC, a firm that helps small- and medium-sized businesses make their Web sites and online marketing more effective. Rick has 10 years of experience improving online businesses, including improving Web site design, information architecture, usability, e-commerce sales, content management, and Internet marketing.

Prior to starting his consulting company, Rick worked at Circuit City and Crutchfield Corporation where he led each company's Web site design team. Under his direction, both sites were awarded the Bizrate Circle of Excellence in consecutive years.

Rick Whittington Consulting LLC

Richmond, VA

804-363-4861

rick@rickwhittington.com

Tip: Rick Whittington, Rick Whittington Consulting

E-mail Marketing Do's and Don'ts for the Holidays

The holidays are here, and if you're in Internet retail you have hopefully already solidified an online marketing plan for the holidays. That plan probably involves e-mail marketing, so I've devised some reminders of what you should do and avoid doing so your e-mail marketing is as effective as possible during this crucial time of year.

Don'ts:

- Use XHTML code in your e-mails (Use HTML as there are delivery errors with XHTML).

- Do not reference external CSS (cascading style sheets) in your HTML e-mail as most e-mail clients cannot read it. Instead, use inline styles or font tags. You can also reference my earlier guide for using CSS in e-mail campaigns to learn what CSS definitions e-mail clients can handle.

- Send e-mail without validating it. Make sure you close all of your HTML tags so the page renders properly in all e-mail clients. You can validate your HTML e-mail with the W3C Validator.

Tip: Rick Whittington, Rick Whittington Consulting

• Embed forms or surveys in your e-mail marketing campaign. Instead, create a landing page on your Web site with the form or survey and include a link to this page in your e-mail campaign.

• Send an all-graphical e-mail. Some e-mail clients will hide images by default, and your customers won't see your message at all when accessing it through a preview pane.

• Use javascript. This will trigger all kinds of spam filters.

Do's:

• Include some "administrative" text at the top of your e-mail containing your company name or Web site address.

• Post the HTML e-mail on your Web site and offer a link to it at the top of your e-mail campaign. The text should read, "View this e-mail at our Web site" or something similar. "Having trouble viewing this e-mail? View it on our site" is also a popular option.

• Link all of your images back to your Web site.

• Include heights, widths, and ALT tags on all images. Some e-mail clients that hide images by default may assign a value to the height and width of your images, pushing content further down the page.

• If you offer a phone ordering line, include it in the e-mail campaign.

• Design all HTML e-mail for a 500-600 pixel width.

• Include your site categories/hierarchy as text links. Again, if your customers' e-mail clients hide images by default, customers will still see the text links to your main site categories. My research has shown that as many as 60 percent of customers click the navigational links to the main categories of your site.

• Check spelling. Not only is a misspelled word unprofessional, it can also increase your spam score.

• Produce a text and HTML version of your e-mail campaign. Multi-part MIME e-mail requires both and not including a text version could increase your spam score.

• Make text versions no more than 60 characters wide.

Tip: Rick Whittington, Rick Whittington Consulting

• If you are looking for a good editor to create your e-mail marketing campaigns, try Macromedia Dreamweaver. Using Word or FrontPage to create HTML e-mail marketing campaigns is not a good idea since they do not render "clean" HTML and assign styles to your campaign that most e-mail clients cannot decipher.

Rick Whittington runs Rick Whittington Consulting LLC, a firm that helps small- and medium-sized businesses make their Web sites and online marketing more effective. Rick has 10 years of experience improving online businesses, including improving Web site design, information architecture, usability, e-commerce sales, content management, and Internet marketing.

Prior to starting his consulting company, Rick worked at Circuit City and Crutchfield Corporation where he led each company's Web site design team. Under his direction, both sites were awarded the Bizrate Circle of Excellence in consecutive years.

Rick Whittington Consulting LLC

Richmond, VA

804-363-4861

rick@rickwhittington.com

Tip: Darren Fell

Getting Into The Inbox

We all know that e-mails successfully drive new and existing customers back to our sites, and that this marketing method is crucial to company revenues. But in the heavily spam-populated world of e-mail, the inbox is getting increasingly difficult to get into.

Worse still, many companies use poor e-mail marketing methods and can seem like spammers themselves. Given the frequency of unsolicited e-mails, many of the typical phrases used are copied by spam filters and if recognized, are used to reject e-mails.

So how do you get your e-mail past the Internet service providers (ISPs), past the junk folders and into your customers' inboxes?

The answer is this: It requires detailed knowledge and constant management to stay within the ever tightening rules of the Internet.

Tip: Darren Fell

Whether you are running your own e-mail operation or outsourcing, this knowledge will help you drastically improve the number of people who see your e-mails and, ultimately, the people who visit your site.

1) Do you have permission?

This is the first area to examine and is critical. Get this wrong, start broadcasting regularly, and you could find yourself in trouble with the Information Commissioner and get a fine for every spam complaint, or rather painfully get yourself blocked by ISPs, thereby preventing all of your e-mails getting out to your customer base.

This blocking process can be very easily achieved if the recipient uses 'Spamcop,' for example, as it gives the users the right to say the e-mail is spam. If enough users make the same comment about certain e-mails, the company sending them is blocked by any spam filter using the Spamcop system. If your spam record is very poor across the Internet your details — IP address and domain name — can be registered on many spam directories, ensuring you would have little chance getting any of your e-mails through.

There are two possibilities here. You could be trying to expand your online customer base, in which case you would probably be buying data or it could be your own, which you have built up directly from your site.

These basic points will ensure you don't fall before you've even got to the first hurdle.

Buying in data: Where have you got it from? If you are running an acquisition program to gain more customers, have you checked how old the list is? If the list is more than nine months old it may be best to look elsewhere. Good list owners ensure that their data is regularly re-called at least every six months. What assurances has the list broker given you? You should expect to find out exactly how it was collected and from which Web sites. Ideally the recipients should have specifically been asked if they were interested in your type of service and of course said that they didn't mind being contacted.

Your own data: It is important to check how you have collected the data. The EU data directive requires that you ask your customer to check a box to agree to receiving communication from you. Make sure this box is not automatically checked — do this the wrong way round and it could lead to customer spam complaints.

2) How do your customers unsubscribe?

Tip: Darren Fell

Again another basic detail check. Is your unsubscribe clear within your e-mail and does it work? I see so many e-mails requiring a detective to find these and in many cases the unsubscribe links do not work.

Get this wrong and your e-mails could lead to numerous spam complaints and there's a danger you will be blocked by ISPs.

3) What sending address are you using?

You may not have thought about this, but if you use a sending address that is different than the actual broadcasting address, this can be perceived as spam. For example, news@brandx.com will appear in the user's inbox, but the broadcasting address will be XYZ123@mailshot.com.

New anti-spam standards such as Sender ID look to compare the address used with the broadcasting address. These can be found in the 'header' file of the e-mail and show how it was sent. This method was introduced to prevent spammers using domains that aren't theirs in an attempt to look like a particular brand.

If you are using an external e-mail broadcasting company, many do not set this up correctly, slapping your reply address over their broadcasting address. Many can provide professional masking that uses your domain correctly in the sending address. If not, look to move to a company that does.

Using professional e-mail masking can also prevent issues with anti-phishing detectors, as the links used within the e-mail come from your domain rather than the e-mail broadcaster's domain. Anti-phishing, if you have not come across this yet, is designed to warn users of potential 'scam' mail often used to dupe recipients into giving their bank details away. The tell-tale sign is that the actual address doesn't match the URLs contained in the e-mail.

If you are broadcasting e-mail campaigns yourself, you need to set up special server configurations so that information is broadcast correctly. Check with your technical department that publishes your Sender Protection Framework (SPF) details, otherwise Sender ID spam filters will reject your mail.

4) The e-mail itself — testing with Spam Assassin

Given the huge number of spam e-mails, it is important you do not use phrases in your e-mails that can make them look like these. Many spam filters are updated regularly with these phrases so it's important to check that your mail is likely to pass before you actually send it.

Tip: Darren Fell

The industry standard is to use a program aptly named Spam Assassin.

This can be downloaded from the Internet and used to test the content of your mails via its live database. It will score anything that looks like spam, but also look at common place items like the legally required 'click here to unsubscribe' link. The idea is to get as low a score as possible as many spam filters themselves will use this same database and filter accordingly.

5) What is the quality of the HTML used to build the e-mail?

Delving into the real detail here, many free e-mail services like Hotmail and Yahoo! test the quality of the HTML of e-mails being received. If poor quality HTML is used, these e-mails are rejected on the basis that the poor HTML may break ISPs Web-based user interfaces. For example, columns and tables may be misaligned and page design destroyed.

Again, HTML checkers can be sourced from the Internet to easily check the quality of the HTML used to build your e-mails.

6) White listing

This is the service undertaken by major ISPs to ensure trusted content can be delivered through their spam protection systems. It is one of the most difficult tasks to undertake if you are broadcasting yourself, given that ISPs do not publicize the process and it normally is only ever managed by the 'top-end' e-mail broadcasters.

If you want an 'assured' deliverability through the key ISPs, the best route is to outsource.

7) Risk analysis monitoring

This is probably the most complex route to take, but ensures that you always maintain a clean record with every ISP and their free e-mail accounts — so deliveries should never be an issue.

Risk analysis monitoring follows the simple theory that if you understand the rules of each of the ISPs, then not breaking them will allow you to continue delivering straight into your customers' inboxes.

For you to undertake a system like this you will need to have real-time monitoring of the following levels: number of opt-outs, hard bounces, soft bounces, and blocked e-mails.

Tip: Darren Fell

If any of the tolerances are broken, say exceeding 10 percent of hard bounces on a single send, the delivery will be paused to examine the reasons why.

This system is the ultimate method of ensuring your deliverability is kept at the highest levels. Although it can be implemented on your own broadcasting system, if e-mail is this important to online gaming companies' revenue it is worth outsourcing to a specialist e-mail provider.

So How on Earth Do You Make Your E-Mail Campaigns Truly Successful?

Does it take a set of pyrotechnics to wiz and bang like the 5th of November fireworks night to get your customer to open it and click through to your site? Well if the technology was there then that would be great; as long as we were prepared for a few law suits from the people who had heart attacks after opening their inboxes. But back to current capabilities, there is much we can do to get what we all want — action from the e-mail.

Setting goals and targets — First and foremost, there is absolutely no point doing anything without a goal. So if you set the goals — exactly what you want to achieve with your e-mails — you instantly have something to measure against.

There is a lot of e-mail marketing that starts off so well, but over the course of six months it turns into drudgery with falling open and click through rates. To you that means less interest and therefore much less revenue.

So rather than allowing your e-mails to turn into a village newsletter without the gossip (boring), every single campaign should be created with a unique target in mind.

Fundamentals are the following:

i)   Open Rate — Who is actually looking at your e-mails

ii)   Click Through Rate — The amount of people clicking through to your site

iii)   The Unsubscribe or Opt-out Rate — A key indicator, if this rises above 1% your e-mails are either getting boring or the frequency of them is over the top, for example more than once a week

iv)   Top Links — Which links are being clicked on (and by whom). Which area is grabbing the most interest?

v)   Post Click Tracking — Are customers performing the actions desired on your site, such as buying more items or playing more games?

Tip: Darren Fell

Most in-house systems cannot provide detailed levels of reporting and rely on a Web analytics system to show movement around Web sites, but clearly these statistics are incredibly important to understand how to continually 'tweak' this area of marketing, and get customers starting to put their hands in their pockets.

PureResponse system showing all key statistics; open rate through to unsubscribe level:

Getting the e-mail opened — Ok, now down to business. How do we get customers to open the e-mail amidst an overcrowded inbox? Well, the only thing we have in reality is the subject line.

Getting it close to an impactful tabloid front page title should always make a difference, but if combined with the customer's name, surely that would have an even greater effect?

The answer is a resounding yes. Adding personalization to the subject line can often increase the open rate by eight to ten percent and in some cases by much more. Few people wouldn't respond to this: "Darren, here's a $10 token, you cannot miss our latest sale / game / etc!"

Tip: Darren Fell

Now of course if you have your customers' details, use them to personalize the actual body of the e-mail.

Preview windows — The other factor within our control that can affect open rates is what appears in what is known as the preview window. This is the small area at the top of the e-mail that shows, say, the first 10 to 15 lines.

This area certainly touches on the creative design of the e-mail, but make this top area look exciting with the key 'calls to action' and together with a powerful subject line, it will be all too alluring for the customer not to click through and see the whole thing.

Creative: keep the e-mails looking sexy — Maybe not the right adjective in your mind, but as so many companies follow such a boring brand design within their e-mails, how do they expect people to read them month in, month out and not become immune.

The answer is to have crisp, clean graphics that literally punch their way out of the screen. Imagine a girl with big red boxing gloves on, throwing a punch through the screen. "You'll be knocked out! Our products / games / etc. have far more punch than the rest!"

So strong, vibrant colors and good graphics can make all the difference. Try not to make the mistake of getting a template and following this format all the time though. Recipients quickly get bored and even if the subject line is alluring, will want to see something that renews their interest in your brand.

Another mistake often made with e-mails is packing too much in. Although it may look fantastic to, say, make it look like a magazine with numerous little columns and articles, doing this probably overplays its function. The job of an e-mail is to get users so interested that they perform an action — and that means getting them to your site to buy.

The power of great copy — Until a little company by the name of innocent drinks came along, I'm not sure anyone had really thought about the power of making their written word any different than the rest. Sure, everyone had their own in-house style. But innocent developed its own unique style of writing. Many articles have been written about innocent since, claiming their copy has set the brand apart.

In short, do not try and write the copy yourself. Get a copywriter and not only will your creative standout, you will see the copy equally leap from the page.

Tip: Darren Fell

Relevance: only talking about things that interest the customer — Gone are the days of 'spray and hope' marketing, the sort where a company sends out a few million e-mails and hope someone comes back interested. Customers expect to only be spoken to about things that actually interest them. Do not send them an e-mail about bingo if they only like poker.

Given the power of certain e-mail marketing tools, if you can see what customers click through on, you can then get a deeper understanding of their interests. Then talk to them only about what gets them excited. If it's what they really want to hear, they will be far more likely to do what you suggest.

PureResponse system showing the ability to see which areas are of most interest and exactly who is clicking through:

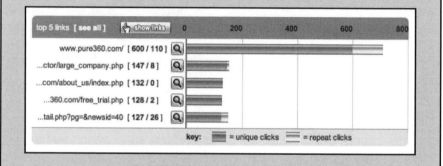

When you start to collect data prior to beginning your e-mail marketing, it is worth noting that a good exercise is to find out what people most like when they sign up and tailor any communication to this. But don't make the mistake of turning data capture areas on your site into a full survey, otherwise you will end up collecting only a pitiful amount of people who would like to receive your e-mails.

This whole area is called segmentation. It allows you to easily divide up your customer or prospect base by whatever criteria you want. You can then marry the content and creative of each e-mail specifically for them. Making them far more susceptible to buying into your services, don't you think?

About the Contributor Darren Fell, Founder of Pure

Darren Fell is the founder of e-mail marketing company Pure **www.pure360.com**. *Award-winning Pure is one of the top e-mail and SMS marketing companies in the UK*. Founded in 2000, over 450 brands, including innocent drinks and Levis Europe, use the company's PureResponse and PureUnlimited technology. Pure is the first*

Tip: Darren Fell

e-mail service provider in the UK to offer a fully managed, bespoke e-mail server system which eradicates per-e-mail charges for top-end brands sending millions of e-mails. PureUnlimited is saving big brands thousands of pounds each month, and dedicated bandwidth enables e-mail campaign send-outs to benefit from unparalleled delivery speeds.

*Recommended by respected online marketing publisher E-consultancy's E-mail Marketing Buyers Guide 2006

Contact:

+44 (0)1273 647882,

darren.fell@pure360.com

AUTHOR BIOGRAPHY
AND DEDICATION

This book is dedicated to my wife, Vonda, — For being there with me the past 22-plus years and being supportive of my coast guard career. I could not have done it without you!

Bruce C. Brown is the best selling author of *How to Use the Internet to Advertise, Promote, and Market Your Business or Web Site with Little or No Money* and recently published his third book, *The Ultimate Guide to Search Engine Marketing: Pay Per Click Advertising Secrets Revealed.* Bruce is finishing his 23rd year as an officer in the United States Coast Guard and is looking forward to retirement when he can concentrate on helping others succeed with their online businesses and marketing campaigns. He uses his 20+ years of expertise in financial management in conjunction with more than 12 years as a Web designer, business owner, e-marketing consultant, and hardware and software specialist. He completed college during his military career, earning degrees from the University of Phoenix and Charter Oak State College. He currently splits his time between Washington, DC and Land O Lakes, Florida, with his wife Vonda and youngest son, Colton. His oldest son, Dalton, is a full-time student at the University of South Florida in Tampa (Go Bulls!), and his middle son, Jordan, is a full-time student at the University of Florida in Gainesville (Go Gators!).

GLOSSARY

Ad: For Web advertising, an ad is almost always a banner, a graphic image or set of animated images (in a file called an animated GIF) of a designated pixel size and byte size limit. An ad or set of ads for a campaign is often referred to as "the creative." Banners and other special advertising.

Ad impression: An ad impression, or ad view, occurs when a user pulls up a Web page through a browser and sees an ad that is served on that page. Many Web sites sell advertising space by ad impressions.

Ad rotation: Ads are often rotated into ad spaces from a list. This is usually done automatically by software on the Web site or at a central site administered by an ad broker or server facility for a network of Web sites.

Ad space: An ad space is a space on a Web page that is reserved for ads. An ad space group is a group of spaces within a Web site that share the same characteristics so that an ad purchase can be made for the group of spaces.

Ad Stream: the series of advertisements viewed by the user during a single visit to a site.

Ad view: An ad view, synonymous with ad impression, is a single ad that appears on a Web page when the page arrives at the viewer's display. Ad views are what most Web sites sell or prefer to sell. A Web page may offer space for a number of ad views. In general, the term impression is more commonly used.

Affiliate: the publisher/salesperson in an affiliate marketing relationship.

Affiliate directory: a categorized

listing of affiliate programs.

Affiliate forum: an online community where visitors may read and post topics related to affiliate marketing.

Affiliate fraud: bogus activity generated by an affiliate in an attempt to generate illegitimate, unearned revenue.

Affiliate marketing: revenue sharing between online advertisers/ merchants and online publishers/ salespeople, whereby compensation is based on performance measures, typically in the form of sales, clicks, registrations, or a hybrid model. Affiliate marketing is the use by a Web site that sells products of other Web sites, called affiliates, to help market the products. Amazon. com, the book seller, created the first large-scale affiliate program and hundreds of other companies have followed since.

Affiliate merchant: the advertiser in an affiliate marketing relationship.

Affiliate network: a value-added intermediary providing services, including aggregation, for affiliate merchants and affiliates.

Affiliate software: software that, at a minimum, provides tracking and reporting of commission-triggering actions (sales, registrations, or clicks) from affiliate links.

Affirmative consent: An active request by a reader or subscriber to receive advertising or promotional information, newsletters, etc. Generally affirmative consent does not included the following—failing to uncheck a pre-checked box on a Web form, entering a business relationship with an organization without being asked for separate permission to be sent specific types of e-mail, opt-out.

Authentication: An automated process that verifies an e-mail sender's identity.

Banner: A banner is an advertisement in the form of a graphic image that typically runs across a Web page or is positioned in a margin or other space reserved for ads. Banner ads are usually Graphics Interchange Format (GIF) images. In addition to adhering to size, many Web sites limit the size of the file to a certain number of bytes so that the file will display quickly. Most ads are animated GIFs since animation has been shown to attract a larger percentage of user clicks. The most common larger banner ad is 468 pixels wide by 60 pixels high. Smaller sizes include 125 by 125 and 120 by 90 pixels. These and other banner sizes have been established as standard sizes by the Internet Advertising Bureau.

Bayesian filter: An anti-spam program that evaluates header and content of incoming e-mail messages to determine the probability that it is spam. Bayesian filters assign point values to items that appear frequently in spam, such as the words "money-back guarantee" or "free." A message that accumulated too many points is either rejected as probable spam or delivered to a junkmail folder. (Also known as a content-based filter.).

Beyond the banner: This is the idea that, in addition to banner ads, there are other ways to use the Internet to communicate a marketing message. These include sponsoring a Web site or a particular feature on it; advertising in e-mail newsletters; co-branding with another company and its Web site; contest promotion; and, in general, finding new ways to engage and interact with the desired audience. "Beyond the banner" approaches can also include the interstitial and streaming video infomercial. The banner itself can be transformed into a small rich media event.

Behaviorally Targeted Advertising: a method of compiling data on Web visitors, such as surfing history, gender, age and personal preferences, to later target them with tailored ads.

Blacklists: Lists of IP addresses that are being used by or belong to organizations or individuals that have been identified as sending spam. Blacklists are oǸen used by organizations and Internet Service Providers as part of their filtering process to block all incoming mail form a particular IP address (or block of addresses).

Block: An action by an Internet Service Provider to prevent e-mail messages from being forwarded to the end recipient.

Booked space: This is the number of ad views for an ad space that are currently sold out.

Bounces: E-mail messages that fail to reach their intended destination. "Hard" bounces are caused by invalid e-mail addresses, whereas "soft" bounces are due to temporary conditions, such as overloaded inboxes.

Brand, brand name, and branding: A brand is a product, service, or concept that is publicly distinguished from other products, services, or concepts so that it can be easily communicated and usually marketed. A brand name is the name of the distinctive product, service, or concept. Branding is the process of creating and disseminating the brand name. Branding can be applied to the entire corporate identity as well as to individual product and service names. In Web and other media advertising, it is recognized that there is usually some kind of branding value whether or not an immediate, direct response can be measured from an ad or campaign. Companies like Proctor and Gamble have made a science out of creating and evaluating the success of their brand name products.

Bulk folder (also junk folder): Where many e-mail clients send messages that appear to be from spammers or contain spam or are from any sender who's not in the recipient's address book or contact list. Some clients allow the recipient to override the system's settings and direct that mail from a suspect sender be sent directly to the inbox. E.g., Yahoo Mail gives recipients a button marked "Not Spam" on every message in the bulk folder;

Caching: In Internet advertising, the caching of pages in a cache server or the user's computer means that some ad views won't be known by the ad counting programs and is a source of concern. There are several

techniques for telling the browser not to cache particular pages. On the other hand, specifying no caching for all pages may mean that users will find your site to be slower than you would like.

Campaign: A campaign consists of one or more Ad Groups. The ads in a given campaign share the same daily budget, language and location targeting, end dates, and distribution options.

Challenge-Response: An authentication method that requires a human to respond to an e-mail challenge message before the original e-mail that triggered the challenge is delivered to the recipient. This method is sometimes used to cut down on spam since it requires an action by a human sender.

Click: According to ad industry recommended guidelines from FAST, a click is "when a visitor interacts with an advertisement." This does not apparently mean simply interacting with a rich media ad, but actually clicking on it so that the visitor is headed toward the advertiser's destination. (It also does not mean that the visitor actually waits to fully arrive at the destination, but just that the visitor started going there.)

Click stream: A click stream is a recorded path of the pages a user requested in going through one or more Web sites. Click stream information can help Web site owners understand how visitors are using their site and which pages are getting the most use. It can help advertisers understand how users get to the client's pages, what pages they look at, and how they go about ordering a product.

Click-through: A click-through is what is counted by the sponsoring site as a result of an ad click. In practice, click and click-through tend to be used interchangeably. A click-through, however, seems to imply that the user actually received the page. A few advertisers are willing to pay only for click-throughs rather than for ad impressions.

Click rate: The click rate is the percentage of ad views that resulted in click-throughs. Although there is visibility and branding value in ad views that don't result in a click-through, this value is difficult to measure. A click-through has several values: it's an indication of the ad's effectiveness and it results in the viewer getting to the advertiser's Web site where other messages can be provided. A new approach is for a click to result not in a link to another site but to an immediate product order window. What a successful click rate is depends on a number of factors, such as: the campaign objectives, how enticing the banner message is, how explicit the message is (a message that is complete within the banner may be less apt to be clicked), audience/message matching, how new the banner is, how often it is displayed to the same user, and so forth. In general, click rates for high-repeat, branding banners vary from 0.15 to 1 percent. Ads with provocative, mysterious, or other compelling content can induce click rates ranging from 1 to 5 percent and sometimes higher. The click rate for a given ad tends to diminish with repeated exposure.

Co-branding: Co-branding on the Web often means two Web sites or Web site sections or features displaying their logos (and thus their brands) together so that the viewer considers the site or feature to be a joint enterprise. (Co-branding is often associated with cross-linking between the sites, although it isn't necessary.)

Cookie: A cookie is a file on a Web user's hard drive (it's kept in one of the subdirectories under the browser file directory) that is used by Web sites to record data about the user. Some ad rotation software uses cookies to see which ad the user has just seen so that a different ad will be rotated into the next page view.

Conversation Rate: The key metric to evaluate the effectiveness of a conversion (often, sales) effort, reflecting the percentage of people converted into buyers (or subscribers, or whatever action is desired) out of the total population exposed to the conversion effort. For Web sites, the conversion rate is the number of visitors who took the desired action divided by the total number of visitors in a given time period (typically, per month). For e-mail marketing, the conversion rate is the number of people who take an action divided by the total number of people who received the e-mail.

Cost-per-action: Cost-per-action is what an advertiser pays for each visitor that takes some specifically defined action in response to an ad beyond simply clicking on it. For example, a visitor might visit an advertiser's site and request to be subscribed to their newsletter.

Cost-per-click (CPC): The amount of money an advertiser will pay to a site each time a user clicks on an ad or link.

Cost-per-lead: This is a more specific form of cost-per-action in which a visitor provides enough information at the advertiser's site (or in interaction with a rich media ad) to be used as a sales lead. Note that you can estimate cost-per-lead regardless of how you pay for the ad (in other words, buying on a pay-per-lead basis is not required to calculate the cost-per-lead).

Cost-per-sale: Sites that sell products directly from their Web site or can otherwise determine sales generated as the result of an advertising sales lead can calculate the cost-per-sale of Web advertising.

CPA: cost per action. The cost of one impression (the action of displaying a banner ad).

CPM: CPM is "cost per thousand" ad impressions, an industry standard measure for selling ads on Web sites. This measure is taken from print advertising. The "M" has nothing to do with "mega" or million. It's taken from the Roman numeral for "thousand."

Creative: Ad agencies and buyers often refer to ad banners and other forms of created advertising as ""the creative." Since the creative requires creative inspiration and skill that may come from a third party, it often doesn't arrive until late in the preparation for a new campaign launch.

Conversion rate: The percentage of site visitors who respond to the desired goal of an ad campaign compared with the total number of people who see the ad campaign. The goal may be, for example, convincing readers to become subscribers, encouraging customers to buy something, or enticing prospective customers from another site with an ad.

CTR: click-through rate. The cost of one click-through for a banner ad.

Database Segmentation: Upon successfully sending a campaign that reaches your recipients' inbox instead of their spam folder you will be inundated with open and click statistics. A good ESP will have reports that show which recipients clicked on which links. A great ESP will not only give you a report, but the ability to automatically send follow-up e-mail to recipients who clicked on a specific link so timely opportunities are not missed. Automated database segmentation based on recipient behavior is the key to understanding how to generate additional interest using e-mail.

Data Collection: E-mail marketing is not a one way street. Your recipients want to respond to your e-mail and without providing them a systematic way of doing so, you lose the ability to capture valuable data. From surveys to landing pages, an ESP should have integrated forms to help you maximize your feedback collection. The information you collect should serve as a guide not only for future e-mail campaigns but other marketing efforts as well.

Demographics: Demographics is data about the size and characteristics of a population or audience (for example, gender, age group, income group, purchasing history, personal preferences, and so forth).

Domains: registered domain name (with name server record)

Double Opt-In: A message is automatically sent to the person who's been signed up for a mailing list, asking if he or she really wants to be added to the list. Unless he or she actively replies positively, his or her name is wiped from the list and they never get another message.

DNS: Domain Name Server (or system) – An Internet service that translates domain names into IP addresses.

DNS Configuration: DNS Configuration as it relates to e-mail marketing allows you to send e-mail from your domain name instead of your ESP's domain. This is important for both branding and credibility. In addition, many anti-phishing filters will block your e-mail or warn e-mail recipients not to click on a link if a link in your e-mail does not match the domain from where the e-mail is sent. A credible e-mail service provider will help you with the DNS setup process so you can send e-mail from yourdomain.com instead of youre-mailserviceprovider.com.

Domain Keys: An anti-spam soŇ ware application being developed by Yahoo and using a combination of public and private "keys" to authenticate the sender's domain and reduce the chance that a spammer or hacker will fake the domain sending address.

Dynamic Ad Placement: the process by which an ad is inserted into a page in response to a user's request.

Electronic Mailing Lists: also referred to as listservs; sometimes used to send advertising messages because they reach a list of subscribers who have already expressed an interest in a topic.

E-mail harvesting: The disreputable and often illegal practice of using an automated program to scan Web pages and collect e-mail addresses for use by spammers.

Enhanced whitelist: A super-whitelist maintained by AOL for bulk e-mailers who meet strict delivery standards, including less than one spam complaint for every 1,000e-mail messages. E-mailers on the enhanced whitelist can bypass AOL 9.0's automatic suppression of images and links.

Entertainment Polls: unscientific polls appearing on any manner of web sites representing the collective opinions of people taking the poll.

ESP (E-mail Service Provider): the operator of the mail server whether it is the corporate IT department, a small independent domain with its own mail server, or an e-mail service provider that delivers on behalf of a client base.

False positive: A legitimate e-mail message that is mistakenly rejected or filtered by a spam filter.

Filtering: Filtering is the immediate analysis by a program of a user Web page request in order to determine which ad or ads to return in the requested page. A Web page request can tell a Web site or its ad server whether it fits a certain characteristic such as coming from a particular company's address or that the user is using a particular level of browser. The Web ad server can respond accordingly.

Firewall: A program or set of programs designed to keep unauthorized users or messages from accessing a private network. The firewall usually has rules or protocols that authorize or prohibit outside users or messages. In e-mail, a firewall can be designed so that messages from domains or users listed as suspect because of spamming, hacking or forging will not be delivered.

Fold: "Above the fold," a term borrowed from print media, refers to an ad that is viewable as soon as the Web page arrives. You don't have to scroll down (or sideways) to see it. Since screen resolution can affect what is immediately viewable, it's good to know whether the Web site's audience tends to set their resolution at 640 by 480 pixels or at 800 by 600 (or higher).

Footer: An area at the end of an e-mail message or newsletter that contains information that doesn't change from one edition to the next, such as contact information, the company's postal address or the e-mail address the recipient used to subscribe to mailings. Some software programs can be set to place this information automatically.

Hard bounces: E-mail messages that cannot be delivered to the recipient because of a permanent error, such as an invalid or non-existing e-mail address.

Harvesting: using automated scripts known as "bots" to identify the correct syntax of e-mail addresses on Web pages and newsgroup posts and copy the addresses to a list.

Header: Routing and program data at the start of an e-mail message, including the sender's name and e-mail address, originating e-mail server IP address, recipient IP address and any transfers in the process.

Header Analysis: identifies headers that don't conform to RFC's, a strong indication of spam

Hosts: a computer system with registered ip address

Hit: A hit is the sending of a single file whether an HTML file, an image, an audio file, or other file type. Since a single Web page request can bring with it a number of individual files, the number of hits from a site is a not a good indication of its actual use (number of visitors). It does have meaning for the Web site space provider, however, as an indicator of traffic flow.

Image Scanning: Filters out offensive images before a user sees then

Impression: According to the "Basic Advertising Measures," from FAST, an ad industry group, an impression is "The count of a delivered basic advertising unit from an ad distribution point." Impressions are how most Web advertising is sold and the cost is quoted in terms of the cost per thousand impressions (CPM).

Insertion order: An insertion order is a formal, printed order to run an ad campaign. Typically, the insertion order identifies the campaign name, the Web site receiving the order and the planner or buyer giving the order, the individual ads to be run (or who will provide them), the ad sizes, the campaign beginning and end dates, the CPM, the total cost, discounts to be applied, and reporting requirements and possible penalties or stipulations relative to the failure to deliver the impressions.

Internet: the millions of computers that are linked together around the world, allowing any computer to communicate with any other that is part of the network

Inventory: Inventory is the total number of ad views or impressions that a Web site has to sell over a given period of time (usually, inventory is figured by the month).

IP address: An IP address is a unique identifier for a computer on the Internet. It is written as four numbers separated by periods. Each number can range from 0 to 255. Before connecting to a computer over the Internet, a Domain Name Server translates the domain name into its corresponding IP address.

Keyword Matching Options: There are four types of keyword matching: broad matching, exact matching, phrase matching, and negative keywords. These options help you refine your ad targeting on Google search pages.

Joe job: A spam-industry term for a forged e-mail, in which a spammer or hacker fakes a genuine e-mail address in order to hide his identity.

"Junk" E-mail: e-mail messages sent to multiple recipients who did not request it and non in the right target audience

Keyword: A word or phrase that a user types into a search engine when looking for specific information.

Keyword Searches: searches for

specific text that identifies unwanted e-mail.

List hygiene: The act of maintaining a list so that hard bounces and unsubscribed names are removed from mailings. Some list owners also use an e-mail change of address service to update old or abandoned e-mail addresses (hopefully with a permission step baked in) as part of this process.

Maximum cost-per-click (CPC): With keyword-targeted ad campaigns, you choose the maximum cost-per-click (Max CPC) you are willing to pay.

Maximum cost-per-impression (CPM): With site-targeted ad campaigns, you choose the maximum cost per thousand impressions (Max CPM) you are willing to pay.

Media broker: Since it's often not efficient for an advertiser to select every Web site it wants to put ads on, media brokers aggregate sites for advertisers and their media planners and buyers, based on demographics and other factors.

Media buyer: A media buyer, usually at an advertising agency, works with a media planner to allocate the money provided for an advertising campaign among specific print or online media (magazines, TV, Web sites, and so forth), and then calls and places the advertising orders. On the Web, placing the order often includes requesting proposals and negotiating the final cost.

Meta tags: Hidden HTML directions for Web browsers or search engines. They include important information such as the title of each page, relevant keywords describing site content, and the description of the site that shows up when a search engine returns a search.

Networks: registered class A/B/C addresses

Newsgroups: topic-specific discussion and information exchange forums open to interested parties.

Non-Permission Marketing: an e-mail message which is or appears to be sent to multiple recipients who did not request it, even though they may be in the right target market

Opt-in e-mail: Opt-in e-mail is e-mail containing information or advertising that users explicitly request (opt) to receive. Typically, a Web site invites its visitors to fill out forms identifying subject or product categories that interest them and about which they are willing to receive e-mail from anyone who might send it. The Web site sells the names (with explicit or implicit permission from their visitors) to a company that specializes in collecting mailing lists that represent different interests. Whenever the mailing list company sells its lists to advertisers, the Web site is paid a small amount for each name that it generated for the list. You can sometimes identify opt-in e-mail because it starts with a statement that tells you that you have previously agreed to receive such messages.

Page impressions: a measure of how many times a web-page has been displayed to visitors. Often used as a crude way of counting the visitors to a site.

Page requests: a measure of the number of pages that visitors have viewed in a day. Often used as a crude way of indicating the popularity of your Web site.

Paid Search: the area of keyword, contextual advertising, often called Pay-Per-Click

Page view: A common metric for measuring how many times a complete page is visited.

Pay-per-click: In pay-per-click advertising, the advertiser pays a certain amount for each click-through to the advertiser's Web site. The amount paid per click-through is arranged at the time of the insertion order and varies considerably. Higher pay-per-click rates recognize that there may be some "no-click" branding value as well as click-through value provided.

Pay-per-lead: In pay-per-lead advertising, the advertiser pays for each sales lead generated. For example, an advertiser might pay for every visitor that clicked on a site and then filled out a form.

Pay-per-sale: Pay-per-sale is not customarily used for ad buys. It is, however, the customary way to pay Web sites that participate in affiliate programs, such as those of Amazon.com and Beyond.com.

Pay-per-view: Since this is the prevalent type of ad buying arrangement at larger Web sites, this term tends to be used only when comparing this most prevalent method with pay-per-click and other methods.

Payment threshold: the minimum accumulated commission an affiliate must earn to trigger payment from an affiliate program.

Phishing: An attempt to trick recipients into giving out personal information (i.e. credit card numbers or account passwords) by sending e-mail pretending to be from a legitimate source such as the user's bank, credit card company or online Web vendor.

Proof of performance: Some advertisers may want proof that the ads they've bought have actually run and that click-through figures are accurate. In print media, tear sheets taken from a publication prove that an ad was run. On the Web, there is no industry-wide practice for proof of performance. Some buyers rely on the integrity of the media broker and the Web site. The ad buyer usually checks the Web site to determine the ads are actually running. Most buyers require weekly figures during a campaign. A few want to look directly at the figures, viewing the ad server or Web site reporting tool.

Psychographic characteristics: This is a term for personal interest information that is gathered by Web sites by requesting it from users. For example, a Web site could ask users to list the Web sites that they visit most often. Advertisers could use this data to help create a demographic profile for that site.

Reporting template: Although the media have to report data to ad agencies and media planners and buyers during and at the end of each campaign, no standard report is yet available. FAST, the ad industry coalition, is working on a proposed standard reporting template that would enable reporting to be consistent.

Reverse DNS: The process in which an IP address is matched correctly to a domain name, instead of a domain name being matched to an IP address. Reverse DNS is a popular method for catching spammers who use invalid IP addresses. If a spam filter or program can't match the IP address to the domain name, it can reject the e-mail.

Rich media: Rich media is advertising that contains perceptual or interactive elements more elaborate than the usual banner ad. Today, the term is often used for banner ads with popup menus that let the visitor select a particular page to link to on the advertiser's site. Rich media ads are generally more challenging to create and to serve. Some early studies have shown that rich media ads tend to be more effective than ordinary animated banner ads.

ROI: ROI (return on investment) is "the bottom line" on how successful an ad or campaign was in terms of what the returns (generally sales revenue) were for the money expended (invested).

Run-of-network: A run-of-network ad is one that is placed to run on all sites within a given network of sites. Ad sales firms handle run-of-network insertion orders in such a way as to optimize results for the buyer consistent with higher priority ad commitments.

Run-of-site: A run-of-site ad is one that is placed to rotate on all non-featured ad spaces on a site. CPM rates for run-of-site ads are usually less than for rates for specially-placed ads or sponsorships.

Search engine marketing (SEM): Promoting a Web site through a search engine. This most often refers to targeting prospective customers by buying relevant keywords or phrases.

Search Engine: a special site that provides an index of other Web site addresses listed according to key words and descriptions in the original page.

Search engine optimization (SEO): Making a Web site more friendly to search engines, resulting in a higher page rank.

Soft bounces: E-mail messages that cannot be delivered to the recipient because of a temporary error, such as a full mailbox.

Sophisticated Personalization: Instead of mass produced e-mail, this is the ability to create mass personalized e-mail. This ability goes beyond basic merge fields to create mass personalized automatically tailored based on interests and recipient behavior.

Spam: an unwanted e-mail message sent in bulk to thousands of addresses to try to advertise something. (Also known as unsolicited commercial e-mail): Unwanted, unsolicited junk e-mail sent to a large number of recipients.

Spam Posts: messages posted to an e-mail discussion group, chat rooms or bulletin boards that are "off topic" or distinctly promotional.

Splash page: A splash page (also known as an interstitial) is a preliminary page that precedes the regular home page of a Web site and usually promotes a particular site feature or provides advertising. A splash page is timed to move on to the home page after a short period of time.

Spoofing: The disreputable and often illegal act of falsifying the sender e-mail address to make it appear as if an e-mail message.

Sponsor: Depending on the context, a sponsor simply means an advertiser who has sponsored an ad and, by doing so, has also helped sponsor or sustain the Web site itself. It can also mean an advertiser that has a special relationship with the Web site and supports a special feature of a Web site, such as a writer's column, a Flower-of-the-Day, or a collection of articles on a particular subject.

Sponsorship: Sponsorship is an association with a Web site in some way that gives an advertiser some particular visibility and advantage above that of run-of-site advertising. When associated with specific content, sponsorship can provide a more targeted audience than run-of-site ad buys. Sponsorship also implies a "synergy and resonance" between the Web site and the advertiser. Some sponsorships are available as value-added opportunities for advertisers who buy a certain minimum amount of advertising.

Targeting: Targeting is purchasing ad space on Web sites that match audience and campaign objective requirements. **Techtarget.com**, with over 20 Web sites targeted to special information technology audiences, is an example of an online publishing business built to enable advertising targeting.

Unique IP Address: An IP address physically identifies a computer or server on the Internet. It is similar to a social security number in that no two IP addresses are the same and each IP address carries a reputation. Black lists, Internet Service Providers (ISPs) and corporate network administrators routinely fight spam or unwanted mail by blocking IP addresses. E-mail Service Providers (ESPs) that group multiple clients per IP address are cheating them out of building a good reputation. Just as you would never blindly share your social security number, there is no reason why you would want to share your IP address with other marketers who are less scrupulous than you. Based on independent study by Jupiter Research, Marketing Sherpa and Return Path, almost 30% of all bulk e-mail gets blocked. It is fact that marketers who send e-mail using a shared IP address experience lower deliverability rates than marketers who send using a unique IP address.

Unique visitor: A unique visitor is someone with a unique address who is entering a Web site for the first time that day (or some other specified period). Thus, a visitor that returns within the same day is not counted twice. A unique visitors count tells you how many different people there are in your audience during the time period, but not how much they used the site during the period.

User session: A user session is someone with a unique address that enters or reenters a Web site each day (or some other specified period). A user session is sometimes determined by counting only those users that haven't reentered the site within the past 20 minutes or a similar period. User session figures are sometimes used, somewhat incorrectly, to indicate "visits" or "visitors" per day. User sessions are a better indicator of total site activity than "unique visitors" since they indicate frequency of use.

View: A view is, depending on what's meant, either an ad view or a page view. Usually an ad view is what's meant. There can be multiple ad views per page views. View counting should consider that a small percentage of users choose to turn the graphics off (not display the images) in their browser.

Visit: A visit is a Web user with a unique address entering a Web site at some page for the first time that day (or for the first time in a lesser time period). The number of visits is roughly equivalent to the number of different people that visit a site. This term is ambiguous unless the user defines it, since it could mean a user session or it could mean a unique visitor that day.

White Lists: A list of pre-authorized e-mail addresses from which e-mail messages can be delivered regardless of spam filters;

Yield: the percentage of clicks vs. impressions on an ad within a specific page.

INDEX